FALL GUYS

FALL

False
Confessions
and the Politics
of Murder

Jim Fisher

SOUTHERN ILLINOIS UNIVERSITY PRESS

Carbondale and Edwardsville

Library of Congress Cataloging-in-Publication Data

Fisher, Jim, 1939 –
    Fall guys : false confessions and the politics of murder / Jim
Fisher.
        p.   cm.
    Includes index.
        1. Homicide investigation — United States.   2. Murder —
United States — Investigation.   3. Confession (Law) — United
States.   4. Scapegoat — United States.   I. Title.
HV8079.H6F57   1996
363.2′59523′0973 — dc20   96–13138
ISBN 0-8093-2069-x (alk. paper).   CIP

The paper used in this publication meets the minimum
requirements of the American National Standard for Information
Sciences — Permanence of Paper for Printed Library Materials,
ANSI z39.48–1984. ∞

To Jerry Pacek and
to the memory of Chuck Duffy,
men of uncommon strength
and courage

CONTENTS

Acknowledgments

Special thanks to my friend and Edinboro colleague E. Ernest Wood who, as he has done before, provided valuable editorial advice and encouragement.

I'd also like to thank Doris Lessig who typed two versions of the manuscript and made several important suggestions regarding the organization of the book. Doris was the first to read what I'd written, and I value her opinion. My thanks as well to Kathryn Koldehoff for an outstanding and helpful job of editing.

I'd also like to thank Greg Lessig, my friend and fellow member of Edinboro's Political Science Department. Greg went over the manuscript carefully and caught my errors. His suggestions were also helpful.

Thanks also to the following people: Mike Ahwesh, Ken Arnold, Catherine Asperger, Dan Barber, David S. Bayne, Irene Belfiore, Jim Booth, Ted Botula, Russ Broman, Walter R. Brooks, Nick Bruich, John Casciato, Norma Chase, Claudia Coates, Floyd Coles, John Collins, Bob Colville, Bert Cook, Eugene L. Coon, Fred Cooper, Karen DePalma, Olga DeRamo, Robert W. Doty, Susan Pehon Dragosljvich, Jim Drane, Chuck Duffy, Rick Elia, William Fera, Jerry Fielder, James D. Fisher, Leslie Fisher, Sue Fisher, Jim Flevaris, John Gaydos, Yolanda Glasso, Gail Glenn, Harlan Gorman, William Gustafson, Harold Gwin, Chuck Hanna, Steve Hanus, Joe Hatten, Betty Henchar, John Henchar, Joseph Hergenroeder, Richard Hoyga, Bernice Hummert, Anna Jaworski, John Kelly, Lydia King, Elaine Klaich, Tony Klimko, Karen Kovatch, Jack Legett, Darla Lynn, Pam Mansell, Susan Mayes, John McMahon, John M. McNamara, Dorothy Moore, Robert K. Morehead, Paul Moses, John Nee, Marilyn Fergason Nestor, Steve Oppenheim, Jerry Pacek, Peg Pacek, Marie Passmore, Ed Peters, Brian Pitzer, Fran Pratt, Mrs. George Puff, Amy Reynolds, Msgr. Charles Owen Rice, Art Sabulsky, Nick Schifino, Richard Schwab, Russell Scott, Genevieve Settino, Ron Shaulis, B. G. Shields, Fritz Skiles, Pat Smiley, Bernice Smith, Vanessa Smith, Ross H. Spencer, Joe Start, Mary Sudik, Nick Sudik,

John Syka, Janet Tamaro, Dave Templeton, John Thompson, Kay Thompson, Janice Todd, John Todd, William J. Vorcheck, Ed Vrotney, Harry Weber, William Weichler, Linda Wilson, Ralph Yovetich, Lisa Zompa, Gene Zorn, Harry Zubryd, Marjorie Zubryd, and Maureen Zubryd.

FALL GUYS

PROLOGUE

The girls ran to the outhouse through the cold drizzle and the dark. The older one, Darla, who was eight, noticed the flashing red lights and heard men's voices and the slamming of car doors down the street in front of Helen Zubryd's house. It was nine o'clock, an hour beyond their bedtime.

The girls were out in their backyard this time of night on a ruse. They had told their mother they had to go to the bathroom but really wanted to play outside. They had been playing in the outhouse about ten minutes when they heard a terrible banging on the outhouse door. The pounding was so loud and furious that Darla's sister — "Little Hunky" — began to whimper. Darla got up on her toes to peek out the half-moon in the door and came face-to-face with a pair of wild-looking eyes. She tried to scream but had no voice. The man outside was talking crazily to himself. Darla couldn't make out what he was saying and had no idea who he was or what he wanted. Trapped, the girls huddled against the back wall of the outhouse. They were certain this man would force his way into the shed and kill them both. The pounding stopped, and the man grew silent, but he was out there. Darla saw his eyes and part of his face through the little window. She could hear him breathe. There was nothing they could do but wait.

Suddenly, in the distance, Darla heard a familiar sound. It was her dog, Flash. Her mother must have let him out to fetch them in. The barking grew louder; the man shouted something, then ran off, heavy-footed, into the night. From the sound of it, Flash was hot on his heels.

The girls stood frozen in the outhouse until they could no longer hear the man or the dog. That's when they made a dash for the house.

That night, when Darla finally got to sleep, she dreamed of the man and what might have happened. In the morning, Darla's mother told her about the police cars down the street and what had happened to Helen Zubryd. For the next thirty-one years, Darla would see those eyes a thousand times and would live in constant fear that one day, when she wasn't dreaming, she would see them again.

1 Introduction

THE CREATOR OF SHERLOCK HOLMES, SIR ARTHUR Conan Doyle, said that a first-class investigator had to have a good mind, exact knowledge, and the powers of observation and deduction. That's true, as far as it goes, but he forgot to mention persistence, audacity, objectivity, and, above all, integrity. And a little luck never hurt anyone.

I was (and still am) a criminal justice professor at Edinboro University in northwestern Pennsylvania, twenty miles south of Lake Erie. I had been teaching courses in criminal law and criminal investigation for seventeen years, but I didn't think of myself as a college professor. Having a law degree instead of a Ph.D. and six years in the Federal Bureau of Investigation (FBI), I didn't fit the mold. My Bureau experience led me into private investigations; then four years later, I stumbled into teaching, starting as a part-time instructor, lecturing to cops who attended college at night. With my background, no one was going to mistake me for an egghead.

In 1982, I became interested in the Lindbergh case, the celebrated kidnapping and murder of Charles and Anne Lindbergh's firstborn son. I spent four years researching the 1932 crime, its investigation, the trial, and all that followed up to the execution of Bruno Richard Hauptmann in 1936. Late in 1987, Rutgers University Press published my book on the case.

Because I had written the Lindbergh book, people assumed I knew something about celebrated crimes. In fact, I knew very little about this kind of history. It had therefore been stupid of me to accept an invitation to give a lecture on the history of celebrated

5

crimes in western Pennsylvania. In desperation, I asked one of my criminal justice students, Linda Wilson, to go over to the microfilm machine in the Baron-Forness Library and look back through old newspaper files for some headline cases. For no particular reason, I asked her to start in 1959 and work backward. A few days later, she brought me a folder crammed with microfilmed newspaper clippings. She had dozens of headline cases, but the article that caught my eye was a short piece about a murder that had taken place near Pittsburgh. After reading the article, I immediately lost interest in the other cases. This March 15, 1959, clipping had to do with the murder of Helen Zubryd in Sewickley Township back in November 1956.

I didn't know it then, but this article would change my life and the lives of others in ways none of us could have imagined.

2 "Yes, I Killed My Mother"

THE NEWSPAPER ARTICLE THAT HAD CAUGHT MY EYE IN 1989 had to do with an eleven-year-old boy named Charlie Zubryd who had told homicide detectives that, twenty-eight months earlier, he had murdered his mother with a hatchet. He would have been eight.

The district attorney (D.A.) in charge of the case, Edward C. Boyle, said that, according to the boy, his mother was about to punish him with an army belt that contained a big buckle. The belt had been his father's. The boy told detectives that his mother had chased him into the basement with the belt, and that's when he had hit her in the head with the hatchet—first with the blunt end and then with the sharp edge. When the police arrived at the scene, the hatchet, normally kept on the workbench, was embedded in her forehead.

The newspaper article ended with the following quote from District Attorney Boyle:

> We have questioned about 1,500 persons in this (case) and it always comes back to the home. Detectives were always puzzled by the belt found near the body. They never felt it was an instrument to protect herself . . . from an attacker.

This was incredible. I had never heard of a child this young committing so brutal a murder, and I couldn't imagine such a crime. And there was something else: Why had it taken the detectives so long to solve the murder? According to the article, they had questioned fifteen hundred people over a period of twenty-eight months. If the boy had done it, wouldn't that have been obvious earlier? How could an eight-year-old child have gotten away with this? Where was the physical evidence? According to the article, county detectives had been questioning the boy "periodically" since the crime. If the boy was the killer, why had it taken so long to get him to confess? None of this made any sense. The way I figured it, the detectives were idiots, the boy was some kind of child monster, or he had been framed.

I read the article several times, and the more I did, the more questions I had. Was Charlie Zubryd ever charged with murder? Was he "treated" as a juvenile offender? Was he nuts? Where was he now? I had never been so worked up or so interested in something I had read in the paper. That all of this had happened more than thirty years before made it all the more intriguing.

A few days later, I went to the library and started reading about the case in Pittsburgh's three daily newspapers. I started with November 21, 1956, the day after the killing, and worked my way forward as though I were living in Pittsburgh then and following the case day by day in the papers. From reading all of the newspaper accounts, I learned the following:

The murdered woman, Helen Zubryd, had been a forty-one-year-old widow. Her husband, Joe, had died fourteen months earlier of Bright's disease. Helen Zubryd had been a simple woman, a housecleaner who had worked hard to support and raise her only child, a precocious eight-and-a-half-year-old boy named Charlie. The boy and his mother lived in the tiny white frame house Joe had built in 1952. Not much larger than a boxcar, with a large picture window in front, the two-bedroom house sat on a three-acre lot 400 feet off Barley Road, a rural, unpaved street in Allegheny County, Pennsylvania, one mile south of Ambridge, an Ohio River factory town fifteen miles north of downtown Pittsburgh.

When the police got to the house that night, they had found Helen lying faceup on her basement floor, the hatchet buried deep in her forehead. Her blue jeans and sweater, according to the papers, were in "disarray." At first the detectives thought she had been raped. According to the neighbors, Charlie had discovered his mother's body when he arrived home from Catherine Asperger's house next door, where he had been playing with Mrs. Asperger's eight-year-old daughter Elaine. A few minutes later, he was back at the Asperger home crying for help.

From the news clippings, I learned that the man in charge of the investigation was Sergeant Ted Botula. Botula ran the homicide bureau for the Allegheny County detective's office. In 1956, county detectives worked directly under the D.A.; as political appointees, they served at his pleasure as long as he kept getting elected.

Less than an hour after the corpse was carried in a canvas body bag to the coroner's truck, a man named Elmer Skiles fell dead in Helen Zubryd's front yard. Mr. Skiles, a sixty-two-year-old resident of Barley Road, suffered a heart attack while leading a TV crew and a group of newspaper reporters and photographers up the hill to Helen's house. He suddenly stopped, stood up straight, then fell flat on his face in the wet grass. He was dead when he hit the ground. Elmer Skiles had lived across the street from Catherine Asperger in a squalid basement foundation, which had never been completed into a house. He had lived there with his wife, Margaret, and four of his eight children.

The next day, Helen Zubryd's murder made the front page of every newspaper in southwestern Pennsylvania. All the papers reported that, during the early morning hours following the murder, county detectives had arrested "two members of a neighborhood family." In custody were James Skiles, twenty-three, and his thirty-six-year-old brother, Elmer, Jr., both retarded. According to the papers, neither man had been able to account for himself at the time Helen Zubryd was killed.

Sergeant Ted Botula, notwithstanding the arrests of the Skiles brothers, told reporters that he had no leads in the case. In his opinion, the brutal slaying had been committed by a "big powerful man," a man who "had to have tremendous strength to bury an ax like that."

On Thanksgiving Day, a couple days after the murder, the Skiles brothers were released from custody. They had been held in the county jail in downtown Pittsburgh across the street from the Allegheny County Courthouse, which housed, on the fourth floor, the county detective's office and the crime laboratory. The Skiles brothers, according to newspaper accounts, had been interrogated at length and had passed lie detector tests.

Dr. Theodore R. Helmbold, the deputy coroner and forensic pathologist who had performed Helen Zubryd's autopsy, told reporters she had died from "multiple fractures of the skull." The doctor said "six blows had been inflicted on her left temple and forehead by the hatchet, and one blow on top of her head had apparently been inflicted by the hammer end." Dr. Helmbold noted that, while Mrs. Zubryd's body was "partially unclad of her dungarees she had been wearing, she had not been sexually attacked."

Detective Botula had told reporters that, in his mind, Helen Zubryd had been lying on the basement floor when the murderer had delivered the blow that had left the hatchet embedded four or five inches in her head. Botula also made it clear that Pat McCormick, the identification man, had not recovered any latent fingerprints from the hatchet. According to Botula's estimation, Helen Zubryd had been slain sometime between 6:45 and 7:25 in the evening.

Saturday, November 24, 1956, Helen Zubryd was buried following a brief funeral service at St. Mary's Byzantine Rite Church in Ambridge. On that same morning the *Pittsburgh Post-Gazette*, under the subheadline "AX KILLER CLUES POINT TO 'FRIEND'," listed the reasons why Detective Botula was now thinking that Helen Zubryd had known her killer. These reasons, which made little sense to me, were as follows:

> 1. The geographical fact that the County Detective's investigation is fanning out from the Zubryd home to the surrounding area.
> 2. The fact that County detectives are known to be re-checking the original stories told them by neighbors and others.

3. The fact that while Mrs. Zubryd's clothing was in disarray, there was no evidence a struggle had taken place in the orderly basement.

4. The fact that Mrs. Zubryd's body was not found near the cellar door or the stairway through which she might have tried to escape.

5. The fact that Mrs. Zubryd apparently was not warned by the barking of her dog Spot who was tied in the back yard and would have been able to notice the arrival of any stranger.

On Monday, November 26, six days after the murder, Sergeant Botula assigned six detectives to the investigation full-time. The officers would set up a field headquarters in Helen Zubryd's house and work from there until they solved the case. Botula told reporters he was still working under the assumption that she knew her slayer, a theory he based on the fact that her dog hadn't barked that night. Several reporters, however, had noted in print that Mrs. Zubryd's dog was so friendly he was almost fawning.

One week after the crime, the Zubryd murder dropped out of the news. The last article that would appear for several weeks was a short piece under the heading "KILLER'S MOTIVE IN WOMAN'S DEATH RE-MAINS OBSCURE." The article contained nothing new, and it was clear that, at this point, despite all their efforts, Botula and his detectives had hit the wall. Hundreds of people had been questioned — neighbors, relatives, Helen's fellow workers, her employers, and a couple dozen unfortunate souls who just happened to be in the wrong place at the wrong time. More than twenty suspects had been put on the lie box, including relatives, Helen's closest neighbors, and men who were in custody on charges of rape and lesser sexual offenses.

As a former investigator myself, I could identify with Ted Botula and felt his frustration. As an experienced homicide cop, he probably realized that, when an innocent person like Helen Zubryd is brutally murdered in her own house, citizens get scared. A madman was on the loose, and it was Botula's job to catch him. This murder must have put Botula's boss, District Attorney Boyle, on the spot. If Botula solved the case, he would be a hero. If he didn't, he would look like an incompetent political appointee. The heat was on because, if the county detectives looked bad, so did the D.A., and if the D.A. came off looking ineffective, they might all be looking for jobs after election day.

The Zubryd murder popped back into the news, for one day, in January 1957. That was the day the coroner's inquest was held, a routine hearing to establish officially that Helen Zubryd's manner of death was homicide. The hearing, held before a coroner's jury of six men, featured the testimony of Dr. Helmbold, the forensic pathologist who had performed the autopsy; Detective Botula; Pat McCormick, the identification and crime scene technician; Mrs. Catherine Asperger, Helen Zubryd's next-door neighbor; a handful of county detectives; and Charlie Zubryd, who had little to say when he took the stand. The murder was still unsolved, and by now the county detectives had other, more pressing cases on their hands. The Zubryd case had been back in the news for one day, then it was history.

❏ ❏ ❏

Two years following the Zubryd inquest, the case exploded back into the news: the case was solved. Detective Ted Botula had finally — after twenty-eight months — caught the slayer. Newspaper headlines across the state proclaimed the news that Helen Zubryd had been brutally slain by her little boy, Charlie, who had confessed to the crime. Detective Botula announced to reporters that Charlie's legal guardian, his Aunt Marge Zubryd, had called his office to report that the child had been acting strangely. According to the March 15, 1959, edition of the *Pittsburgh Press,* "the boy's relatives decided yesterday to inform county detectives of the boy's strange behavior. They suggested that Charles be brought in for 'a little talk.'"

Botula's version of who had called whom didn't jibe with Marge's. The story in the *Pittsburgh Sun-Telegraph* reflected her version of how it had started:

> I want no credit for bringing him into the detective bureau. They kept checking with us regularly over the past two years.
> When they called the other day and asked about Charlie I told them I was worried. Charlie needed help, psychiatric help.

Someone was lying, and although I had no way of determining who was telling the truth, I tended to believe Marge's version. Telling it Botula's way made it seem that Charlie's behavior had made Mike and Marge Zubryd suspicious, that Botula had simply acted on their information. This version suited Botula because it made Charlie look guilty, legitimized the interrogation, and lent credence to the confession.

Regardless of who had called whom, Mike and Marge put Charlie in the car at three o'clock on Saturday, March 14, and headed for Pittsburgh. Charlie was excited because he thought they were taking him downtown to see the St. Patrick's Day parade. But when Mike drove through the tunnel that led to the courtyard in the center of the Allegheny County Courthouse, he realized that he wouldn't be seeing any parade and that he had been lied to. Charlie had been to this place before, and he suddenly realized what was going on.

Charlie's confession made headlines in all the Pittsburgh area newspapers and dominated the news on radio and television. The story took up the entire front page of the *Pittsburgh Sun-Telegraph* under a huge headline that read "BOY ADMITS KILLING HIS MOTHER WITH HATCHET." According to the *Sun-Telegraph:*

> Charlie started chewing at his finger nails.
>
> He was sullen and quiet for two hours. Occasionally Botula or Francis Flannery (Botula's Homicide partner) would look at him in the eye. Finally Botula said, "Son, we know you killed your mother, but we don't know why you did it. Do you want to tell us now?"
>
> For an instant Charlie raised his head with what detectives call "a sparkle in his eye." He replied:
>
> "Yes, I killed my mother. Now I'll tell you why I did it."

The *Pittsburgh Press*'s account of how the confession came about was slightly different:

> Homicide Detectives Ted Botula and Francis Flannery, after a bit of small talk, asked Charlie why he was so moody.
>
> "Do you have something to tell?" they asked him.
>
> After a moment or two of shifting in the chair, Charlie said, "Yes, I killed my mother. She was going to whip me with an Army belt. I ran to the cellar, and she came after me. That's when I picked up the hatchet."

The entire text of Charlie's signed statement wasn't in any of the newspapers. Charlie, in addition to confessing to Detectives Botula and Flannery and their boss, Chief Henry Pieper, had reenacted the crime for District Attorney Boyle. In Boyle's office, with Botula on the floor playing the role of Charlie's mother, the boy took a position over Botula and swung an imaginary hatchet into the detective's face. Following this, Mike and Marge Zubryd were escorted into Boyle's office where Charlie confessed to them. Charlie's Aunt Marion and her husband, Tom Stetter, were also brought before the confessing boy. Charlie spilled the beans to everyone.

Charlie must have been an excellent confessor because his Uncle Mike said this to reporters afterwards:

> He sounded awfully convincing. It's not for me to say whether he did it or not.
>
> He looked like a different boy after the confession. He said he was relieved. He looked relieved – like a different boy.

District Attorney Boyle had more to say about Charlie and his confession than anyone:

> The boy doesn't remember what his mother was going to discipline him for. His father had used the same belt on him. The hatchet was taken from a workbench. The boy had used it to chop trees around their place.
>
> After he told the story, he brightened up and seemed to be very happy. He reminded me of a boy getting a new toy. He was relieved of tremendous pressure.
>
> I believe the boy's story. I have no reason to doubt him because he told us the first blow was on the back of the head with the blunt end of the hatchet. This confirms what Doctor Helmbold had found in his autopsy, information that had never been made public.
>
> I am weighing everything and taking every precaution before determining whether he will be tried (for murder) or turned over to juvenile authorities.

District Attorney Boyle went on to explain that Charlie could be charged with murder because in Pennsylvania the law only required that the child be over seven years old and know the difference between right and wrong.

Detective Botula, calling the Zubryd case a "heartbreaker particularly for any fellow who has children," outlined for reporters why he was convinced Charlie was the killer.

> 1. The time factor. By the boy's original story the murder must have occurred during the 20 minutes he was out of the house.
>
> 2. The murderer was left-handed. Charlie is left-handed.
>
> 3. There was no mud or signs of wet footprints in the house even though it had rained outside and the family dog, Spot, made no fuss.
>
> 4. The Army belt found near the body seemed more of a weapon a woman would choose to punish a boy rather than to defend herself against an intruder.

On March 16, 1959, two days after the confession, the local Sewickley Township newspaper, the *Daily Citizen*, published a long article about the Zubryd case that contained a few lines that caught my eye: "*Fingerprints on the weapon were obliterated when a neighbor pulled the hatchet from Mrs. Zubryd's skull*" (italics mine).

What was that about? There had been nothing along these lines reported in the other papers, nor had this been said back in 1956. How did the detectives know there were any latent fingerprints on the hatchet in the first place? Pat McCormick had said that he hadn't found any prints on the hatchet. McCormick mentioned nothing about obliterated prints. There had been nothing in the other papers about the hatchet being removed. What neighbor had done this and when? It had been my understanding that when the police arrived at the scene the hatchet was still embedded in Helen's head.

I saw something else in the *Daily Citizen* that raised my eyebrows. It had to do with the condition of Helen's clothing. If Charlie had killed his mother to avoid a spanking, why had he fooled with her clothing? According to the article in the *Daily Citizen*, District Attorney Boyle had an explanation for that: "Mrs. Zubryd's clothing had been disarranged, apparently to indicate she was the victim of a sex attack."

Boyle was implying that eight-year-old Charlie had "disarranged" his mother's clothing to throw investigators "off the trail," to make the police think she had been murdered by a man who had sex on his mind. In an article that began, "Apparently little Charlie didn't have a safety valve for letting off emotional steam," a reporter for the *Pittsburgh Sun-Telegraph* wrote: "A written statement will be taken from the boy. He also will be given another lie detector test. *The one he took two years ago proved inconclusive because of his age and nervous condition*" (italics mine).

In the *Daily Citizen* article, Boyle reported that "at no time was the boy a suspect in the slaying."

If the boy had never been a suspect, why had they given him a polygraph test? What would an eight-year-old boy who had found his mother murdered have to lie about?

This was a strange case, and Charlie Zubryd was one hell of a kid: savage, cold-blooded, cunning, and cool under pressure.

Something didn't fit. And then it hit me. In all the newspaper accounts of the case up to Charlie's confession, there was no mention of the army belt found near Helen's body. That belt figured prominently in Charlie's admission and was one of the principal reasons, according to the first article I had read, why Ted Botula had been suspicious of the boy from the beginning. According to his confession, Charlie had bludgeoned his mother to the ground then sunk the hatchet into her forehead to avoid being spanked by that belt. If Detective Botula had suspected this right off, why had it taken twenty-eight months to get Charlie to confess? If the belt was such a big clue, why was it not mentioned until after Charlie's confession? How could an eight-year-old child commit such a brutal, bloody crime? According to newspaper reportage of the case prior to the confession, the police were looking for a powerful sex offender. To believe Charlie, one had to accept that he had the fury and the strength to attack and murder his mother. The boy also had to be calm and collected, because to throw off the police he had "rearranged" his mother's blue jeans before running next door for help. The boy could act as well; and sometime during all of this he managed to clean up, otherwise he would have been covered with his mother's blood.

Nothing made sense in this case. How could Charlie's aunts and uncles have bought his confession? Something was missing. Who was Charlie Zubryd, and who was his mother? How did this case turn out? The Zubryd murder — this thirty-three-year-old crime, reminded me of a novel you couldn't put down. So I did what anyone would do; I kept turning the pages.

3   "Charge the Boy,
     or Release Him"

EARLY ON IN MY STUDY OF THE ZUBRYD CASE, I DE-veloped an interest in District Attorney Edward C. Boyle, the head prosecutor of Allegheny County. Boyle told reporters he was certain Charlie Zubryd had murdered his mother. I wondered if the D.A. of a large metropolitan county would allow his detectives to frame a nearly eleven-year-old boy. It seemed unlikely, but I didn't know Boyle. Before going any further on the case, I decided to check on Mr. Boyle. He had died in 1981, so I started my inquiry with his obituary.

Boyle was elected district attorney in November 1956, the month and year Helen Zubryd was murdered. He had previously served eight years as the United States attorney for the Western Judicial District of Pennsylvania, the federal equivalent of a county prosecutor. Boyle served two, four-year terms as D.A., then he was voted out of office in 1964. His opponents accused him of being "weak on crime," and they hired a private investigator to "put the clock on him," that is, to follow Boyle around to determine how he filled his workday. It seemed that Mr. Boyle — nicknamed "Easygoing Eddie — spent three hours a day on the job. If he wasn't at home, he spent the rest of the day hanging out at the Moose Club, the Knights of Equity Lodge, or downtown at the William Penn Hotel where he was a member of the prestigious Varsity Club. As Irish as they came, appearing regularly on KDKA radio's "Mike Folan's Irish Hour," Boyle never missed a political convention, banquet,

big-time wedding, or important funeral. Known for wearing pin-
stripe suits, heavily starched shirts, ad polka-dot bow ties, he could
eat, drink, and tell stories with the best of them. When asked about
his priorities as D.A., Boyle would tell of his fight to prevent juvenile delinquency and mention his concern about "communist
infiltration."

Irish-Catholic Eddie, the shrewd politician, had appointed Henry
Pieper — a Protestant and an active member of the Masons — as his
chief detective. He had done this to broaden his political base, a
maneuver referred to in Pittsburgh as the "Balkan system."

The Allegheny County detective's office functioned as the district attorney's fact-finding arm; as such, it handled criminal investigations in townships and boroughs too small to have police
departments staffed by trained detectives. The agency occupied
the fourth floor of the historic Allegheny County Courthouse, a
massive, granite-block structure that took up an entire city block
in downtown Pittsburgh. The courthouse and county jail, located
across the street, had been built in 1888 in the style of a great Re-
naissance palace. The courthouse and jail were connected by an en-
closed, stone bridge — the Bridge of Sighs — that arched twenty-six
feet over Ross Street, a busy downtown thoroughfare.

Boyle's chief detective, Henry Pieper, a rumpled, easygoing bear
of a man who looked more like a college professor than a cop, had
retired in 1940 after twenty-five years with the Pittsburgh Police Department. Pieper had started out as a traffic cop; then he had
moved up through the police bureaucracy to the superintendent's
office, where he had worked until his retirement as an administrative aide. Although Pieper was not a professional investigator, he
was a fairly competent administrator who got along with his detectives by keeping out of their way and not asking too many questions.

County detectives without rank sat at desks in the big squad
room. Actually they sat at gray worktables — thirty in all — lined up
ten rows deep, three across. Private offices were reserved for Pieper
and certain other officers, including Sergeant Botula, head of the
homicide unit. Every weekday morning at eight-thirty, some forty
detectives gathered for roll call in the green squad room. Except for
Ted Botula and his partner, Francis Flannery, only a handful of the
detectives in that room knew the first thing about criminal investigation: they were all political appointees.

I returned to the newspaper accounts of Charlie's confession and what had happened afterward. Early Saturday morning, following his confession and the crime scene reenactment in Boyle's office, Botula and Flannery drove Charlie to the Oakland section of Pittsburgh where they booked him into the Juvenile Detention Center. The juvenile facility was housed in an ordinary, two-story stone building that sat between Fifth and Forbes Avenues at Craft Street. Charlie was taken downstairs to a large room, a lounge, where a couple dozen other boys, all older than Charlie, were sitting around watching TV.

The next morning, Charlie's Aunt Marion, whom he called Aunt "Mamie," telephoned Marge Zubryd to express her doubts regarding Charlie's guilt and to see about getting him an attorney. Marge had also begun to question the soundness of the confession, although not as much as Marion. Mike, on the other hand, was having a hard time believing that the boy was innocent. Marge said that if Marion wanted to get a lawyer for Charlie it was all right with her. The women agreed that Genevieve Settino, the attorney in Ambridge who had handled Helen's estate, would be a good place to start.

Later that Sunday morning, Marion Stetter called Genevieve Settino who recommended Louis C. Glasso, explaining that it was customary, and wise, to appoint an attorney from the county in which the crime had occurred. Miss Settino practiced civil law in Beaver County and had no desire to take on a murder case. Louis Glasso, who specialized in criminal defense work, was an experienced and capable lawyer who crusaded tirelessly for his clients. He would also take the case for nothing because of the great injustice involved — and the publicity.

That Sunday, Lou Glasso went to the Juvenile Detention Center in Oakland to introduce himself to Charlie. Glasso, a bony, sallow-complexioned six-footer, had been born and raised in the eastern part of the state. After graduating from Dickinson Law School in Carlisle, Pennsylvania, Glasso moved to Pittsburgh to practice law. Like many full-time defense attorneys, the thirty-five-year-old was a lone wolf professionally. He lived in Glenshaw, a suburban community on the northern fringe of greater Pittsburgh, in a large house with his wife, Yolanda, and their three children. Although he was an aggressive advocate, Glasso was by nature easygoing and friendly.

Glasso found Charlie exhausted and confused. The boy spoke highly of Ted Botula, who had been so nice to him, and he seemed reluctant to contradict the detectives who had assured him he had killed his mother.

On Monday, March 16, the *Sun-Telegraph* came out with a pair of large front-page headlines — "PENT EMOTIONS BLAMED FOR BOY TURNING KILLER" and "BOY SHOWS HOW HE KILLED MOM." According to the *Sun-Telegraph*, "Detectives learned during their investigation that Charlie liked to dress in girls clothing. They said he strutted around the house in his mother's high-heeled shoes and carried a parasol."

There was also a quote from Charlie's Aunt Marion, who said, "I felt Charles knew more about the case than he told us before, but I never thought he was involved. I don't know which has been the bigger shock — the mother's death or his confession."

Charlie's crime scene reenactment was also chronicled: "10-year-old Charlie Zubryd swung his empty hand in an arc about County Detective Ted Botula's head. The man let himself fall. Charlie pounced on the fallen detective lying face up. He swung the empty left hand four more times."

Later that afternoon, Lou Glasso stopped by the Juvenile Detention Center to tell Charlie he had been to court, where he had filed a motion to get Charlie released from custody. The hearing had been set for the following day. The late edition of the *Pittsburgh Press* came out with the following headline stretched across the front page: "BOY AWAITS DECISION IN HATCHET DEATH"; and under that a smaller headline read "10-YEAR-OLD CALM AFTER CONFESSING HE KILLED MOTHER." According to the article, the D.A. and county detectives "said yesterday they are convinced the boy was telling the truth when he confessed to the murder four times Saturday."

Tuesday afternoon, March 17, downtown in the City-County Building, a handful of newspaper reporters, a couple of photographers, and a TV crew waited for Charlie in the hallway outside Judge John Duff's courtroom. When Charlie saw the reporters and cameramen, he took off his red hunting cap and covered his face with it; then he turned and started walking backwards. Botula turned the boy around so he wouldn't fall down, then he guided him into the courtroom.

Charlie sat at the defense table between Botula and Glasso. Botula draped an arm around the boy's shoulders. Detective Flannery and the assistant D.A.s took up their positions at the prosecution table. Everyone rose when the judge strolled in and climbed to the bench. "Sit down," he said, as he sat. "This is an informal hearing. Is everybody present?"

"Yes, sir," Glasso and the prosecutors replied.

"Well then," the judge said, looking toward the prosecution table, "has this boy been charged with anything?"

"No, sir," replied James Dillon, the lead prosecutor.

Lou Glasso got to his feet. "Your Honor — "

"Mr. Glasso, please sit down," the judge said.

"Sorry, Your Honor," Glasso mumbled as he lowered himself into his chair. "Your Honor, this boy has not been charged with any crime. The police took him into their interrogation room and grilled him — without his relatives or an attorney present. They got him alone in that room and somehow put the idea into his head that he had killed his mother."

"Wait a minute," one of the prosecutors said, "Mr. Glasso doesn't know what went on in that room."

"Sir," Glasso interrupted, "this child has been illegally held — incommunicado — against his constitutional rights. He hasn't been charged with a crime. How can they hold him? Mr. Boyle cannot declare himself a benefactor of this child despite his best motives. Charge the boy, and set bail, or release him."

Judge Duff switched his attention to the prosecution table. "What about that? Have there been any charges filed against this boy?"

"No, sir," said Mr. Dillon. "But I'd like to say, Your Honor, that we are as deeply concerned about his welfare as anyone in Allegheny County."

"But are there no charges?" the judge asked.

"No, sir, but this child is not in police custody. We turned him over to the juvenile authorities because the boy's relatives didn't want him."

A moment later, the judge asked, "What about the child's legal guardians? Are they in the courtroom?"

"No, sir, they're not," Glasso replied. After another exchange, Glasso offered to send his secretary to fetch Mike Zubryd. "I can have him in court within an hour."

"Then I would like you to do that," the judge replied. "We will adjourn until Mr. Zubryd arrives."

"Thank you, sir."

"Court adjourned."

❏ ❏ ❏

At four o'clock Mike Zubryd, accompanied by Glasso's secretary, walked into the courtroom. Then he and Glasso went through the door that led to the judge's chambers. The secretary sat down in Glasso's chair and put her arm around Charlie.

Following a ten-minute conference in the judge's office, the three returned to the courtroom. The judge climbed to his chair and said, "I want the boy released from custody and turned over to his attorney, Lou Glasso." Judge Duff looked down at the two men at the prosecution table and asked, "Are you planning to file formal charges against the boy?"

"That is under consideration," replied Earl Adair, the second prosecutor.

"I also order," the judge said, "psychiatric examinations for the boy."

"That will be done," Adair said, "by the juvenile court."

"Your Honor," Glasso bellowed, "I have two psychiatrists who have volunteered to give the child immediate treatment."

"Who are they?" Judge Duff asked.

"Dr. William McCabe and Dr. Bernard Barish, Your Honor. They are affiliated with the Western Psychiatric Institute in Oakland. The boy will be placed into a small, private hospital in East Liberty where the doctors are prepared to give him a series of psychiatric, psychological, and neurological examinations."

"Do you have any objections to that?" the judge asked the prosecutors.

"No, sir," Adair replied.

"And does his legal guardian, Mike Zubryd, have any objections to this plan?" asked the judge.

"No, Your Honor," Glasso replied.

"What kind of hospital are you taking him to?" the judge asked. "Is it a psychiatric facility?"

"No, sir, it's a forty-room, general hospital on Paulson Street. The owner and administrator, Dr. Robert Alvin, is a friend of mine. There will be no charge. Charlie will have a private room."

"How long will he be hospitalized?" asked the judge.

"Two, possibly three weeks, Your Honor."

"Then it's so ordered," the judge said. "Court adjourned."

Detectives Botula and Flannery and the assistant D.A.s looked on as Lou Glasso, Charlie and Mike Zubryd, and Glasso's secretary got up and started for the door. When the small group stepped into the hallway, they were surrounded by newspaper and TV reporters. "What was it like at the juvenile center?" a reporter asked.

"I was afraid," Charlie replied. "I thought about going home."

"Are you sad because you're not going home now?"

"Yes."

4 Strangers Bearing Gifts

THE *PITTSBURGH SUN-TELEGRAPH*, ON TUESDAY, MARCH 17, 1959, the day of Charlie's hearing, carried this bold front-page headline: "BOY'S RELEASE IS DEMANDED." A most interesting article, however, appearing in the same paper, was entitled "DID CHARLIE KILL HIS MOTHER? AUNT DOUBTS BOY'S STORY." The article began:

> Mrs. Thomas Stetter, Charlie Zubryd's "Aunt Mamie," was convinced her 10-year-old nephew told the truth about killing his mother two years ago.
>
> Now, in her East End home, she has had time to think about it. She's not so sure anymore. She said:
>
> "I can't believe, in the first place, that Charlie would do it, although he certainly seemed convincing enough when he confessed Saturday.
>
> "But my sister-in-law wasn't afraid of a little squirt of a kid, and that's all Charlie was — is.
>
> "He couldn't have weighed more than forty

pounds soaking wet at the time of the murder. Helen was a big woman. She did a lot of work building that house.

"Why, in September, just two months before the killing, she dug the trench for her own gas line when they converted her furnace — 200 feet."

The more Mrs. Stetter talked, the more she recalled. She said:

"Helen wasn't afraid of anything. When we'd visit her and then go to leave at night, we had to walk through a hollow to the car.

"We'd tell her to stay in the house but she'd laugh and tell us there wasn't anything to be afraid of there.

"She certainly wouldn't be afraid of Charlie, even with a hatchet. Not if she had a belt in her hand.

"Charlie had the Zubryd trait. He'd get sullen and pout or sulk. But he never threw a tantrum. He'd just go to his room and sulk. He and his mother were real close."

They were so close that Charlie loved to dress up in his mother's high-heeled shoes, her aprons, and her lipstick, Mrs. Stetter recalled. She said:

"We used to kid him about it. We even dressed him in one of my daughter Karen's dresses one time and he reveled in it."

Charlie helped his mother nurse his father through his last illness until he died fourteen months before the murder. Mrs. Stetter said:

"Charlie loved to cook and sew — anything that girls like. He used to play house and dolls with my girls and he was a model of behavior. Never once did he get out of line."

Charlie didn't want to go to school when he started first grade, Mrs. Stetter recalled. She said:

"He was just like the Zubryds — pretending to be sick. He could make himself sick — just like that."

> She snapped her fingers.
>
> "He'd get sick every morning until Helen took him to the doctor. He told her there was nothing the matter with him. For a while she carried him bodily to school."
>
> Mrs. Stetter added:
>
> "He was always saying he wanted to be a priest. He was an altar boy for Father Josh at St. Mary's Church in Herminie. He went to confession. Since his mother's death, though, he got sick every time he took communion."
>
> Mrs. Stetter recalled the scene in District Attorney Boyle's office again. She shook her head and said:
>
> "I can't believe he'd do it, or that Helen feared him enough to run away!"

Dr. William McCabe, a swarthy hulk of a man with a brooding face and dark, haunting eyes, was one of the best-known psychiatrists in Pittsburgh. He was affiliated with the Western Psychiatric Institute, a facility in Oakland near the University of Pittsburgh where he lectured at the medical school as a professor of psychiatry. Over the years he had taken the stand in dozens of murder trials to testify that the defendant was insane. An obvious eccentric, with body language that bordered on the bizarre, McCabe was well-known to the police who, to a man, considered him crazy. Drs. Bernard Barish and Yale Koskoff would be assisting Dr. McCabe in evaluating Charlie. McCabe had also asked child psychologist Robert T. Glenn to help on the case. During the next two to three weeks, McCabe and his associates would be giving Charlie a battery of psychiatric, neurological, intelligence, and psychological tests. When finished, they'd know Charlie Zubryd better than Charlie Zubryd knew himself.

Toward the end of his first week in the hospital, Charlie had his first visit with Marilyn Fergason, a young reporter for the *Pittsburgh Sun-Telegraph*. Dr. McCabe had asked Marilyn to come to the hospital where she would have full access to Charlie and his physicians. Charlie and the reporter, a striking redhead who specialized in crime features and had on several occasions accompanied Pittsburgh vice cops into gambling joints and after-hours clubs, hit it off immediately. Following their first visit, Marilyn wrote about Charlie and the murder of his mother. During the next several days, Marilyn would stop by regularly to talk to Charlie and his doctors.

Dr. McCabe doubted that Charlie, as an eight-year-old, would have had the physical strength to plant the hatchet as deeply as it had been found in his mother's skull. To test his theory, he had asked Charlie to squeeze a pair of bars that measured the strength of his hands. The instrument, called a "gripometer," showed that Charlie was a relatively weak eleven-year-old; from this, Dr. McCabe concluded that, at eight, Charlie would have been physically incapable of committing the murder.

On Saturday, March 28, twelve days after Charlie's admission to the hospital, Dr. McCabe called a press conference to announce the results of Charlie's tests and to state that he and the other doctors were absolutely convinced of his innocence. McCabe told reporters there was nothing wrong with the boy neurologically. Charlie was also very intelligent; and although extremely sensitive, his emotional range was normal:

> What we have here is a bright young boy who is emotionally sound, and normal. He's having a little difficulty at the moment because the police have told him he killed his mother. Since he's only a child, he believed them. Other than that, the boy is fine. He didn't murder anyone, and to suggest otherwise is outrageous.

Late Sunday afternoon, March 29, thirteen days after Lou Glasso had taken Charlie to the hospital, some of his relatives visited him. Mike and Marge had brought his grandmother, Katherine Zubryd, and his aunt Olga Zubryd, one of Mike's younger sisters. Tom and Marion Stetter had driven over from Shadyside. Marge, Tom, and Marion hadn't seen Charlie since the day he had confessed to them in Eddie Boyle's office. Lou Glasso had come to the hospital to be with Charlie during the visit. Charlie hadn't looked forward to this, and by the time Marge Zubryd led the group into his room, he was jittery and a little apprehensive. Marge carried a grocery bag full of Charlie's underwear and socks and put it on the floor at the foot of his bed.

Charlie sat with his feet hanging over the edge of the bed wearing the blue robe Marilyn Fergason had given him for the occasion. Several comic books, gifts he had received from Glasso and the doctors, were scattered on the bed behind him. No one came forward to give Charlie a hug or a kiss, and no one, including Charlie, knew what to say.

❑ ❑ ❑

Dr. McCabe stayed with Charlie after his relatives left the hospital. The visit had left the boy depressed and on edge, so it wasn't a good time to tell him that Mike and Marge didn't want him back. Dr. McCabe did tell Charlie that a nice couple he knew wanted to meet him. Would that be okay? Charlie didn't object. Grown-ups had always treated him as a pest; now people he didn't know were coming to visit him. Dr. McCabe did not mention that this couple had been shopping for a child.

The next day, Dr. McCabe showed up at the hospital with the couple, who brought gifts, and the get-together went well. Later that night, several hours after the visit, the man called Dr. McCabe to tell him that he and his wife were interested in the boy and would like to see more of him. Dr. McCabe said that he thought Charlie liked them, too. He would talk to Charlie, and if the boy was willing, he'd arrange another visit. Charlie said he'd enjoyed the visit and seemed eager to see them again, so Dr. McCabe made the arrangements, and the people came back, every day.

A week later, on April 6, the day before Charlie was to be released from the hospital, Marilyn Fergason's article appeared in the *Pittsburgh Sun-Telegraph*. The piece, entitled "CHARLIE INNOCENT, TESTS SAY," featured several quotes from Dr. McCabe and Charlie. In explaining Charlie's confession, Dr. McCabe said: " You might say it approached brainwashing that they gave him. You take any intelligent being and keep telling him something over and over again with a promise of a reward at the end and he'll finally comply."

Referring to his electroencephalographic exam, Charlie said: "It wasn't bad, taking it. It was a whole lot of wires connected on my head and it registered what I did. See? Here's where I swallowed. I think I moved once here."

According to the article, a childless couple had asked to adopt Charlie. They were waiting for Mike Zubryd's consent. "I'll have a whole new family," Charlie said.

5 Helen and Joe

THE ZUBRYD CASE DROPPED OUT OF THE NEWS FOR good following Marilyn Fergason's article. I spent a week going through Pittsburgh's three newspapers hoping that the story had resurfaced in 1959. It hadn't; not a trace. I even checked the microfilm files on the tenth and twentieth anniversaries of the murder and Charlie's subsequent confession on the chance that some reporter had found Charlie or one of his relatives, or even Lou Glasso, and conducted a follow-up interview. No such luck. The story had vanished into thin air as though it had never existed.

Did Charlie Zubryd really kill his mother, or had he been framed by the police? If he had been framed, why? Why would a detective like Ted Botula frame an eleven-year-old boy? I had to know, and I was now ready to get out of my office and out of the library and start talking to people. I vacillated between knowing that the boy couldn't have killed his mother and the tantalizing notion that perhaps he had. Since most murder investigations begin with a thorough check of the victim, I decided to drive out to Hawk Run, Pennsylvania, to look for Helen's relatives. Maybe one or two of her brothers — the Sudik men — would still be alive and willing to provide a picture of her life, at least up until her move to western Pennsylvania and her marriage to Joe Zubryd.

On a beautiful Saturday morning, my wife, Sue, and I drove into central Pennsylvania headed for Hawk Run, and by the end of the day, we had learned quite a bit about Charlie Zubryd's murdered mother. We had talked to several of Helen's relatives and had seen her wedding picture, a small black-and-white photograph taken in somebody's backyard shortly after the marriage ceremony: Helen, wearing a simple white dress that fell below her knees, stood next to her husband, a thin, athletic-looking man in a dark double-breasted suit. They were about the same height, and Joe, wearing steel-rimmed eyeglasses, had a gaunt, stern face and a head of thick brown hair combed straight back.

Helen, although twenty-eight when the wedding photograph was taken, looked young, innocent, and fresh. She was tall for a woman and slender, and she had dark, shoulder-length hair, a roundish face, and teeth that were perfectly straight. Her thin, delicate lips formed a cautious smile.

❑ ❑ ❑

Helen Zubryd, born on June 25, 1915, was her mother's tenth and final child. Helen's parents, John and Mary Sudik, and their firstborn son, Wash, had emigrated from Austria-Hungary in 1895. They settled in the bituminous coal region of central Pennsylvania, where John found a job at the Morrisdale Mining Company in Hawk Run, a woodsy, coal-mining village nestled in the mountains a few miles from Philipsburg. Mary raised her ten children in a tiny frame house on an acre of land, while John labored seven days a week in the ground beneath them. A vegetable garden and a cow provided much of what they ate; and as soon as a child was old enough to hold down a paying job, he or she went off to work, but the money came back to the household.

Though she would like to have had a chance to, Helen didn't attend school beyond the eighth grade — none of the Sudik children did — high school was a luxury the family couldn't afford. When Helen was fourteen, her father, disabled by a lung disease at the age of sixty-two, had to quit the mine and was out of work for good. A hard drinker all of his life, John Sudik stayed on the booze, got sicker, and grew increasingly morose.

Both Helen and her brother Pete, the only children still living at home, had to find work to support the family, destroying Helen's dream of a high school education. One morning at dawn, Helen sat up in bed with a start. She thought she had heard a gun go off. Her brother must have heard it too because he was out of his bed and heading toward the door. Helen followed him outside, and that's where they found their father. He was sprawled dead in the grass next to his shotgun. John Sudik had shot his head off at the neck. Helen was sixteen.

Following the suicide, Pete left home, but Helen stayed behind to help her mother. She washed, sewed, tended the garden, and worked for pay cleaning other people's houses and taking care of their children. She even got a job as a housekeeper at the Philipsburg estate of a wealthy man who had once been a state senator.

In 1941, almost ten years after Helen's father had killed himself, Mary Philips, one of Helen's older, married sisters, moved to Ambridge in the western part of the state, where she landed a good-paying job in a steel factory. By the end of that year, the United States was in the war, and Ambridge blossomed into a railroad and manufacturing boomtown. Because of the shortage of young men, women like Helen were needed in the mills. The jobs were tough and gritty, but the pay was good; and an ambitious and strong woman like Helen could get all the hours she wanted. So, in 1942, at age twenty-seven, Helen climbed aboard a Greyhound bus for Pittsburgh and, carrying her worldly goods in a borrowed suitcase and a brown paper bag, said good-bye to her old life in Hawk Run and finally began her own life.

The Wycoff Steel Company was in Ambridge. With its smoky factories, noisy freight trains, sooty air, and bustling downtown, Ambridge was a far cry from the quiet, mountain life of central Pennsylvania. Moving to a factory town was a big adjustment, but for the first time in her life, Helen Sudik was getting paid what she was worth. She hated to leave her ailing mother, but at twenty-seven, she had come to a point in her life when she had to start thinking about her future.

At her new job, Helen met and started dating Joe Zubryd, a handsome young man who had an ethnic, social, and economic background similar to hers. Joe came from a large Polish family made up of his parents and nine children — four boys and five girls. As with John Sudik, his father, Charles Zubryd, had been a coal miner. Joe had been born and raised in Keystone, a coal-mining patch that was nothing more than a street lined with company-owned houses a mile from Herminie, a coal town fifteen miles southeast of Pittsburgh. Because he was the oldest son and his parents needed his help in supporting the family, Joe was exempt from war service. In July 1943, he and Helen took off work and drove to Hawk Run where they got married in a small Catholic church. That was, perhaps, the happiest day in Helen's life. Nine days later her mother died.

Helen and Joe rented an apartment a few miles from Ambridge in the blue-collar town of Sewickley and worked as much overtime as they could to save money for a house. When the war ended and the soldiers came home, Helen and Joe were laid off. Joe found a job driving a cement truck; then a few months later, he was hired as an auto mechanic at the Buick dealership in Ambridge. Shortly after the war, Joe's father died, leaving his wife and three of his boys still at home; and, although Joe was working hard to raise money for his own house, he continued to support them.

Helen gave birth to Charlie in April 1948 when she was thirty-three. When she and Joe tried to get the baby baptized at the St. Mary's Byzantine Rite Church in Ambridge, they ran into a problem. Because of some denominational rift between St. Mary's and the little Catholic church in Hawk Run where they had been married, the Ambridge church would not recognize the marriage. In order to get Charlie baptized, Helen and Joe had to get married again, this time in Ambridge.

In the spring of 1949, when Charlie was a year old, Helen and Joe bought a three-acre lot on Barley Road in Sewickley Township. On that property they built, with their own hands, a tiny wooden house comprised of four rooms and a basement. They couldn't afford indoor plumbing, and that meant an outhouse and drinking water drawn from a well. Four years later, a natural gas explosion set off by an electric water pump blew the little house off its foundation. No one was hurt, but Helen, Joe, and Charlie had to move in with Janice and John Todd who lived in nearby Bell Acres. Janice Todd was the daughter of Mary Philips, the older sister who had gotten Helen her factory job at the Wycoff Steel Company.

Helen and Joe rebuilt their house on the same lot, and this time they added indoor plumbing. However, they still couldn't afford a garage, which they had planned to add later. They never did. On September 17, 1955, shortly after they had moved back into their re-built house, Joe, suffering from a severe case of nephritis, died when his kidneys gave out. He had been bedridden for months and in terrible pain. He died in agony at the age of forty.

Joe had some life insurance, but the cost of the funeral took up most of that. Helen abhorred the idea of taking welfare because she considered it charity, so she went back to work doing what she had done for fourteen years in Hawk Run: she cleaned other people's houses.

Mike Zubryd, the oldest of Joe's younger brothers and one of the Zubryd children Joe had helped his mother support, had married a nurse named Marjorie. Mike and Marge lived with Mike's mother, Katherine, at the Zubryd family house, a place formerly owned by the coal company in Keystone. Following Joe's death, Mike spent many Saturdays driving to the other side of Pittsburgh to help Helen maintain her house and keep up the yard. His wife didn't mind because she worked Saturdays at the hospital.

Helen had worried and fretted about what would become of Charlie if something happened to her. She didn't want him raised in an orphanage, so one day she asked Mike if he and Marjorie would become Charlie's legal guardians in the event of her death. Helen knew that Mike and Marge were physically incapable of having children of their own and believed they would make good parents for the boy.

After Joe Zubryd's death, Helen had remained close to her older sister Mary, who lived in Ambridge, and she had kept in touch with Mary's daughter, Janice Todd. Her brother John lived in the Pittsburgh area, but the rest of the Sudik's — five brothers and two sisters — still resided in Hawk Run. For this reason, Helen had been closest to the Zubryd side of the family and had been particularly friendly with her sister-in-law, Marion Stetter. An hour or so before she had been murdered, Helen had been on the phone with Marion, Charlie's Aunt Mamie, talking about the Thanksgiving trip she and the boy would have taken to Marion's house in the Shadyside section of Pittsburgh. Overworked and lonely, Helen had been looking forward to this holiday with her family.

❏ ❏ ❏

Helen Zubryd was an unlikely murder victim, and it seemed even more unlikely that her son Charlie had been her killer. Was it possible that Ted Botula, the man in charge of the case and the detective who had taken credit for getting the confession, actually believed that Charlie had done it? I figured that in 1959, the year Charlie had confessed, no one had ever heard of a killer so young. I went back to the library and found I was wrong, but it was very rare before 1957.

Prior to 1957, America's idea of a bad kid was a teenager who played hooky from school, ran away from home, got knocked up, or stole a few hubcaps. Even in New York City, where they had gangs, it was still zip guns, chains, and street fights over "turf." Dope, automatic weapons, and mass murder for the most part came later, much later. This was the era of *Gidget Goes to Hawaii*, the "Mickey Mouse Club," and Annette Funicello. This was a time when teenagers were expected to be respectful, polite, and responsible. But in 1957, more youngsters started killing people, and that had everyone scared. Child murderers were popping up all over the country, and in September 1957, near Pittsburgh, a ten-year-old boy named Mickey Chervenak shot his dad in the chest with a 12-gauge shotgun. The father was beating the boy's mother when the kid blew him away. Coroner William McClelland's inquest jury found the shooting justifiable, so no charges were filed. It wasn't murder, but the old man was just as dead.

Two months later, over in Westmoreland County near Greensburg, another ten-year-old boy shot his father to death. This kid, Harry Geyer, Jr., used a .22 rifle under circumstances frighteningly premeditated. The boy said he'd been thinking about killing his dad for a month because he had gotten tired of being bossed around. After the shooting, the boy was turned over to juvenile court; and two months later, he was sentenced to an indefinite term at George Junior Republic, a reform school in Grove City, Pennsylvania. Both cases made headlines in Pittsburgh.

The following year, in January, a nineteen-year-old garbage man named Charles Starkweather, with his girlfriend in tow, went on a killing spree in Lincoln, Nebraska. It was an outrageous crime that made TV news and front-page headlines everywhere. People weren't accustomed to such brutal and senseless killing, especially committed by people so young. Starkweather had shot and stabbed seven people, and in 1959 he died in the electric chair. His girlfriend, Caril Ann Fugate, got life. She was fourteen.

In the spring of 1958, an eleven-year-old boy confessed to drowning two of his friends in the Hudson River; Lana Turner's fourteen-year-old daughter stabbed the movie star's boyfriend to death; and, in a case that must have made Ted Botula sit up and take notice, a fifteen-year-old boy in Moundsville, West Virginia, hit his mother in the head with a hatchet then hid her body under his bed for six days.

6 The Aspergers

BEFORE I COULD CONTINUE MY INVESTIGATION, I WOULD have to find out if any of the detectives on the Zubryd case were still alive. I knew the Allegheny County detective's office as an arm of the district attorney's office had been abolished in 1974. County-wide investigations were now conducted out of the Allegheny County Police Department. Under the new arrangement, politics would be kept out of police work, at least in theory.

In reading through the Zubryd news clippings, I had come across the names of some of the Allegheny County detectives who had worked on the case: Henry Pieper, Francis Flannery, and Ted Botula. I didn't know any of these men, and I didn't know if they were still around, so I called a friend, John Nee, a retired Pittsburgh police detective. "Yeah, I knew all of those guys," he said. "Pieper and Flannery are dead, but as far as I know, Teddy Botula is still here." I then asked about Lou Glasso and Dr. William McCabe. "They're gone," he said. "McCabe went nuts and killed himself. Lou Glasso retired to Florida and died there in 1977."

That left Ted Botula. "What about Ted?" I asked.

"Oh, I remember Teddy," my friend replied. "He was quite a guy — and, man, what a dresser. That guy was dapper. Old Teddy loved to get headlines — they used to say he was on TV more than Bill Burns [a local TV anchor]. Nice guy, though. Everybody liked Teddy — I mean the cops did. He was kind of tough on the bad guys. If somebody said the wrong thing to Teddy — he'd go right to his fists. Hell, that's the way cops were then."

I found Botula's name in the telephone book and thought about calling him right away, but then I wondered if I should wait until I had more information about the case.

❏ ❏ ❏

I remembered reading in the old newspapers about Catherine Asperger, the forty-three-year-old widow who lived in the little

Cape Cod next door to Helen Zubryd. On the night of the murder, Charlie Zubryd had been at her house playing with Mrs. Asperger's eight-year-old daughter, Elaine. At eight o'clock, Charlie said that it was time for him to go home, so Mrs. Asperger put down her ironing and stepped outside to turn on the light so the boy could see. It was already dark and had started to drizzle.

"Be careful on the grass," Mrs. Asperger said, as Charlie began the fifty-foot trek down the rain-dampened slope to his house. Moments later, Mrs. Asperger watched him climb the steps to his front stoop and disappear into his house. With Charlie safely home, she returned to her ironing. Less than five minutes later, Charlie was back, banging on her door.

I called the number listed in the phone book for Mrs. Asperger, and a woman answered the phone. "Are you the lady who used to live on Barley Road next to Helen Zubryd?" I asked.

"Yes," she replied. "What do you want?"

"I'm sorry to call you out of the blue like this, but I'm interested in the Zubryd murder. I am a college professor at Edinboro University, and I am studying the case. Could I come down sometime to talk to you about it?"

"Huh?"

"Do you remember anything about the case?"

Mrs. Asperger sort of giggled, then said, "Yes, I remember — of course. He came back and knocked on my door. 'She's bleeding,' he said. 'Hurry up, a hatchet fell on Mommy.'" Mrs. Asperger broke into a nervous laugh. "How could I forget?" she said, in her heavy Eastern European accent. "I went over and saw this stick over her head. 'Mommy — don't touch her!' Elaine — my daughter — yelled. 'Don't touch her.' I was gonna pull it out — but didn't — you can get in trouble for that," she said, then nervously laughed.

Mrs. Asperger was talking about the murder as if it had happened yesterday. She continued nonstop for at least five minutes before I jumped in to ask if I could come to her house and talk to her in person. She said I could, and we made a date for the following afternoon. Mrs. Asperger had mentioned that she was a widow and lived alone, so I thought it would be a good idea to take my wife, Sue, along on the sixty-mile trip.

Catherine Asperger lived in a small one-story house overlooking a four-lane highway that ran along the Ohio River. She answered the door; and when my wife and I stepped into her living room, we were greeted by her daughter, Elaine, and Elaine's husband, Allan Klaich. Catherine explained that she had called Elaine after talking to me, and Elaine had been concerned about who I might be. Elaine spoke up and said she had called a county detective she knew and told him I was coming to see her mother. She handed me a piece of paper with the detective's phone number on it and asked if I would call him. I went to the telephone, dialed the number, and talked to the officer. Lucky for me, he happened to be an Edinboro graduate who knew who I was. I handed the phone back to Elaine, and when she hung up, she said she hoped I understood — they were just being careful. The Zubryd case was not a subject they took lightly.

Catherine was a short, stocky woman in her mid seventies with a round face and short, tightly curled hair that was almost white. She wore old-fashioned glasses — the kind women wore in the fifties — and talked extremely rapidly, her words coming out in bursts, punctuated by a sound she made that resembled a nervous giggle or guffaw. I had never been around a woman so tightly wound. Her hands, eyes, and facial muscles were never at rest, and her neck would get red in a flash then go white just as quickly. She spoke in paragraphs, so if you didn't listen closely, you'd miss a lot. She reminded me of a boiler that needed immediate tending. Elaine was just the opposite. Also short, but not as round, Elaine was calm, collected, and still — at least on the surface.

The five of us went to Catherine's kitchen, where we took seats around her table. She poured soft drinks and brought out a plate of cookies. Before I could ask my first question, Elaine and her mother asked me to tell them everything I knew about Charlie. I said that I only knew what I had read in the papers. They were obviously disappointed, and so was I; I had hoped they would be telling me about him.

Catherine got up from the table and walked out of the kitchen. A few seconds later she was back carrying an old *True Detective* magazine. The tattered magazine contained, she said, an account of Helen's murder. She had saved it for thirty years and wanted me to have it. Resisting the urge to open it and start reading, I thanked her and slipped it into my briefcase.

She was quite open about her life story, a rather sad tale, I thought. Her parents were Yugoslavian, but she was born in the United States. In 1915, when Catherine was a year old, her family returned to Europe for a visit; while there, her father was drafted into World War I by the Yugoslavian army. She didn't get back to America until she was thirteen, which explained her heavy Yugoslavian accent.

Catherine's husband, Vincent, had been dead thirty-eight years. He had worked in a steel mill, had been injured on the job, then came down with tuberculosis and went to a sanatorium. Prior to his death, he had been unable to work for twenty years. Mrs. Asperger had for forty years been a cook at the Watson Home, a hospital that treated polio patients. Working full-time and raising two daughters on her own, life for Catherine had not been easy.

Amid bursts of nervous laughter, giggles, and guffaws, and between digressions and side conversations with Elaine, Catherine told me what happened the night Helen Zubryd was murdered.

"He came back—I went and opened my door and he says, 'Mrs. Asperger, hurry up, come over and help me with my Mom.' I says to him, 'What's the matter with your Mom?' And he says, 'She's bleeding,' I said, 'What did she do?' And he says, 'I don't know what she did—the hatchet fell on her. She's bleeding.'" Catherine burst into a fit of laughter, then said, "I thought maybe she got her finger cut or something."

She then went on to relate, in great detail, what had transpired following Charlie's return to her house that November night in 1956.

With Charlie leading the way, Catherine and Elaine stepped quickly but clumsily through the wet grass between the two houses. "Mommy," Elaine cried, "my feet are getting soaked."

"Hurry up," Charlie pleaded. "She's bleeding!"

The Zubryd and Asperger houses sat on the same street, but they faced different directions. That's because Barley Road made a ninety-degree turn at Catherine's place; and her house, a modest white one-story frame affair with a detached, single-car garage, faced a part of the road that would have been a cross street had it intersected. This meant that her house backed up to the Zubryd's front yard.

Catherine and the kids had walked a distance between the two dwellings and were approaching the front of the Zubryd house when Charlie said, "She's in the cellar." As Catherine and her little girl walked past the front of Charlie's place en route to the basement door at the far side of the building, Charlie climbed the front steps and entered the house through the main door.

Catherine and Elaine turned the corner at the end of the house and found the basement door standing wide open. The cellar light was on, but it was weak and cast a murky, yellow glow amid the black shadows. Catherine considered entering the basement alone but decided not to leave Elaine outside by herself, so she took the little girl by the hand and led her inside.

"I looked over there and there she was, laying down on the floor and stretched out. Her arms were stretched and her legs were stretched out, you know, laying straight on her back. I went over there and thought maybe she'd fallen and hit her head or something. I was gonna go pick her up — [laughs] when I bent down — you know — I stepped over her, one foot on one side, one on the other — because I thought that would be the only way I could pick her up [laughs]. I seen that there was some kind of stick on her face. But it seemed like somebody had pushed it through under her eye, you know, in her head. And I thought, I wonder, what's that? No wonder the blood is going over her face. Before I even got the chance to straighten up — Elaine — my daughter — hollers — 'Mom — don't touch her!' And whenever she said that I got even more scared."

Startled, Catherine straightened and stepped back. As she stood there, half frozen in fear and confusion, she heard footsteps. When she looked up, she saw Charlie walking up the stairway from where he had been standing on the basement steps. It suddenly occurred to her that she and Elaine were in the presence of a woman who had been beaten to death. From the look on Elaine's face, the little girl had also figured this out and was frantic to get out of the basement. "We're calling the police," Catherine said as she turned Elaine around and ushered her up the stairs.

The stairway led to the kitchen, and when Catherine and Elaine got to the top, Catherine heard Charlie's high-pitched voice. He was speaking into the telephone that sat on the stand in the living room near the kitchen doorway. "Are you talking to the police?" she asked, as she lumbered through the kitchen.

"I'm telling Aunt Mamie about Mommy," he replied. "I told her she's bleeding and needs a doctor." Into the phone he said, "A hatchet fell on Mommy!"

Catherine grabbed the phone book from under the table and

turned to the page where emergency numbers were listed. "Give me the telephone," she said. Charlie kept talking as though he hadn't heard her. "Charlie, get off the phone!" Charlie didn't respond, so Catherine jerked it out of his hand. "I'm calling the police," she blurted to the person on the line, then she hung up. A second later, she dialed the number of the Ambridge Police Department.

The officer who answered in Ambridge couldn't make any sense out of what Catherine was trying to tell him. Her thick Yugoslavian accent and her machine-gun delivery made it difficult, particularly over the phone. The officer kept asking Catherine to repeat herself, and she did, but to no avail. Finally, the policeman realized that something had taken place in Sewickley Township, outside the jurisdiction of the Ambridge police. He got rid of her by telling her to call the township.

Abandoned by the Ambridge cop, Catherine called the police in the town of Sewickley and got the dispatcher, a man who quickly cut her off by announcing that the town police didn't respond to township calls. He then hung up. Desperate to get in touch with someone in law enforcement, anyone, she called the borough building in Fairoaks, a village located a mile down the main highway from Barley Road. No one answered. She telephoned the police in Leetsdale, another nearby borough, but no one was there. Having run out of police departments and on the verge of panic, Catherine thought of Jim Flevaris, a part-time Sewickley Township patrolman who lived a few hundred yards from her house. Up to then she hadn't called Flevaris because she didn't consider him a real cop. But at this point, she was frantic and would settle for anyone. Since Flevaris didn't work out of an office, she telephoned his house, but when no one answered, she slammed down the handpiece. "Jesus God," she cried.

Charlie and Elaine, standing next to each other in their yellow raincoats, had been watching all this from the kitchen on the other side of the archway. Although some color had seeped back into Charlie's face, he still looked like porcelain and was a little dazed. Both of their heads were soaking wet, and that normally would have sent Catherine running for a towel; she thought that was how kids got polio. But with Helen Zubryd lying dead in the basement, she wasn't thinking about that kind of thing.

"When is the doctor coming?" Charlie asked, matter-of-factly.

Catherine gave the boy a long, blank look; then she muttered, "Doctor. Who is your doctor? Do you know his name?"

"Dr. Gaydos," Charlie replied.

Catherine picked up the phone directory and turned to the Yellow Pages. "Here it is," she said. "I'm calling the doctor." She dropped the book to the floor and started to dial Dr. John Gaydos' number. "Oh, God," she moaned, "if he's not there, I'll go crazy."

"I'm scared," Elaine whispered to Charlie. "I want to go home." Charlie put his hand on Elaine's shoulder. "Don't cry," he said.

Dr. Gaydos answered the phone and agreed to come to Helen's house, but he didn't know the way. Catherine said she'd drive down Barley Road to Big Sewickley Creek Road and meet him at the Pine Inn Tavern. Did the doctor know where that was? He did, and that's where they agreed to meet. Before Catherine headed off to get the doctor, she took Elaine and Charlie back to her house, where she locked them in and told them not to open the door for anyone.

She got to the Pine Inn Tavern first and had to wait for the doctor. When he finally arrived and they were on the way back to Helen's, he fell so far behind Catherine that she had to pull off the road a couple of times so he could catch up. When they got to Helen's basement door, Dr. Gaydos told Catherine to wait outside for the ambulance. The doctor said he had called it before he had left Ambridge. Catherine was insulted and angry. She yelled, "I'm the one who found her, why don't you go wait for the ambulance!" But Dr. Gaydos insisted, and Catherine stomped angrily back to her house and the children.

This was the first time I had heard of Dr. Gaydos and his presence that night at the scene of the murder. Catherine said he was still practicing medicine in Ambridge.

As she talked, she mentioned a name I had seen in the newspapers but had forgotten: Charlie had also called Janice Todd, Helen's niece. Janice, Charlie's Aunt "Nin," lived in Bell Acres, a village not far from Barley Road. While Catherine was off meeting Dr. Gaydos, Janice and her husband, John, had driven to the house.

"I heard on the radio that Charlie confessed," Catherine said. "Then we saw it on the television. I said, 'Oh, my God, I left Elaine in the kitchen with an ax killer!' Then we read about it in the papers. Little Charlie—we couldn't believe it!"

I asked her if she believed that Charlie had killed his mother.

She said, "I don't know. He wasn't very strong to do such a thing. But then we heard he confessed; we thought he must have. We didn't know what to think. That's all we talked about. We were shocked. We read in the papers that the person who killed Helen was left-handed. We said, 'Charlie is left-handed.'"

"Did Helen keep a hatchet in her house?" I asked.

"They had one, I seen Charlie play with it. One time he made cuts in a tree out in their backyard."

I was about to follow up on the hatchet when she said, "After supper that night, I went over to Helen's, but she was in no mood to talk. She was laying on the couch and didn't want to talk, so me and Elaine went home."

"Why didn't she want to talk?" I asked.

"I knocked on the door and she opened it, but she didn't say 'hello' or nothing like that; she just went over to the couch and laid down. She didn't even ask me and Elaine to come in. She was taking a nap."

"Was she sick?"

"No, she just didn't want to talk. She didn't ask us to leave, but she wanted to be alone."

"Was she mad at you?"

"No. Helen was like that sometimes. She couldn't talk to you. She looked tired. Maybe she had trouble at work."

"She was a cleaning lady, right?"

"Yeah, she had a good job."

"Do you know where she worked?"

"At some house in Sewickley Heights or Edgeworth. Some big place."

"Who were the people she worked for?"

"I don't know."

"You don't remember?"

"She never told me. She said they was rich. They had a fancy yard, with a garden."

"You don't know where?"

"No. Helen never said."

A minute or so later, I asked, "So, you saw Helen on the night she was murdered?"

"Yeah, me and Elaine."

"What time was that?"

"We went over there at five o'clock. Elaine talked to her on the phone after that."

"When?"

"I don't know. About a quarter to seven. Elaine called to see if Charlie could come over."

"What time did Charlie come to your house?"

"Just before seven."

"Did his mother bring him?"

"No. He always came over by himself."

"How long did he stay?"

"About an hour."

"So, at five o'clock you saw Helen?"

"That's right. Elaine wanted to see if Charlie could come over. She had a board game she had just gotten for her birthday, and she wanted Charlie to help her figure out the rules. He was a real smart kid. And I had taken some bones over for their dog."

"What time did Helen usually get home from work?" I asked.

"Three-thirty in the afternoon."

I asked if Helen had worked that day, and Catherine said yes. Asked how she knew that, she answered, "She always worked on Tuesdays."

"Did she tell you she had worked that day?"

"No, but her car was gone when I left for work that morning."

"What time was that?"

"Eight-thirty."

After another short exchange, Catherine said, "After Helen got killed, I was afraid of everyone. I moved out the next day, never spent another night in that house." She giggled and looked at Elaine, who was sitting at the table motionless, as though spellbound.

"After the murder, did people think the retarded boys [the Skiles brothers] had done it?"

"Yes, some did. A lot of people thought it was Mr. Skiles. They arrested the boys, you know."

"I read about that in the papers," I said. "Did you think someone from the Skiles family murdered Helen?"

"I wasn't sure; then Charlie confessed," she said, as if the two events were not separated by more than two years' time.

"After the murder, did the police come around and ask you about Charlie's Uncle Mike?"

"Yes. They wanted to know why he had been at Helen's house so much."

"Why was he?"

"I don't know!" Catherine gushed. "He was fixing things — you know, helping out."

"Was he there a lot?" I asked.

"Uh huh. He came every Saturday."

"Was his wife with him?"

"No. She worked on Saturdays. She was a nurse."

"Was there something going on between Helen and Mike?" I asked.

"Don't ask me!" Catherine exclaimed. "I don't know!"

"Back to the Skileses," I said. "Charlie played over there?"

"Yeah. They had a grandson living there about his age. He was over there that afternoon."

"The day of the murder?"

"Yes."

When I asked Catherine if the subject of Charlie and his mother still came up in family discussions, she said, "Not much. But I still think about it, and I still get scared."

"What do you know about Charlie?" I asked.

"He got adopted by some people in Ohio, and he goes by their name," she said. "He came back to some funeral — someone related to Janice Todd. I went over there but didn't get to see him. He came back with his adopted mom. They said he wasn't very big. I thought he was going to be tall. They said he had nice clothes, but he never got married."

"How long ago was that?" I asked.

"Um — I don't know."

"Maybe ten years," Elaine said. Taking this opportunity to switch my attention to her, I asked Elaine what she remembered of that night, and she said she recalled seeing the handle of the hatchet and the blood on Mrs. Zubryd's face. Elaine also recalled being in the kitchen with Charlie while her mother was off getting the doctor. She said she had been haunted all of her life by these memories — and by the idea that someday Charlie might come back and murder her. She knew that was silly, but the idea was there, in the back of her mind, and she couldn't get rid of it. When I started asking her questions about Charlie, she said she wasn't sure she ought to talk about him. "Are you going to write about this?" she asked.

"I might," I replied.

"I was wondering, you know, how he would take it if he read this." Elaine was obviously afraid of Charlie Zubryd, but as we talked, she seemed to forget her fear.

When describing what kind of kid he had been, she emphasized that he was good in school, moody, and, she said, "very possessive of me. He wanted to be with me all of the time. I didn't like that. I was a little afraid of him, but I didn't know what it was about him I didn't like. He always wanted to pull me aside to be with me, and I wanted to be with everybody. He was smart; he always knew what was going on in school. When he used to play, he always wanted to be the mother. He always made a point of that. He wanted to be the girl. I can remember that he used to know about his mother's undergarments. I remember that he wore them, too. I remember thinking how strange that was. He was preoccupied with this kind of thing. One time he called me into his bathroom when he was taking a bath — he wanted me to see him."

Elaine said she had heard that Helen had taken Charlie to a psychiatrist not long before the killing. She said, "In those days ethnic people didn't do that — if there was a problem, they kept it in the family. They kept it quiet. There must have been something very wrong with him. At the coroner's inquest, my mother said Charlie got up and left the room when she took the stand. By doing that, my mother thought Charlie was insinuating she had killed his mother. She felt really bad for him to say that — to pin it on her — when he knew she couldn't have done it. It made her suspicious. For just a little boy, Charlie was wary — he was always prepared to say the right thing. Charlie was also very close to his mom; I knew that, and I knew that he loved her very much. They had a wonderful relationship — I never heard Mrs. Zubryd even holler at him. My mom and I always felt he wouldn't have killed his mother because he loved her too much. But then he confessed — he said he had. We didn't know what to think. Then we got to wondering."

I asked Elaine if she had heard anything about Charlie as an adult. She said she hadn't. A year or so after the murder, his Aunt Marge had brought him back to the area to visit Janice Todd in Bell Acres, and the Aspergers went to see him. While there, Charlie told Elaine that he hated his Uncle Mike and had hated living in Herminie with them after the murder. He said his uncle had taken away all of his photographs of his mother. He said that, when he grew up, he'd catch the man who had killed her. That was the last time Elaine had seen him.

Two hours after my wife and I had walked into Catherine Asperger's house, the interview ended. Just before we left, Elaine gave me three black-and-white snapshots in which she and Charlie were posing with some of the other kids in the old neighborhood. The photographs had been taken less than a year before the murder.

In return for the photographs, Elaine made me promise to tell her everything I found out about Charlie Zubryd. She seemed fascinated but a little puzzled that I was looking into the case. "Helen Zubryd," she said, "was a nobody. I didn't think people wrote books about folks like her."

7 *True Detective*

AFTER TALKING TO CATHERINE AND ELAINE ASPERGER, I realized that there is no statute of limitations on fear. Some thirty-three years after the murder, Catherine Asperger was still frightened by the memory, and Elaine was still afraid of Charlie. Although Helen Zubryd's murder was history, to those affected by it, the wounds were still fresh. I wondered how many others were still suffering from the events of that night.

As a former criminal investigator with a special interest in physical crime scene evidence, I was struck by the fact that so many people had visited Helen's body before the police arrived. Besides Charlie, Catherine, and Elaine, there had been Janice Todd, Dr. John Gaydos, and possibly John Syka — the man who owned the funeral home in Ambridge and ran the ambulance service. John Syka and Dr. Gaydos were alive, and I hoped they'd talk to me about that night and what had happened to Helen Zubryd.

The newspaper accounts of the crime scene and the physical evidence were meager and vague. To fully understand the crime, I'd have to get my hands on the crime scene photographs — assuming they had been taken — if they were still around.

Starved for more information, I read the article in the *True Detective* magazine Catherine Asperger had given me. Although it was a long, detailed account of the case, I couldn't be sure of its accuracy. I had read magazine stories like this before and had found stupendous errors and omissions. But for now, I would take what I could get; and in the article, I discovered much that I hadn't known, including details about the scene of the crime.

> **The police contingent, consisting of photographers, fingerprint men, and other officials, was headed by Allegheny Detectives Ted Botula and Francis Flannery. . . . Helen Zubryd lay on her back on the cement floor, her feet near the cellar stairs, her head close to the furnace.** *The hatchet was so firmly embedded in her skull that it took two police officers to pull it out* [**italics mine**].

That couldn't be correct. Detectives would not remove a fatal bullet at the scene of a shooting, and they would not pull a hatchet out of a murder victim's head. That's the kind of thing left to experts, such as forensic pathologists. If the police had removed the hatchet, *they* would have ruined any chance of getting latent fingerprints off the murder weapon. If that had been the case, it wouldn't have mattered if someone else had touched the hatchet first.

The article I was reading, called "Pennsylvania's Incredible Axe Murder," published in the July 1959 issue of *True Detective* (which that month featured "Beatnik Brunette in the Baby-Doll Nightie") had more information about the crime scene: "The bodice of her dress appeared to be intact. But a zipper at the side had been ripped from the cloth, and the skirt was raised so that she was nude from the waist to the knees." That couldn't be right, either. According to all of the newspaper accounts and Catherine Asperger's memory, Helen had been wearing blue jeans. The papers had described Helen's clothing as being in "disarray," and Catherine had said nothing about Helen being nude. I continued reading:

> **On the floor by the body lay a stout leather Army belt with a large brass buckle. It was**

picked up carefully and taken to the police laboratory for examination. . . . [A]ccording to Charles Zubryd, the belt had belonged to his father. The boy said he hadn't seen it for a long time. He supposed his mother had kept it in a closet where she stored most of his late father's effects. It seemed odd that Mrs. Zubryd would pick up this long-unused belt in an effort to ward off an attacker with a hatchet.

The laboratory men, after a thorough examination of the Zubryd basement and the position in which the dead body had lain, had come to the conclusion that the killer was, in all likelihood, left-handed. If he had not been, they reasoned, because of the spot where the body had lain, he would have struck the furnace with the uplifted hatchet. Thus, it appeared that Mrs. Zubryd had been struck from the left side.

According to the *True Detective* account, Botula had called Charlie's aunt and had asked to have the boy brought in for questioning. This didn't square with Botula's version, in which the aunt had called him for help.

A large portion of the *True Detective* article dealt with Dr. William McCabe's psychiatric evaluation of Charlie.

"All the tests," said McCabe, "proved to be within normal limits. Not that he could fool me, but I had all those tests done just to make sure.

The doctor said, further, that the boy was highly intelligent with an IQ of 116, that he was extremely sensitive and registered normal emotions.

"His confession," said Dr. McCabe, "was a simple case of brain washing, whether consciously or unconsciously done — plus the fantasy which all children, and particularly bright ones, indulge in.

"The boy," he said, "has built up this fantasy of murder from things he has heard and from reading the newspapers. He is most intelligent. He not only reads the papers but is interested in history and geography. He is able to read adult

texts in these subjects, and he reads other adult
books."

The doctor added that he thought it most
important that the boy be moved to another
section of the community where he would no
longer be subject to questioning or criticism
concerning his mother's death. Meanwhile, a
childless couple had made a request that they
be permitted to adopt the boy. This is for his
present guardian to decide.

There was nothing more in the article regarding the identity of
the couple who wanted Charlie and no indication that he had in fact
been adopted. The most fascinating part of the article had to do
with Charlie's behavior following his mother's murder, behavior
that had supposedly made Mike and Marge Zubryd — and Botula —
suspicious:

Some of the detectives, had, at one time, actually considered 8-year-old Charles the slayer of
his mother. On one occasion they interviewed
the boy in front of his parish priest, Father
[Josephat] Popovich. During that conversation
one officer had stated flatly that he believed little
Charles was [guilty of] matricide, however, at
the time, no one had given this theory much
credence. . . .

"He is often sullen and moody," said Harold
Kratsky [the magazine's fictitious name for
Mike Zubryd]. He won't talk to anyone. He acts
as if he's got something on his mind. He's a
queer kid."

They learned of another, and in the eyes of
the investigators, a far more suspicious circum-
stance. Charles, it appeared, was a religious
boy, a devout Catholic. But, according to the
Kratskys, since his mother's death he often appeared reluctant to receive Holy Communion
and when he did, he often became ill.

Now, before Holy Communion may be given,
the recipient must be shriven. In other words,
it is necessary for him first to attend the con-
fessional and rid himself of whatever sins may

lie upon his soul. It had occurred to the Kratskys—and it now occurred to the detectives—that Charles had hesitated to take communion primarily because he had been reluctant to go to confession.

Charles, it appeared, had always wanted to be a priest. He had been an altar boy at St. Mary's Church in Herminie. He went to confession regularly. "But," said Mrs. Stetter thoughtfully, "since his mother's death, he'd become sick sometimes before receiving communion."

There it was again—the sudden fear of a religious child before taking Holy Communion. The detectives took their report back to Chief Detective Pieper and District Attorney Boyle. It was decided to question Charles Zubryd again.

I didn't know what to make of Charlie's reluctance to receive Holy Communion and, upon doing so, becoming sick. I needed help and got it from Dr. Jim Drane, a member of Edinboro's Philosophy Department. I told him what I had learned about the case so far and gave him the *True Detective* article about Charlie and the murder. Dr. Drane, scholar, author, and teacher in the medical ethics field, is a former Jesuit priest who, earlier in his career, had studied violent behavior with Karl Menninger at the renowned Menninger Foundation.

I asked him if he thought a boy so young could have committed such a violent act, and he said it was possible but unusual. He talked about a "pool of hostility" that could build in a child who was in some way abused or abandoned. Normally, children repress their anger and their desire to strike out at a parent. They don't act on these impulses because they are afraid. Dr. Drane noted that Charlie may have felt abandoned during his father's illness and subsequent death, and his mechanism for repressing his anger could have eventually broken down. Dr. Drane said that Dr. McCabe's evaluation of Charlie seemed rather superficial with all of that talk about brainwashing and fantasizing. I asked Dr. Drane to assume for a moment that Charlie had murdered his mother and then asked him if Charlie, as a forty-year-old adult, could still be dangerous. He pointed out that psychiatry, as a model for understanding and explaining human behavior, had its weaknesses, and when it came to predicting future behavior, it was even more unreliable. He said it was quite possible that Charlie could have matured into a normal adult, particularly if he had received professional help along the way. But there was no way to know this for sure.

Dr. Drane suggested that, in my investigation of Charlie, I look for evidence of sexual abuse, abandonment, or both, events in Charlie's life that may have produced a "pool of hostility" that could have led to the murder of his mother.

❑ ❑ ❑

The day after my visit with Catherine and Elaine Asperger, I called Dr. John Gaydos, and he agreed to see me the next day. Sue and I drove to the doctor's spacious ranch-style home in an upper-class neighborhood nestled in the woods on the side of a hill near Sewickley. He greeted us like old friends and led us into his den where we could talk.

The seventy-one-year-old physician, who reminded me of a small-town doctor right out of a Norman Rockwell painting, re-membered getting a call that November night from a woman who said that Helen Zubryd had just hurt herself and was lying on the floor in her basement bleeding from the wound. The doctor didn't know how to get to Barley Road, so he agreed to meet the caller at the Pine Inn Tavern on Big Sewickley Creek Road. He then tele-phoned John Syka at his funeral home in Ambridge and asked him to rush to the Zubryd house in his ambulance. The doctor didn't know Helen was dead; nor did he know the identity of the person who had called him from the Zubryd house. About twenty minutes after getting the call, Dr. Gaydos met the caller at the tavern and fol-lowed her back to Barley Road.

Dr. Gaydos found Helen lying faceup on her basement floor with the hatchet stuck into her head. "I reached for that hatchet," he said, "and tried to pull it out, but it was in there too tight. It wouldn't budge."

I asked him to describe Helen's body, and he said, "Someone had pulled down her dungarees – she was fully exposed. I could see her pubic hair. Then all of a sudden I said to myself – 'What in the hell am I doing here?' That's when I picked up my bag and ran out of the basement. I ran straight to my car and drove home. I didn't wait for the ambulance or the police, and I didn't talk to anyone. I was scared to death. All I could think about was getting out of that place. I didn't tell the police I had touched the hatchet. No one had told me I was walking into a murder! I don't know how many times I've told that story at parties. I'll never forget it—I was scared to death."

I asked Dr. Gaydos if he knew who had called the county detective's office, and he replied that he didn't know. "It wasn't me," he said. "I didn't hang around there long enough to call anyone."

Dr. Gaydos said he hadn't known Helen Zubryd as well as he had known Helen's sister Mary and was also acquainted with Mary's daughter, Janice Todd, who had told him that, after Charlie Zubryd's father died, the boy insisted on sleeping with his mother. She also told him that the boy seemed preoccupied with sexual things—menstruation, reproduction—subjects of that nature, and that he had asked to see his mother naked. Janice Todd said that Helen had expressed concern over this.

I told Dr. Gaydos that I hadn't talked to Janice Todd. I'd like to, I said, but I wasn't sure how to approach her. I didn't want to call her up out of the blue. He said that Janice Todd wasn't the kind of person who would talk with a stranger about something so personal. "I'll call her for you," he said, "to break the ice. Give me a ring in a couple of days and I'll let you know what she says."

I thanked the doctor for his time and said I'd get back to him about Janice Todd. As we were leaving, I asked him what he had heard about the boy, Charlie Zubryd. "Not a thing," he replied. "But I'll tell you this: a lot of his relatives think he did it."

"What do *you* think?" I asked.

"Well, the police believed he did it; they made a pretty good case. He was a very strange boy."

"Did he do it?"

"He may have, yes."

❏ ❏ ❏

In an effort to get my hands on the police file on the case, I got in touch with a homicide detective in Pittsburgh who said he'd come check on it for me. He said the old Allegheny County detectives' case files had been moved to the county police department. He said he'd call me.

A couple of days later I called him. "Oh, yeah," he said. "I checked it out, and we don't have any of those old files. Our files only go back to 1960. The Zubryd stuff must still be over in the courthouse — probably up on the sixth floor. That's where they keep all of the old files. It's like an attic. If I were you, I'd call someone down at the D.A.'s office."

I called the D.A.'s office and talked with the chief deputy D.A., who said he would send someone up to the sixth floor to look for the Zubryd papers. The assistant prosecutor said he wasn't optimistic that they would still be there because he had heard that all of the old records had been destroyed in 1974 when the old county detective's office was dismantled and replaced by the new system. He said he'd get back to me. He didn't call me back, so the next day I called him. "Bad news," he said. "There's nothing up there. Those old files, including the Zubryd case, are gone."

I was more than a little disappointed, but I was also skeptical. I wasn't ready to give up on those files and realized that, if they were truly gone, it would be virtually impossible for me to get to the bottom of the Zubryd case. I needed to meet with the D.A. himself; the problem was, I didn't know him. But I did know someone who did, someone who might be able to arrange a meeting between myself and the D.A. I had known all along that getting those files wouldn't be easy, but I still hoped they were around somewhere. Since I wasn't a cop, and I didn't have access to police files — even old ones — I'd have to rely on others. I had always found this frustrating and, more often than not, disappointing.

8 John Syka

AMBRIDGE, PENNSYLVANIA, GOT ITS NAME FROM THE American Bridge Company, the first and one of the largest industrial plants built along the eastern bank of the Ohio River. In 1956, the town was a snake-shaped cluster of factories, power plants, slag piles, railroad yards, office buildings, stores, bowling alleys, beer joints, churches, schools, and homes — all squeezed between the river and the hills that lay fifteen miles north of Pittsburgh. The melting-pot city of 20,000 Poles, Hungarians, Czechoslovakians, Romanians, Russians, Greeks, and Italians, to name a few, called itself "the City of Churches"— there were twenty-five in all. Ambridge wasn't a clean town or very pretty, but it was a friendly place, and there were jobs; and if you didn't mind a little dirt and a smell in the air, it was a good place to live, work, and raise a family.

Syka's Funeral Home, two stories of brown brick, with a green shingled roof and a green twenty-foot aluminum canopy extending from the main entrance to the curb, sat on Lattimer Avenue at the south end of town. Lattimer Avenue paralleled Pennsylvania Route 65, which runs north and south along the river; if you follow Route 65 south, it takes you right into Pittsburgh. (In 1960, when John F. Kennedy came to western Pennsylvania to campaign for president, his motorcade rolled down Lattimer Avenue past Syka's Funeral Home. Following Kennedy's assassination, Lattimer Avenue became Kennedy Avenue. So much for Mr. Lattimer, whoever he was.)

John Syka and his family lived on the second floor of the big house, above the casket display room, embalming chamber, business office, lobby, and four viewing rooms. When he looked out his front windows, he saw Route 65, a half dozen factory buildings, four sets of Pennsylvania Railroad tracks, the brown waters of the Ohio River, and on the other side of the river, the tree-covered hills that stood between Ambridge and the town of Aliquippa. In November, with the leaves off the trees and without snow, the hills would have been as black as the giant mound of slag that ran between the river and the railroad tracks.

Mr. Syka owned one of the town's five funeral homes and operated an ambulance service, the one Dr. Gaydos had sent to the Zubryd house that night.

On a freezing day in February, Sue and I drove to Ambridge, where we talked with John Syka, a tall, lean, distinguished man in his seventies. He invited us into the funeral home and there, around a large conference table, told us what he remembered about the Zubryd murder.

He had received a telephone call about a quarter past eight that night from Dr. John Gaydos who said a woman who lived on Barley Road in Sewickley Township had cut herself in the head and needed emergency treatment. Dr. Gaydos didn't know the way to the house, so he had arranged to meet the victim's neighbor at the Pine Inn Tavern on Big Sewickley Creek Road. The neighbor said she would lead him back to the injured woman's house. Syka told the doctor that he knew how to find Barley Road and would get there with his ambulance as soon as he could. Twenty-five minutes after he spoke with Dr. Gaydos, John Syka drove his ambulance up Barley Road to the Zubryd house.

As he slowed to a stop where the street turned sharply to the right, a short, bony man approached his vehicle. Syka lowered his window and said, "I'm looking for the woman who's hurt. Is that the house?" He nodded in the direction of Mrs. Asperger's.

"I'm Elmer Skiles," the man replied. "I live over there," he said, pointing to his basement-foundation home. "The woman you wanna see lives down there." He gestured broadly with his arm. "She's got no driveway, so you'll hafta park it up here."

Syka asked if anyone had seen Dr. Gaydos.

"He ain't here no more," Skiles replied.

"What?"

"He was here, but he left."

"Did he see the woman?" Syka asked.

"Yeah, he went down, but he come running out of there like he seen the devil. He got into his car and took off like a bat out of hell. He didn't say nothin' to no one."

The mortician took a different route to Helen's basement than that taken by Catherine Asperger and the kids. Instead of walking across the front of Helen's house to her basement door, he strode through her backyard. He kept close to the house, and when he got a few feet from the end of the dwelling, he heard a sharp noise. It sounded like a chain rubbing against metal, and it gave him a start. He looked to his left and immediately relaxed — it was a dog that had wrapped his chain around the pole so many times he had virtually lashed himself to it. The hound stood there wagging his hind end and whimpering. Syka didn't have time to unwind the dog, so he rounded the corner and walked into the basement.

The moment Syka laid eyes on Helen, he knew that she had been murdered. However, unlike Dr. Gaydos who had apparently fled for his life, Syka — a mortician and accustomed to all manner of death — stood and calmly contemplated the scene. He knelt beside the body and looked closely at her forehead, where the knob-shaped hammer end of the hatchet poked out. The blade was buried completely into her skull. He noted the position of Helen's arms and legs and observed how the killer had ripped open and pulled down her blue jeans and panties, exposing her lower stomach, pubic triangle, and thighs. Helen Zubryd's dungarees and underwear, pulled to her knees like that, produced a savage and vulgar sight, one that even a mortician wouldn't likely forget.

It was clear that Helen never had a chance. This was not a medical emergency; it was a matter for the coroner and the police. With this in mind, Syka climbed the basement steps to Helen's kitchen, where he telephoned the Allegheny County coroner's office. He next dialed the local state police barracks and talked to a trooper who told him the murder fell within the jurisdiction of the Allegheny County detective's office. Syka hung up and called the county authorities. The officer who took his call said that he would immediately notify Henry Pieper (the chief county detective) and that homicide investigators would be dispatched to the scene at once.

❏ ❏ ❏

John Syka told us that he had been in Helen's basement with the county detectives and the crime scene technicians, who took photographs and combed the place for clues. His most vivid memory of that night was the hatchet. Someone at the scene had decided to take the tool out of Helen's head before she was hauled to the morgue. The job had fallen to the fingerprint technician, Pat McCormick, who tried but couldn't yank the tool out of her face. That's when Mr. Syka volunteered to hold Helen's head so McCormick could get both hands on the handle. After much tugging and pulling, the blade slipped out, leaving an angry gash in the victim's forehead. "That thing was really in there," Mr. Syka said.

I asked him if he thought Charlie could have been strong enough to sink the hatchet that deeply. Mr. Syka responded by telling us how difficult it had been for McCormick to pull it out. "The boy couldn't have done it," he said. "I don't think the boy could have ripped her blue jeans and panties either."

Since Mr. Syka didn't believe Charlie had killed his mother, I asked him if he had any idea who had. "No," he replied, "but whoever killed her must of been crazy."

Before we left the funeral home, Mr. Syka gave me, among other things, an old *Inside Detective* magazine that contained a story about

Helen Zubryd at 20. (Author's collection.)

Charlie Zubryd, at 2, with his parents, 1950. (Author's collection.)

Helen (at 28) and Joe Zubryd on their wedding day, July 1943. (Author's collection.)

Charlie Zubryd, at 7, with friends one year before his mother's murder. *Back row to Charlie's right,* Elaine Asperger, his best friend and next-door neighbor. (Author's collection.)

Helen Zubryd's house on Barley Road, Sewickley Township.
(Courtesy Allegheny County Detective's Office.)

Allegheny County detective Joe Start.
(Author's collection.)

Charlie Zubryd with his uncle Mike after the boy
testified at the Mar. 17, 1957 inquest into his
mother's death. (Courtesy *Pittsburgh Sun-Telegraph.*)

Chuck Duffy, at 14, with his adopted mother, Florence Duffy, 1962. (Author's collection.)

The Zubryd house, 1990. (Photo by author.)

The remains of the Skiles residence. (Photo by author.)

Chuck Duffy, 1989, at 41, his mother's age when she was murdered.
(Photo by author.)

Sixth Ave. and Morgan St., Brackenridge. Jerry Pacek found Lillian Stevick's body lying next to the cement steps running up the hill next to the DeLeonardis house, which is on the left corner. (Courtesy Allegheny County Detective's Office.)

Jerry Pacek at the corner of Seventh Ave. and Morgan St., Brackenridge, Nov. 19, 1958. Pacek is wearing the clothes he wore 36 hours earlier when Lillian Stevick was murdered down the street. (Courtesy Allegheny County Detective's Office.)

Stevick crime scene reenactment, Brackenridge, Nov. 19, 1958. Jerry Pacek is with Uldine Large, an Allegheny County detective who is playing the murder victim. (Courtesy Allegheny County Detective's Office.)

Stevick crime scene reenactment, Brackenridge. Jerry Pacek is showing the police how he had supposedly dragged the victim's body off the sidewalk into the DeLeonardis backyard. (Courtesy Allegheny County Detective's Office.)

Jerry Pacek is depicted showing detectives where he had found the hatchet, supposedly the Stevick murder weapon. When this photograph was taken (Nov. 24, 1958), Detective Botula knew the hatchet was not the murder weapon. (Courtesy Allegheny County Detective's Office.)

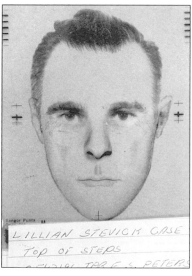

Police drawing of the man Jerry Pacek saw near Lillian Stevick's body on the night of her murder. (Courtesy Ed Peters, Pennsylvania State Police.)

Author Jim Fisher. (Photo by Ernest Erdeky.)

the Zubryd case. As Sue and I drove home that night, I thought about Mike and Marge Zubryd and wondered if they would talk to me about the case. They had heard Charlie confess and would know where he was and what he was doing. I had already looked them up in the phone book, but I was afraid to call. If I didn't go about it just right, I could lose them. Their cooperation was essential to my investigation. I felt that, without their help, I would never get to the bottom of this case.

9 Marge Zubryd

THANKS TO JOHN SYKA, I NOW KNEW THAT THE HATCHET had been pulled out of Helen at the scene by Pat McCormick, the man who was supposed to get the killer's prints off the hatchet handle. It was possible that McCormick had dusted the handle before yanking out the hatchet, but I doubted that. McCormick would probably have known that a porous, wooden surface, such as a hatchet handle, wouldn't respond well to fingerprint powder. The best way would have involved spraying the handle with a solution of silver nitrate then exposing the surface to ultraviolet light, a technique in existence since 1892 (though back then they used the sun). If there had been latents on the handle, they would have become visible as brown stains. Silver nitrate stains aren't lifted like dusted prints, they are photographed. Silver nitrate is usually applied in a crime lab not at the crime scene. If McCormick had dusted the handle, or if he had removed the hatchet without processing it with silver nitrate, which I suspected he had done, he had mishandled a vital piece of physical evidence.

I also had confirmation from Mr. Syka that Helen had been wearing blue jeans — not a dress as reported in the *True Detective* magazine Catherine Asperger had given me. The magazine had been correct about the hatchet, however, so the writer had gotten at least some of it right.

I read the June 1959 edition of *Inside Detective* magazine John Syka had given me. The Zubryd article was entitled "He Could Stare a Hole Through You" and painted Charlie as a spooky little kid who had suddenly turned murderous: "For two years after his mother was found brutally hatcheted to death, the boy seemed okay – going to school, watching TV, doing chores. The only funny thing was how he stared a hole through you."

I was becoming familiar with Ted Botula's style, and the article, a carefully put-together case against Charlie, had Ted Botula written all over it. For example, Catherine Asperger had this to say about the Zubryd dog: "Spot? I believe he was tied up outside. Come to think of it, I didn't hear him barking while Charlie was over here. Not even once, that I remember. I wonder why?" And this:

> While the hatchet was being wrapped up for its trip to the crime laboratory, and the fingerprint men carefully finished their job of covering the cellar, Botula was noting a curious fact; although it had been raining, there appeared to be no footprints outside except those which could be attributed to persons arriving after the murder.

I couldn't help but wonder how had Botula been able to make such a distinction among the footprints? I also noted that Botula's version of the events leading up to Charlie's confession were reflected in this article; it said that, in March 1959, "the aunt and uncle asked for advice from the County detectives who had worked on the murder. The detectives suggested that Charlie, ten years old by now, be brought in for an interview."

According to the article, "Police suffered a setback when lab tests produced no fingerprints or other helpful evidence from the murder weapon." I wasn't surprised.

The *Inside Detective* article mentioned Jim Flevaris, the Sewickley Township constable. Flevaris had been the part-time cop Mrs. Asperger, as a last resort, had tried to call that night. Flevaris lived on Barley Road, right up the street from the Asperger and Zubryd homes. According to the article, Flevaris had his own theory about who may have killed Helen:

> Sewickley Chief Flevaris believed that a sex ma-
> niac had entered the home with the purpose of
> attacking Mrs. Zubryd, and had started up the
> cellar stairs. She heard the noise and went to
> investigate its cause, the chief theorized.
>
> A neighborhood boy had once stolen some-
> thing from the Zubryd home, Flevaris learned.
> "She may have thought it was the same boy
> again," he commented. The chief felt the in-
> truder might have hidden behind the furnace to
> strike an initial blow from behind, and then
> had rained more blows on his unsuspecting vic-
> tim as she fell.
>
> The murderer might have been scared off by
> Charlie returning to the house.

Flevaris's theory made more sense to me than Botula's, but the writer of the article apparently didn't see it that way. He finished up the piece by laying out all of the evidence that supposedly pointed back to the house and Charlie. As far as he was concerned, it was cut-and-dried.

❏ ❏ ❏

I didn't know how Charlie's Uncle Mike and Aunt Marge would react to a stranger calling about Charlie and the murder of his mother. If they had put the case behind them, they wouldn't want some nosy college professor stirring up bad memories. I figured there was a good chance they wouldn't talk to me, particularly if I called up and hit them cold.

Zubryd is a rather unusual name. I checked the phone book for greater Pittsburgh and found only one Zubryd listed—a Harry Zubryd. I called that number and got lucky. Harry happened to be one of Mike's younger brothers, and he didn't mind talking about Mike or the murder.

Harry told me he was twenty-six when Helen was murdered and had been living with Mike and Marge at the Zubryd duplex in Keystone. Like Mike, he'd been attending trade school. Harry said that he heard about Charlie's confession on television and that he had never believed that Charlie killed his mother. Harry Zubryd and Charlie had lived under the same roof for a year, and there was no way, according to him, that Charlie could have killed anyone.

I asked Harry if his brother Mike thought that Charlie had killed Helen. He replied that he was certain Mike considered the boy innocent as well.

"Do you think Mike will talk to me?" I asked.

"Sure," Harry replied. "He'll be glad to."

"Do you and Mike ever talk about Charlie?"

"No. I can't remember the last time."

"Do you know where Charlie is?"

"The last I heard, Charlie was living in Columbus, Ohio. He has another name now." Harry paused for a moment then said, "It's Duffy. The people who adopted him are Duffys. I think one of his doctors took him after he confessed."

"Charlie Duffy," I said, trying out the name.

"He goes by 'Chuck'."

"Have you seen him since the adoption?"

"I saw him at my sister's funeral. That was the only time."

"When was that?" I asked. "And which sister?"

"Marion, about ten years ago."

So Marion Stetter was dead. "Did you talk to him?"

"Just to say hello."

"And you haven't heard anything about him since?"

"No."

"What kind of life was he living?"

"I don't know. He was alone at the funeral, and I don't think he said much to anyone. He didn't hang around to talk afterward."

"Have any of his relatives seen him since the funeral?"

"Not that I know of."

"Is there anything else you can tell me about Chuck?"

"Someone told me that the man who adopted Charlie, the doctor, died some time back."

"Is that all you know about him?"

"Yes."

"What did Charlie look like?"

"When he was a boy?"

"No, when he came back to the funeral."

"He was small and had blond hair. He was quiet — shy. He was nervous. It was embarrassing."

"Why was that?"

"Because people were uncomfortable around him. He was uncomfortable, too."

"Because of the murder?"

"Yes. Because he hadn't seen any of us since the murder."

"Who had told him that his Aunt Marion had died? Did someone from the family call him?"

"I don't know how he found out."

"What about Marion's husband, Tom? Where is he now?"

"I don't know that either. Tom moved somewhere after Marion died. How did you find out about this?" Harry asked.

"I came across the murder in an old newspaper clipping. I then went back and read up on the case. The murder was also written up in a couple of magazines."

"Boy," Harry said, "I'd like to see that stuff."

"I'll send you copies," I replied.

"Okay, and I'll talk to Mike, so when you call, he'll know who you are."

"You're sure he won't mind?" I asked.

"No problem."

I was elated. Mike and Marge Zubryd could tell me more about Charlie than anyone. They could solve many of the mysteries about the boy and the murder. The next day, I made copies of the newspaper and magazine articles and mailed them to Harry. I'd give him time to discuss the matter with Mike. I didn't want to jump the gun and catch Mike by surprise. So I would have to wait. That would be the hardest part — waiting.

❑ ❑ ❑

A week passed, and I resisted the urge to call the Zubryds. In the meantime, I recontacted Catherine and Elaine Asperger and John Syka for additional details. I also visited Helen's old house on Barley Road, looked at the church in Ambridge where her funeral service had been held, and drove down to Keystone to see the Zubryd family duplex where Charlie had lived with Mike and Marge after the murder.

I learned that Jim Flevaris, the part-time township patrolman who had lived up the road from Helen Zubryd and who had been at the murder scene that night, was still living in the Ambridge area, but he was now working in a used appliance store in downtown Ambridge. Sue and I drove down to Ambridge one evening, and the store is where we found him.

I introduced myself and my wife; then I asked him if he remembered the Zubryd murder case. "Hell yes," he said. "The boy did it. I knew the kid did it all along. I knew he was guilty that night."

"How did you know that?" I asked, surprised at his reply. According to one of the true-crime magazine articles, Flevaris had theorized the killer was an intruder.

"Easy. The boy lied."

"Oh?"

"Yeah. He said he saw her on the basement floor, but he couldn't have seen her from where he was standing."

"Where was that?"

"At the top of the steps."

"I thought he'd gone into the basement."

"No. And another thing — the kid said a *hatchet* fell on his mom. Well, I ask you this — how did he know that?"

"How did he know what?" I asked.

"How did he know it was a hatchet?"

"He saw the handle," I said.

"Yeah, but how did he know it was a *hatchet?*"

"What else could it have been?" Sue asked.

"Hell, it could have been anything — a masonry hammer, say. Lookie, if I'm gonna beat you — it's gonna be with the truth." I wasn't sure what Flevaris meant by that, but I later learned he was running for mayor of Bell Acres, and I figured it was one of his political slogans. It must have sounded good to him because he used it eight or nine times in our brief conversation.

"What about the Skiles brothers?" I asked.

"They didn't do it," Flevaris replied. "They lived across the street from me. What a mess. They didn't have no plumbing so they shit into buckets and dumped the slop out back. The wind would carry the smell over to my place. Both of them boys is dead. When their mom died, they were put into a home."

I thanked Jim Flevaris for his time. "What do you think happened to the boy?" I asked as we stepped out of the store and onto the sidewalk.

"I heard he went to prison," Flevaris replied.

❑ ❑ ❑

On a Saturday morning early in March, I picked up the phone and called Mike Zubryd's number. I figured Harry Zubryd had had plenty of time to break the ice. As it turned out, I couldn't have called at a more appropriate time. Marge Zubryd answered the phone, and when I gave her my name and started to identify myself, she interrupted me: "I know who you are, and I know what you want. Harry is standing right here, and he's talking to Mike. He has the articles you gave him, and Mike is telling him he doesn't want anything to do with this. If Mike had answered the phone, he would have hung up on you. He is very upset."

"What about you, Marge?" I asked. "Will you talk to me?"

"Wait a minute," she said. "Harry, get Mike out of here," she said to someone — presumably Harry — on her end. "Take him to the grocery store. After a pause, she came back to me. "I don't mind talking about it," she said. "What do you wanna know?"

I wasn't sure where to start. I knew I wouldn't be having long, casual talks with the Zubryds and felt this might be my one and only chance, so I jumped right in: "How come Mike won't talk?"

"You gotta understand, he went through hell. We both did. At first the police thought Mike did it — they thought he was having an affair with Helen. They fingerprinted him and put him on the lie detector. He's still hurt and angry about that. There's no way he'll talk about it."

"Did Charlie confess the way the papers say he did?"

"Yes. They took us into the D.A.'s office, and we heard him. Marion and Tom did too. He was so *convincing.*"

"You believed him, then?"

"Yes."

"Did Mike believe him?"

"We all did."

"Marion Stetter, did she believe it too?"

"Yes, at first. The next day, she called me and said she wasn't sure."

"What about you? Did you have doubts?"

"Yes, later. But Marion was sure [he was innocent]. I couldn't make up my mind."

"What about Mike?"

"He was convinced Charlie had killed her."

"How does he feel about it now?"

"He still thinks Charlie did it."

"What about the other Zubryds?"

"Except for Harry and Mike's sister Olga, they agree with Mike."

"But you don't?"

"Sometimes I think he confessed just to get away from us."

"So Charlie wasn't happy with you and Mike?"

"He hated us. He wanted to live with Marion. He always liked his Aunt Marion."

"What was Charlie like as a boy?"

"He was difficult."

"In what way?"

"He was moody and had to have his own way. He didn't say he didn't like living with us, he just sulked. Charlie wasn't a devil, but he wasn't an angel either."

"What else do you remember about him?"

"He was a sissy and shrewd. He could pit one of us against the other. He was very good at that."

"You say he was a sissy; what do you mean?"

"He acted like a girl."

"Did that bother Mike?"

"Yes."

"Why?"

"Mike didn't want him to be a queer."

"Is that what Mike thought would happen to Charlie?"

"Yes."

"How did you feel about that?"

"I didn't like the idea any more than Mike did."

"Were you ever afraid of Charlie?"

Marge laughed. "No, there was no reason."

"According to some newspaper accounts, you had telephoned Ted Botula and said you wanted detectives to talk to Charlie—because you thought he knew something about the murder."

"That's a lie," Marge snapped. "Botula had been calling *us,* and finally one day, he said, 'Bring the boy in, so we can talk to him.' We took Charlie that Saturday because we were off work that day."

"So Charlie hadn't made you suspicious?"

"No. When he confessed, it was a bigger shock to us than Helen's murder."

"Then bringing Charlie in for questioning had been Botula's idea?"

"Right. After the confession, Botula said he and his detectives had known all along that Charlie was guilty."

"Did Botula say how they had known that?"

"Botula said his men had found writing on a notepad near Helen's telephone. It read, 'I killed, I have killed, I will kill,' or something like that. Botula said it was Charlie's handwriting. He mentioned Helen's dog and said it didn't bark, so Helen must have known the killer."

"Did you know the dog?"

"The crazy thing never barked."

"How did Lou Glasso, the attorney, get into the case?"

"That was Marion. She had arranged it."

"What was Glasso like?"

"He was a real pain in the ass."

"I thought Mr. Glasso had taken Charlie's case without charging a fee. Didn't he do the work for nothing?"

"Yes. But he did it for the publicity. Glasso was a headline grabber."

"Harry Zubryd told me that a man named Duffy had adopted Charlie."

"That's right. His name was Frank Duffy. He wasn't a doctor, but he was a friend of Dr. McCabe's. He was some kind of psychologist. Lou Glasso had arranged it."

"Where do the Duffys live?"

"Last I heard, Bridgeville. Frank Duffy is dead. I'm not sure where his widow [Florence] is."

"Where is Bridgeville?"

"It's near Pittsburgh."

"Is it in Allegheny County?"

"Yes. It's west of the city."

"Have you kept in touch with Charlie?"

"He goes by Chuck, now."

"Sorry. Have you been in touch?"

"No."

"When's the last time you saw him?"

"We saw him at Marion's funeral."

"Where was that held?"

"In East Liberty."

"When was that?"

"That was in 1979. Marion was only fifty-eight when she died."

"How did Charlie find out about that?"

"Marion was dying and didn't have much time. She had been thinking about Chuck and wanted to see him. Tom got Chuck's number from Florence Duffy, and a month before Marion died, Chuck visited her. Tom invited him to the funeral."

I asked if that was the first time she had seen him since his confession and hospital stay, and she said it was.

"What were your impressions of him?"

"To be honest, he looked gay."

"In what way?"

"The way he dressed."

"How was that?"

"He wore a formfitting coat, tight pants, patent leather shoes, and had a bunch of rings on his hands. I'm not saying I was surprised."

"Was it just his clothing?"

"Oh, no. He acted gay; he was still the sissy."

"What did Mike think of Chuck?"

"Same thing."

"Did Chuck go to the funeral home to see Marion?"

"Yes."

"Did he go to the cemetery?"

"Yes."

"And then what did he do?"

"I think he went home or over to his mother's house in Bridgeville."

"How did Mike respond to Chuck when he saw him?"

"Mike didn't want to have anything to do with him."

"Did they talk?"

"I don't think so," Marge said.

"Mike completely ignored him?"

"Yes."

"Did you and Mike know that Chuck was coming to the funeral?"

"No. It was a complete surprise; we were shocked to see him."

"What about the other relatives?"

"What about them?"

"Were they happy to see Chuck after all those years?"

"No. They felt the same way. Chuck had cousins there who didn't even know who he was."

"How did Chuck react to you?"

"He wasn't very warm."

"Was he nervous?"

"Yes. He didn't have much to say."

"Did he make people uncomfortable?"

"Yes."

"It sounded like Chuck had been thoroughly rejected by his family. Is that correct?"

"Yes, absolutely."

"Have you seen or heard from him since?"

"No."

"Do you know where he is living now?"

"No. A couple of years ago his grandmother, Katherine Zubryd, died. We tried to find him but couldn't."

"Where did you look?"

"We had a number for him in Columbus, Ohio. We tried that number but didn't get any answer. We had heard he owned a store in Columbus, and someone said it had gone bankrupt. We also heard that Chuck had gone to Florida or someplace like that. No one in the family really knew anything about him."

"So Chuck doesn't know that his grandmother is dead?"

"I guess not."

"And you've seen him only once in thirty years?"

"That's right."

"And you don't have any idea whatsoever where he could be now?"

"No idea."

"Is Marion's husband, Tom Stetter, still alive?"

"Yes."

"Where is Tom living?"

"I don't know. After Marion died, he moved away, married again, and has not been in touch with the family."

"Do you expect to hear from Chuck ever again?"

"No."

"Thank you, Marge. I'm sorry I upset Mike."

"He'll get over it. Can I ask you a question?"

"Sure."

"What's your interest in this?"

"What do you mean?" I asked.

"What's in it for you?"

"Nothing."

"Why are you digging all this up now? What's the point?"

"I'm trying to find out if Chuck killed his mother."

"What difference does that make now?"

"It seems to me it would make a lot of difference to Chuck, and if he didn't do it, to the guy who did."

"Harry said you're writing a book on the case."

"I might. It depends on what I find out. If I come across anything, would you want to know about it?"

"Sure."

"Then I can call again?"

"Yes — but don't call when Mike is home."

"When would be a good time?" I asked.

"Around 4:3o in the afternoon — before Mike gets home from work."

"Thanks," I said.

"Bye," she said.

I sat at my desk thinking about Chuck. The rest of the day, I thought of little else. I thought of the day I would find Chuck and make my approach; but first, I wanted a shot at someone else. I was now ready to talk to Ted Botula.

10 Ted Botula

I STARTED MY BACKGROUND INVESTIGATION OF TED Botula by going back to the library and reading old newspaper articles about him and his cases. I looked at the *Pittsburgh Press* from 1956 to 1960, and whenever I came across a Ted Botula murder case, I checked the story in Pittsburgh's other two papers, the *Post-Gazette* and the *Sun-Telegraph*.

In reviewing Botula's cases, I noticed that his investigations seemed thorough and professional. He must have been on good terms with the media because his cases were well covered in the press. In fact, the news articles about his cases contained investigative details not normally found in newspaper reportage. For example, whenever someone confessed, details of that confession would wind up in the papers. I also noticed that Ted liked to have his subjects reenact their crimes in front of relatives, the D.A., the coroner, and in some cases, reporters. In Botula's day, defense attorneys did not always have quick access to the accused; as a result, confessions were easier to obtain, and Ted liked to get as many confessions out of a subject as he could. A person might take back one confession, but repudiating several was much more difficult. When Botula had a suspect dig a hole for himself, he made him dig it deep.

As a result of the confessions, crime reenactments, and Botula's relationship with the press, he was, if not the Pittsburgh area's most successful detective, its most visible.

In 1956, Botula would have been forty-five and employed by the county detective's office eight years, having served under two D.A.s before Edward Boyle. Botula, like everyone else on the county squad, had gotten the job through political pull. He had begun his law enforcement career as a city parks patrolman in Pittsburgh and had caught the eye of the Allegheny County sheriff who had recommended him to the D.A., a Democrat. The next prosecutor had been a Republican, so to save his job, Botula had switched his party registration; then he switched back when Boyle, a Democrat, was elected in 1956. But the reason Botula had been able to stick around so long had as much to do with his ability as his politics. He wasn't a college man, and no one ever accused Teddy of having a brilliant, investigative mind, but Botula was streetwise and knew how to use informants, the polygraph, the crime lab, and if all else failed, bullshit. Botula knew the ropes and did what was necessary to get the job done.

Although only a sergeant, Botula was the county's top homicide detective, and that gave him status and prestige and gained him the respect he needed to control his men. He also knew how to cultivate and take advantage of contacts and friends within the media, in politics, and in other law enforcement agencies, such as the Pittsburgh Police Department and the Allegheny County sheriff's office.

Besides reading about Botula in the papers, I talked to several ex-cops and detectives who had worked with him over the years.

The people I spoke to all remember Botula the same way — there was no disagreement when it came to his personality, motives, and behavior. Botula was many things, but he wasn't an enigma. For Ted Botula, being a homicide detective meant glamor, glory, and romance. Being a detective, a homicide investigator, was his religion, his identity, his whole life. He walked, talked, and dressed the part. In fact, he played the role of detective as effectively as his cinematic counterpart and look-alike, Humphrey Bogart. Blessed with a deep, golden voice, Botula *was* Bogart — Sam Spade with a Pittsburgh accent.

No one in Pittsburgh dressed better than Ted Botula, not even Eddie Boyle. Ted bought expensive clothing. The twenty or so suits he owned, as well as all of his dress shirts, and there were dozens of those, had been carefully fashioned at the Wohlmouth Tailor Shop on Pittsburgh's Fifth Avenue, directly across from the courthouse. Botula preferred Florsheim shoes and, at any given time, possessed ten pairs — half for summer, the rest for winter. His jewelry box was full of silver and gold; and in his closet hung dozens of silk ties, each matching a handkerchief of the same pattern, color, and cloth. His outfits were expensive but not flashy, and he dressed up fully whenever he was called to a crime scene, day or night, because he believed that civilians were impressed by a well-dressed detective.

This wiry, exquisitely attired detective with the thinning brown hair, prominent nose, and fierce, busy eyes, was an ambitious cop climbing the law enforcement ladder two rungs at a time. If there was anyone ready and willing to take on a big case, it was Botula, or "Teddy" as his fellow detectives called him.

Botula quit the county detectives in 1963 to become superintendent of the Allegheny County Workhouse, a prison facility that housed fifteen hundred felons. I wondered how many of these inmates could thank Ted Botula for their living quarters. The prison was torn down in 1971, the year Botula became a member of the Allegheny County Parole Board, a position he held until his retirement in 1976.

During Ted's forty years in Allegheny County law enforcement, he had known hundreds of cops, crooks, lawyers, bail bondsmen, informants, judges, and jailers; and he had been involved, as a city parks patrolman, homicide detective, and corrections official, in hundreds of criminal cases.

He was now seventy-seven, and I wondered what, if anything, he would remember about the murder of Helen Zubryd and the confession of her son Charlie.

❏ ❏ ❏

Early one evening, I called Ted Botula and asked him if I could meet with him at his house to discuss the Zubryd murder. He said he'd be glad to see me. The following afternoon, I was in his living room talking to him about the case.

Ted was extremely friendly and interested in what I was doing. He seemed open and eager to talk about himself, his earlier life, and his long and varied career. He told me about his parents and his own beginning, and I was struck by how similar his background was to Helen Zubryd's.

Botula's father had been a coal miner in Cokeburg, a mining village just off Pennsylvania Route 40 — the old National Pike — in Washington County, twenty miles south of downtown Pittsburgh. Botula's parents had come to America from Austria about the time the Sudiks had come over, and like Helen, he was the youngest in the family with nine brothers and sisters. His mother, a trained midwife, had delivered five hundred babies around Cokeburg. She was rarely paid cash for her services; payment usually came in the form of chickens or apples. In 1924, when Ted was fifteen, at a time when the dreaded "Coal and Iron Police" were cracking the heads of striking coal miners, his father moved the family to Pittsburgh, where Ted attended and graduated from Peabody High School. Ted met his wife in Pittsburgh, a woman with a degree from the University of Pittsburgh, and they had two sons. Life had been kinder to Ted than to Helen. He had gotten an education, a good-paying job, and a spouse who had helped him get ahead.

Although disabled by a bad back and now bald, Botula was still a vigorous, intense man with a mind that was still sharp and a voice that commanded attention. We talked about some of his most famous cases, and I was impressed with how vividly he remembered them. I liked Ted immediately, enjoyed talking with him about the old days, and could sense that he liked me. I wasn't sure, at that point, if Ted or anyone else had framed Charlie Zubryd because I had no way of knowing for certain if Charlie was innocent. And even if he had been innocent, Botula may have honestly believed otherwise. Making a mistake is one thing; framing someone is another story. Still, I was a little uneasy liking Ted so much and getting him to like me. I didn't want to play Joe McGinniss, the author of *Fatal Vision*, to Botula's Jeffrey MacDonald, the army doctor who is serving three consecutive life sentences for the murders of his pregnant wife and two daughters in 1970. MacDonald had been led to believe that *Fatal Vision* would support his claim of innocence. It did not. McGinniss had changed his opinion about MacDonald's guilt but did not inform MacDonald and had portrayed MacDonald as a psychopathic killer. I didn't want to gain Botula's cooperation under false pretenses and promised myself that, if at any point I began to believe that Charlie was innocent, I'd tell Botula and let him decide whether he wanted to continue our relationship.

When Ted got around to discussing the Zubryd case, he started by explaining how he had come to interrogate the boy. "I got an interesting call from the boy's Aunt Marge. She called us and said, 'You better get this little monster out of here!'"

"I take it she was referring to Charlie."

"Yes. He went to live with them after the murder. He was acting strange. They wanted us to have a talk with him."

"About what?"

"Maybe he knew something about the murder."

"Were you surprised?"

"We'd been thinking about him."

"That he did it?"

"I thought about this during the investigation — whether he had the strength to force that hatchet into her head."

"Why did you suspect him?"

"He was cool, he didn't show emotion. He didn't express himself unless you asked him. He never cried."

"Is that it?"

"The dog didn't sound an alarm. There was no disturbance in the house. And we found the belt the late father had used as a disciplinary article."

"What do you think happened?"

"In reconstructing the crime — she went to chastise him, and he ran into the cellar. She chased him and he picked up the ax as she retreated. He hit her on the back of the head. She fell to the floor, and he dragged her to the furnace. We found impressions of a checkered cloth shirt on the furnace. The pattern was similar to what the boy had on that night."

"So you suspected him from the beginning?"

"Yes. We felt right along there was a relationship between the boy and his mother that wasn't aboveboard. He was knowledgeable about reproduction."

"You suspected incest?"

"That may have been it. Neighbors said he slept with her. He was very advanced for his age. He knew how to type, and he was very smart."

"Besides the hatchet, what else do you recall about the body?"

"The only thing we noticed was a tear in her pants — the right leg — up to her knee."

"Any fingerprints on the hatchet?"

"No luck on that. That was completely clear."

"Did you arrest the Skiles brothers?"

"Yes. They appeared to be handicapped mentally. They were taken in and examined then freed. They had a friendly relationship with Mrs. Zubryd."

"They didn't do it?"

"No. I just remembered something funny," Botula said.

"Tell me."

"It's about one of the retarded men — one of the Skiles boys."

"What?"

"We needed pubic hair samples from them, so I asked the county detective if he had gotten any. 'No,' he says, then reaches over and sticks his hand in the suspect's fly — which was partially opened because he was wearing jail coveralls — and pulled out a handful of hair. 'I got some now,' he said." Botula convulsed with laughter. "I told the son of a bitch that wasn't the way to do it — I was really pissed. He didn't know any better."

"I don't imagine the suspect liked it much."

"No, he was scared shitless. Those boys were very, very retarded — both of them. And you should have seen the hole they lived in — it was something."

"You're sure they didn't kill Helen?"

"They didn't do it."

"But you thought Charlie had?"

"Yes."

"Was the hatchet sunk deep into her head?"

"Yes. I go back to the time he chopped a tree in his backyard. Now, the tree didn't fall, but the chop wounds were so accurate you'd think an adult did this. They were very professional chops."

"So he had the strength?"

"Well, my personal feeling is — he did have the strength to chop that ax into her head solidly. I'm thinking of the tissues sealing the ax blade to make it difficult to remove it. Do you follow what I'm saying?"

"Not exactly."

"In other words, it was like vulcanizing that blade into her skull. That would be something to think about."

"Was it Marge Zubryd who called you on that day?"

"Yes. She said the boy was uncontrollable. They brought him in. We called a priest to come over and be with him in the room when we questioned him."

"In the polygraph room?"

"Yes, we used the polygraph room as an interrogation room. Detective Flannery and I talked to the boy about twenty to thirty minutes. The priest was in the room with us. After we talked to him for twenty to thirty minutes, we left him alone in the room. We sat him at a table and gave him a piece of paper and a pencil. Before we left him alone in there, we asked him to write down what he knew about the case, or what was bothering him, or something like that. We left him in there for a little while then came back. He had written one line on the paper. This is what he wrote: 'If I killed my mother I must have blacked out.' That's all."

"Did he confess fully after that?"

"Yes — he told his aunts and uncles what he had done."

"What about Charlie being left-handed? Did that figure into anything?"

"No. No."

"What happened to Charlie after he said he had blacked out and then confessed?"

"Eddie Boyle, the D.A., wouldn't press the case. We heard nothing from him. The psychiatrists — McCabe and them — said Charlie didn't do it. McCabe was nuts himself. McCabe thought the kid made the whole thing up."

"How come Boyle didn't push the case?"

"Eddie Boyle wasn't operating on all six cylinders. He had a bad habit with the booze. After that, I lost interest in the case."

"Do you think Charlie did it?"

"Yes. She had caught him wearing one of her bras. He also wore her lipstick. She got very annoyed over that."

"Did it bother you that the boy was so young when he supposedly did it?"

"We heard about a murder in Long Island where a five-year-old boy killed his parents. You never know."

"Did you keep track of the boy after you closed the case?"

"No. I heard he was adopted. I got a call a few years ago from a guy who said he was Gary Ted Williams. Have you heard of him?"

"No. Why?"

"This guy, Williams, said he wrote songs about famous criminals. He asked me a lot of questions about the Zubryd case. He said he was calling from Los Angeles, and we probably talked for an hour. He wanted to know if the case was still open. Then a week later, this record album comes in the mail." Botula reached down and picked up an album that had been leaning against the side of his chair. He handed it to me. "Read the back," he said, with a smile.

I flipped the album over, and on the back, someone had written: "To Ted Botula — in appreciation of our interesting talks about one of our favorite cases. From your friend, Gary Ted Williams." The album was entitled "Murderers, Mysteries and Man Hunters: Eleven True Ballads Written and Sung by Gary Williams." I handed the album back to Botula.

"I think Gary Ted Williams is Charlie Zubryd," Botula said. He offered me the album, and I took it back with renewed interest. The cover contained photographs of John Dillinger, Jack the Ripper, Black Bart, Al Capone, Lizzie Borden, and Gary Ted Williams himself. On the back of the album, there were two photographs of Williams posing with a couple of old-time outlaws. One of the pictures, showing a younger Williams, at perhaps twenty, was dated 1961. Charlie Zubryd, in 1961, would have been thirteen. I pointed this out to Ted who shrugged his shoulders and said, "Anyone could have fudged that date. Look who he's next to — Lizzie Borden." Botula laughed. "You ought to check this out."

"I will," I said. Charlie Zubryd growing up to be a singer and writer of crime ballads was something I hadn't anticipated.

"He was a strange kid," Botula muttered. "Very cool."

"Whatever happened to Henry Pieper?"

"He died about ten years ago."

"Was he a good detective?"

"No. He was a nice guy, but he didn't know anything about detective work."

"What about Detective Flannery?"

"I called him 'Francy,'" Botula replied. "He's dead."

"What about the fingerprint man — Pat McCormick?"

"We called him 'The Rug.'" Botula laughed. He explained, "Pat was completely bald from some disease he got when he was a kid. He wore this big red wig that was always sliding around on his head — like a rug. He was a nice guy — always happy, always in a good mood."

"Is he —"

"Yeah — they're all dead."

"The polygraph man?"

"Charlie McInerney — him too, and of course Eddie Boyle."

"John Syka is alive," I said to brighten things up a bit. "Do you remember him?"

"Sure — he had the funeral home in Ambridge. I had detectives at the funeral — I even had a guy watching Helen Zubryd's casket."

"What for?"

"To see how people acted — emotionally."

"The detective just stood there and watched?"

"No, he was behind a curtain, peeking out."

"Do you remember who that was?"

"Joe Start. I called him 'Junior.' He was a good one."

That was a new name. "I guess he's dead too?" I asked.

"No, he lives in Sewickley. I'm sure he'll talk to you about the case. Have you talked to the woman who grabbed the hatchet and tried to pull it out?"

"No. I believe that was Janice Todd, the victim's niece."

"Maybe she'll talk to you," Botula said. "I think she lives in Bell Acres."

"Did Pat McCormick — The Rug — take the hatchet out of Helen's head at the scene?"

"Yes — he put a towel around the handle so he wouldn't mess up the prints."

"Why did he do that?"

"It was gonna come out sooner or later. It was stuck in there good. The Rug had a hard time getting it out. There wasn't much blood, though."

"Had Helen been raped?"

"No. There was no evidence of that."

"Who ripped her blue jeans?"

"The boy."

"Why?"

"He was smart."

"You mean he did that to throw you off the track?" I asked.

"Yeah."

"Did Eddie Boyle have a lot of good detectives working for him back then?"

"No. Most of the men had no experience at all—at least not as detectives. One guy had been the mayor's chauffeur. These guys were on the job because they had political pull. Our captain, the guy in charge of investigations, had retired from the city police as head of the patrol division. He was not only the stupidest man I had ever known, he didn't know anything about criminal investigation."

"Only in America," I said, "could a stupid man with no experience in criminal investigations become captain of detectives."

Botula laughed. "That's the way it was."

"You mentioned Joe Start."

"Joe knew what he was doing. He worked with a big, happy-go-lucky guy named Joe Carmody—they were quite a pair. They covered Sewickley Township. That was their district, so the Zubryd case was officially theirs."

"Is Carmody alive?"

"No. He was funny and sloppy—nothing ever fit the guy. He had been a uniformed cop with the city, worked the Liberty Tunnels in Mt. Washington. He was lazy as hell but a nice guy. He was very funny."

"Tell me about Joe Start."

"He was a tall, lean kid with a crew cut, a flattop. People liked him. He'd been on the force about eight years. Before that he had been a military policeman. Joe and I came on the job together, the same year, but I was older, had more experience. So I started as a detective first grade. Joe started as a detective junior grade. That's why I called him 'Junior.'" Botula laughed, "Hell, the guy was six-two. He and Carmody were good friends."

"Was Joe Start present when Charlie confessed?"

"I don't think so," Botula said. "Joe had been shot, you know."

"I didn't know," I said.

"Yeah — he was just a rookie. He and two other county detectives were after a guy named Ed DePofi — a burglar who had shot two Bethel Township patrolmen. Joe and them were at DePofi's house waiting for him when three guys walked up. Eddie Burke, the assistant chief, was inside the house, and Joe Start and his partner were hiding outside. When Start and the other detective jumped out of the bushes, the three guys took off with Joe Start running after them. That's when Eddie Burke opened fire with his Thompson submachine gun. One of the bullets hit Joe in the back. It was a .45. One of the guys Joe was chasing also got shot — by Burke. Everybody thought Joe was gonna die. He was in the hospital a long time but got back on the job within a year. He was okay after that. The bullet never came out."

"I'd like to meet Joe Start," I said.

"Yeah — you'd like him," Botula said. "Hey, you wanna hear something funny?"

"Sure."

"It's about Joe Start."

"Okay."

"One summer Joe Start and Joe Carmody were up in Sewickley looking for a gun this murder suspect had tossed into the Ohio River. They were up there to drag the river with this big magnet we'd gotten from Westinghouse. The thing weighed a ton, and after a day out on the river baking in the sun, Carmody decided to forget the magnet and go out there with a case of beer. I didn't hear from those guys for a week, so I called up there and asked the chief of the Sewickley Police Department to check on them. The chief called me back and said he had a message from Joe Start. I said — 'What is it?' And he says — 'Tell that son of a bitch the air force lost a B-25 in this river, and we're out here looking for a fucking revolver!'" Botula roared.

"I think the B-25 went into the Monongahela," I said; then I felt foolish for saying it.

Botula, still laughing, waved his hand. "What the fuck," he said. "Those guys were a laugh a minute."

I had given Ted a pretty good grilling and was packing up to go. I promised to let him know if Charlie Zubryd had turned into Gary Ted Williams, and as I headed for the door Ted handed me the album. "Don't forget this," he said. "And say hello to Joe Start."

"I will," I replied, as I started down the steps to my car.

Charlie Zubryd a folksinger? I had many questions. To start, I liked Ted Botula and couldn't imagine him framing a boy like Charlie. On the other hand, I couldn't imagine a boy like Charlie murdering his mother. According to Botula, Marge Zubryd had called him up and said, "Get this monster out of here!" This was not how Marge was telling it. Who was lying? Botula had also hinted at sexual abuse. I found this about as likely as Charlie growing up and becoming a singer of crime ballads. But, again, what was the truth? I had a lot to think about.

11 The Futile Paper Chase and Janice Todd

THE DAY AFTER MY TALK WITH TED BOTULA, JOHN Nee, former Pittsburgh police officer and criminal justice professor at Mercyhurst College in Erie, Pennsylvania, the man who had been supplying me with background information on Ted Botula, Eddie Boyle, and the old Allegheny County detective's office, called to say he had managed to get me an appointment with Allegheny County District Attorney Bob Colville. Colville would know where to look for the Zubryd case file and was the only person who could grant me permission to look at it.

The next morning, John and I were in Pittsburgh at the D.A.'s office talking to Colville while two members of his staff were up on the sixth floor of the courthouse searching for the file. They didn't find it. Colville said he wasn't surprised because, when he took office in 1977, he had ordered the closed cases from the old Allegheny County detective's office taken to the morgue and burned. If the Zubryd file was a closed case, it would have been destroyed along with the rest, hatchet and all. So much for that.

A few days later, I drove to Ambridge and talked to Genevieve Settino, the lawyer who drew up Helen Zubryd's will and brought Lou Glasso into the case. I thought maybe Glasso had given Genevieve a copy of his file on Charlie, a file that might have included important police documents. He hadn't; she had no idea where I could find Lou Glasso's papers. In fact, she doubted they existed.

I called Lou Glasso's daughter, Yolanda, who operated a Montessori school on the site of the Glasso family estate in Glenshaw. She remembered that Charlie had stayed with her family for the three months following his release from the hospital, but she knew nothing of her father's papers. Yolanda said her dad lived in Florida for several years prior to his death. She gave me the name of her father's former legal secretary. I called the woman, but she said she quit working for Glasso in 1958. Since Charlie had confessed in 1959, she had no knowledge of the Zubryd case and couldn't even guess where Mr. Glasso's papers would be. She did give me the name of the secretary who had replaced her, but when I checked around, I learned that this woman was dead.

When I tried to get a copy of Helen's autopsy report, the records man at the county morgue told me I was a little late. They didn't keep autopsy files before 1966. When I asked what happened to the old ones, he replied, "Who knows?" then hung up.

❏ ❏ ❏

Having hit the wall on the paper chase, I called Dr. John Gaydos to see if he had asked Janice Todd about talking to me. He said he had, and although Janice was nervous about the idea, I could give her a call. Good news, at last.

I telephoned Janice that evening; and the following afternoon, Sue and I went to her home. The Todds lived in a carefully maintained, red-brick house in a slightly rural, middle-class neighborhood.

Socially and economically, the Todds fit right smack in the middle of the middle class. John, a large-boned, muscular man of average height, was a small-time contractor. He kept his gray hair cropped short and had an open, friendly face that reddened easily. Janice, an impeccably groomed housewife and grandmother with eyeglasses and curly short hair, took care of things at home, including answering the phone and taking business messages for John. Her wide, pleasant face, plumpish physique, and wary stiffness in the presence of people outside her family gave her an old-world quality that was quite common in Ambridge and other towns like it in western Pennsylvania. Janice's life was her family, her church (Catholic), and her home. Although she was Charlie's cousin, she had been more like his aunt. He had called her Aunt "Nin."

Janice *was* nervous, and I couldn't get over the feeling that we were about to discuss some horrible thing that had happened last week. Janice said that she and Helen had been very close — like sisters — and when Helen was murdered like that — in her own house — it was almost too much for her to handle. A couple of years after the murder, when Janice and John heard on the radio that Charlie had confessed, Janice took an emotional spill from which she has never fully recovered. To this day, she cannot think about Helen or Charlie without getting depressed. The decision to talk to me had not come easily and was going to be extremely difficult. Janice still had visions of Helen running from her killer, fearing for her life. She said that a county detective had told her that Helen had died instantly and without pain. Thank God for that.

Since Charlie's confession, thinking about him has been pure agony. Janice said she has never wanted to believe that Charlie had done it, but she has never been able to get over the fact that he had confessed to it. She said she has struggled with this question for more than thirty years.

Charlie's adoption outside the family was another touchy subject. Janice has always felt guilty about that. One day he was family, and the next day he wasn't. He was such a nice little guy, and the next thing she knew, he was gone. When Helen, Joe, and Charlie were living with the Todds while their house on Barley Road was being repaired after the 1952 gas explosion, Charlie, then about four, liked to carry a little red purse and a matching umbrella around the house. Janice said, "It was the cutest thing."

Janice recalled the night Helen was killed as though it were yesterday. After getting a frantic call from Marion Stetter, she, John, and their daughter, Debbie, climbed into their car and drove to Helen's house. That's when Janice walked into the basement and found Helen.

When she saw the hatchet sticking out of Helen's forehead, she instinctively grabbed the handle to pull it out. It was in there so tightly it wouldn't move. Terrified, Janice ran upstairs and bolted out the front door, screaming for help. That's when she saw Mr. and Mrs. Elmer Skiles driving down Barley Road in their pickup truck. "Why are they leaving when people should be coming?" she thought. Janice said she still asks herself that question and wonders if Elmer Skiles, or one of his retarded sons, had anything to do with Helen's murder. Maybe the old man was covering for his boys, and maybe that was why his heart gave out—under the strain. Janice asked me what had become of Elmer, Jr., and James, and I told her Elmer, Jr., was dead. I also said that I'd gotten in touch with a member of the Skiles family who had refused to talk to me about the murder.

Janice said she's lived all this time with the knowledge that she had destroyed valuable fingerprint evidence. I told her that Dr. Gaydos had also grabbed the hatchet and that the police probably wouldn't have gotten anything off of it anyway. Janice said she hadn't known that and fell silent for a few minutes. I wondered what she was thinking, but I didn't ask.

Janice said she has never forgotten what Charlie said the night she and her husband arrived at the house. "He came running out of Mrs. Asperger's and screamed, 'Don't go in there Nin. There's so much blood, it will make you sick!'" Charlie's words had been rambling around in Janice's head for thirty years, and she didn't think she'd ever be able to put the memory of that night behind her.

Sometime after Charlie's confession, Janice got word that a man named Duffy, one of the psychiatrists who had examined Charlie, she thought, had adopted him. The idea of a stranger, especially a psychiatrist, taking the boy—even under those circumstances—didn't sit well with Janice.

Unable to resolve the question of Charlie's guilt or innocence, she had gone to Dr. John Gaydos shortly after the boy confessed to find out if an eight-year-old boy was capable of killing his mother. Dr. Gaydos opened one of his medical journals and pointed to a case in which a boy that young had in fact committed such a crime.

That was *not* what Janice wanted to hear and made her feel worse. A few years later, she ran into Father Josephat Popovich, the pastor of the church in Herminie where Charlie had been an altar boy. Janice pulled the priest aside to ask him whether he thought Charlie had done it. Father Popovich became quite nervous and made it clear that he did not wish to discuss the subject, leaving Janice with the feeling that he thought Charlie was guilty. After that, Janice quit asking questions.

Janice didn't see Charlie or hear from him for the next twenty years, but he was never far from her mind. On January 25, 1980, her father, Nicholas Philips, died. Janice wanted to notify Charlie of his death, but she didn't want to invite him to the funeral without first consulting with her mother and her sisters. A family meeting was held to discuss Charlie, and it was decided that Janice would try to reach him. Although they were doing this for Charlie's sake, they were also curious about him, and the funeral would provide an excellent opportunity to find out what kind of person he had become. It was also decided that, if Charlie did come back, no one would mention Helen or the murder. Those two subjects would be strictly taboo.

Although Janice had no idea where Charlie was or what he had been doing all these years, finding him was easy. She called Florence Duffy, Charlie's adoptive mother, who gave her Charlie's phone number. Charlie had been living and working in Columbus, Ohio, less than 150 miles away. Janice called Charlie, or Chuck, and he said he would come to the funeral. That's all it took, two phone calls.

The next day, Charlie and his mother showed up at Syka's Funeral Home in Ambridge. Charlie's Uncle Nick was in the room Helen had been in. Janice and the others were quite nervous, and when Janice got her first look at Charlie, after all of those years, she felt a sense of relief. He looked like a normal person. He was dressed in a dark, conservative suit; he was a well-mannered and well-spoken man. He had obviously gotten an education and had had a proper upbringing. Charlie was single, had never been married, and according to Janice, seemed a bit effeminate, which didn't surprise her. Janice was also impressed with Charlie's adoptive mother. Florence Duffy was a small, tastefully dressed woman who looked a lot like Nancy Reagan. She spoke softly and had a

slight southern accent. Janice believed she was originally from
Virginia.

Charlie was obviously ill at ease and only spoke when spoken to.
It was an awkward situation for everyone, but otherwise, the funeral
and family reunion went off without a hitch. A couple of days after
the funeral, Janice received a card from Charlie thanking her for
inviting him back. She said she hadn't seen or heard from him in
the subsequent decade.

I was curious to know how Janice had explained Charlie to her
daughters and to others in the family who hadn't been around in
1959 when he had confessed. I was surprised by her answer: none of
her sons-in-law had been told about Charlie. She and her daughters had decided to keep Charlie a secret. As with the Zubryd family, there were some relatives who didn't know he existed.

Janice asked if I still planned to talk to Charlie. I said yes and
wondered if she still had the card he sent her in 1980 after the funeral. She said she had saved the card, and although she didn't
want me to have it—or even borrow it—I could read it and copy
down his phone number. His home number, she said, had been unlisted. Charlie had also given Janice his business number, and that
was on the card as well. Janice got up from the dining room table
where we were sitting. A few minutes later, she came back with the
card. I read it, and from what I could tell, Charlie was part owner of
a "lifestyle store" called "j. Duffy's" in Columbus. Apparently he
was also the store's buyer and lived in an apartment with one of his
partners and his partner's wife. I wrote down both numbers then
handed the card back to Janice. Even though this information was
ten years old, it was a solid lead regarding his whereabouts and a
good starting point.

Janice asked how I planned to approach Charlie. I told her that
I wasn't sure, but I thought I might write him a letter first then follow up with a call. She thought that was the best way to do it; that
way Charlie wouldn't be so shocked. She made me promise to tell
her whether or not Charlie agreed to talk and, if he did, to fill her in
on the details.

On our way home from Janice's house, Sue and I discussed the
best way to break the ice with Chuck. I wasn't sure how to bring up
a matter so personal and so tragic, particularly when I knew so little
about Chuck as an adult. I wondered how he would react to a letter;

then I decided it might be better to call. Of course I'd have to find him first, and when I did, I'd make my move.

12 Joe Start

ALTHOUGH THERE WAS NO TELEPHONE LISTING FOR A Chuck Duffy in Columbus, Ohio, "j. Duffy's," the store was listed, and the number matched the one I had copied from the card Chuck had sent to Janice Todd back in 1980. Marge Zubryd had been unable to locate Chuck two years earlier, but I wondered how hard she had tried. There was a good chance someone at the store could tell me where I could find him. I had decided not to write Chuck a letter. I would call. But before calling the store, I wanted to touch base with Joe Start, the county detective Ted Botula had told me about. I wanted to learn as much as I could about the case before talking to Chuck—assuming of course that Chuck would talk to me.

❏ ❏ ❏

In 1963, Joe Start became head of the Allegheny County Homicide Bureau, replacing Ted Botula, who had taken the top position at the Allegheny County Workhouse. When the Allegheny County Police Department took over the county detective's office in 1974, Joe Start retired as captain.

Every ex-police officer I had spoken to about Joe Start had said he was an outstanding person and a first-class detective. They all remembered that as a rookie Joe had been accidentally shot by another county detective. No one had expected Joe to live, but a year later he was back on the job. Everyone had a good word for Joe and for his partner, Joe Carmody. Both men were subjects of numerous anecdotes — including the one about Start asking Botula how he was supposed to find a handgun in a river that had swallowed up a B-25.

I called Joe Start and asked him if he would talk about the Zubryd case. "Boy, what a coincidence," he said. "My wife and I just got back from vacation, and when I was on the plane I looked out the window and for some reason started thinking about the kid — Charlie. I was wondering whatever happened to him. And now you call. Have you talked to Botula?"

"Yes, I talked to him the other day."

"How is Teddy?"

"He's fine."

"How old would he be now?" Joe asked.

"I think he's seventy-seven."

"That old?"

"Yes."

"Well, I'm sixty-seven. It's been a long time. What did Teddy say about the Zubryd case?"

"He says Charlie did it."

"What do you think?"

"I don't think he did."

"Have you talked to the boy?"

"No, but I plan to. Of course, he's no longer a boy."

"I guess not," Joe Start said. He chuckled. "How old would Charlie be now?"

"He would be around forty-one," I said.

"Well, Charlie Zubryd didn't do it," Joe said. "He couldn't have. He wasn't strong enough to hit her that hard, and he couldn't have ripped her blue jeans that way."

"There was a lot in the paper about Helen's killer being left-handed," I said. "Do you remember any of that?"

"That was Teddy's crap, and so was that stuff about the dog not barking and the army belt. I don't remember seeing the army belt near her body. It was down there in the basement on a shelf or something, but it didn't have anything to do with her murder."

"Are you sure about that?"

"Yes, I remember that well."

"Were you there when the boy confessed?" I asked.

"No, Botula had the kid brought in on a Saturday when me and my partner — Joe Carmody — he's dead now — were off duty. Teddy knew I didn't buy the business about the boy. He had sent me and

Carmody out to question the kid two or three times. Once we talked to him in the priest's office in that little church over in Herminie. Believe me, the kid didn't have any idea what had happened to his mother. That was all in Teddy's head."

"You and Carmody covered Sewickley Township, didn't you?"

"Yeah, it was our district."

"Then wasn't the Zubryd murder your case?"

"It was, but Ted was in charge of all of the murder cases."

"So why didn't he ask you and Carmody to interrogate Charlie on that Saturday?"

"Because Ted knew I wouldn't squeeze a confession out of that kid."

"So you believed that Ted framed the boy?"

"You can make up your own mind about that."

"Why would he do it?"

"You'll have to ask him about that."

"I will," I said.

"Well, anyway—back to that night—me and Carmody found a freshly broken trail through the underbrush in Zubryd's backyard. We figured some man had just run through there, some big guy. We found several sets of shoe impressions outside the basement door, but we had no way of knowing which, if any, had been made by the killer. So many people had been in and out of that basement after the guy fled, his footprints would have been trampled. Then we found out about a man who had gotten on a bus at the foot of Barley Road a little after nine o'clock that night. This man had gotten on the Beaver Valley bus to Sewickley. We interviewed the passengers who saw him, and they said he was sweating, talking to himself, wearing work shoes without socks, and had burrs and jiggers on his army coat. They also said he had scratches on his face. Me and Carmody thought this could be the guy who had killed Helen, the man who'd cut that trail through the bushes. He had gotten on the wrong bus; he wanted to go to Pittsburgh. Did Teddy say anything to you about this guy?"

"No."

"Anyway, this guy was about forty, was powerfully built, had thinning, sandy-colored hair, and a flushed, round face. Me and Carmody called him the 'moon-faced guy.' A couple of years after Charlie confessed, me and Carmody were coming down Beaver Street near the Leetsdale High School—it's now called Quaker Valley—we [cops] drove Plymouth Valiants then. We see this guy running around, trying to hitch a ride. He'd run out into the street between cars and stick out his thumb then run back to the sidewalk. He was acting goofy as hell. I said, 'Hey, Joe, do we have a runner from Dixmont?' Dixmont is a state mental hospital, and I thought maybe this guy got loose. Joe says, 'I'll call in and see if they reported a runaway.' We go by the guy, and he's jumping around out in the street. We're going one way, and he's working the traffic going the other. Our radio dispatcher comes back and says there's no report out of Dixmont. No escapees.

"By now we've driven down the street two or three blocks. We turn around and come back to pick him up. I said, 'Where are you going, sailor?' The guy jumps into the car. 'Good, good, I want a ride to Pittsburgh,' he says. And we started bullshitting him. He says, 'You got anything to eat?' I say, 'So what do you want to eat?' He goes, 'Anything.' So Carmody says, 'We'll get you something to eat.' I don't remember where in the hell we went, but we got him something to eat. I think we went to a coffee shop in Ambridge.

"I'm lookin' at this guy, and I see the son of a bitch isn't wearing any socks. He's got these big work shoes on with no socks. 'Do you ever wear socks?' I asked him. 'No,' he says. 'You never wear socks?' This guy looks at me and says, 'No.' Carmody says, 'What about winter?' The guy says, 'I never wear socks.' So we get his address and drive him up to the north side. We get out of the car go up to his room — it's one of those walk-ups off East Ohio Street near Federal. There was a Hite's Drug Store on the corner, and we go up to his room from the door in the alley behind the place. He had a kitchen and a couple of rooms; the bathroom was down the hall. So we got his name, and we left — but we told him we'd be back in a couple of days. We said we wanted to talk with him some more. He says, 'Yeah — come on back.' We asked him if he'd ever been locked up, and he said he knew what that was. So we left and did this little background on him and found out this guy had a record. He had spent a lot of time at Woodville, an insane asylum outside Pittsburgh.

"We noticed this guy sweated a lot. He talked real fast. We had to slow him down. And I think he told us he was from down around Washington County. We checked with the city, and the city police had a file on him — mostly burglary that had been dropped down from sex offenses, like attempted rape and so forth. The guy would walk into a house and fondle the woman. When he got caught, the police would take him downtown to the [Allegheny] County Behavior Clinic then send him straight over to Woodville. This guy was too nuts to stand trial. This was what he did.

"So I'm sitting there talking to Joe Carmody, and I says, 'Joe, that son of a bitch that rode the bus that night had no socks on. Maybe this fellow is that guy. Let's take a shot at him. There ain't too many people I know who run around wearing work shoes without socks. It's just a hunch, but let's take another whack at him.'

"So we did. We talked to him. We talked to him for, oh, some time. We got his confidence pretty much, and we got around to the incidents where he'd got into those houses and grabbed those women. He was real crude—he'd say, 'That woman wanted to be fucked and then changed her mind and then called the cops because her old man was coming home.' It was just a flimsy, goofy answer.

"We kept working on him. We asked him where he worked—back in 1956—when Helen Zubryd was murdered. It's now about four, maybe five years later. He said he worked at the Katherine Walker estate up near Leetsdale. Well that's not too far from Barley Road, where the murder was. So he had been in the area then. I asked him what he did there, and he says, 'I was a handyman; I cut weeds and I cut trees down and done this and that.' He said he was fired. 'They fired me, them bastards,' he said. Then he went into a tirade about it.

"The next thing we know we got this guy talking about being fired up at the Walker estate. So I asked him, 'When you were fired, did you collect any unemployment compensation?' He says, 'Yeah.' We asked him where he went to get it—to report in for it—and he says Ambridge.

"Then we got around to the day of the crime—this is over some period of interview, you know. I asked him if he knew where he was about that time, and he says, 'Oh, I know where I was.' We say, 'How do you know that?' He goes, 'Cause I was at the unemployment bureau in Ambridge.'

"Well—bingo. We go down and check the unemployment bureau that day, and sure enough, he had reported in that day. It showed that—the exact day of the murder. Now we got us something going here.

"So we talked with the guy some more. 'What did you do after you left the unemployment compensation place in Ambridge?' We were driving in the car with the guy. We drive through Ambridge, and he points out the unemployment bureau. Then he tells us he walked up along the Big Sewickley Creek Road. So we drove along where he said. We got out to the Pine Inn Tavern, and I says, 'You got out this far?' He says, 'Yeah, I walk all the time.' He tells us to stop at this little grocery store near the Pine Inn Tavern. It was more like a fruit stand. He says he went in there to get a half pound of baloney and a loaf of bread. He eats the meat and the bread and continues walking along the highway until he comes to this side road. 'Is this the road?' I asked. 'Yeah,' he says. 'That's the one I went up.' Well, that was Barley Road. 'Why did you go up there?' I asked him. 'I wanted to get a drink of water, I was thirsty.'

"So, our guy goes up this side road. He says it was early evening. It's wintertime. We drive up in the car – Barley Road – and he says, 'That's where I got in trouble.' We stopped the car, and we're right in front of the Zubryd house. 'Is that the place?' I asked. 'Yeah,' he says. 'That's the house.'

"We're sitting there in the car, and I asked the guy, 'Wadaya mean, you got in trouble?' He looks at me and says, 'Well, that woman pissed me off.' I says, 'What woman?' That's when he tells us the story.

"The guy tells us he walked up to the front of the house, and a woman answers, and he says he wants a drink of water. He doesn't remember seeing any kid around. The woman says, 'You go around to the side door.' He goes around to the side of the house, and she meets him there and lets him into the basement. She tells him to come in and she goes and gets him the water. There's a laundry tub down there, and he gets his drink. Incidentally, when we were at the crime scene that night, we saw a glass and had them dust it for prints. They got nothing good off it. Anyway, she said something like – 'You hungry?' He had just eaten the baloney and the bread, but he was that kind of guy; you could never fill him up. She goes upstairs and brings him down a fried-egg sandwich. 'It's cold,' he says. She said it was left over from supper. He eats the sandwich. 'She was just askin' to get fucked,' he tells us. He then says to her, 'You got nice tits.' He then tells us that he reached over and felt her breast. She slapped him. 'That pissed me off,' he said, 'so I grabbed that hatchet and chased her and hit her on the head with it. I was just about to fuck her when I heard a noise upstairs. I got the hell out of there and got scratched up running through her backyard.' That's what he told us. He's the one who brought up the hatchet –

we didn't. How would he have known about this murder four, five years later? We believed him.

"The guy said he caught a bus on Beaver Road in Fairoaks — down by the Duquesne substation — two miles from the house. He wanted to go to Pittsburgh, but he got onto the wrong bus. He was on the one to Sewickley. He got off in Sewickley on the corner of Walnut and Beaver Streets — at the drugstore. The bus driver told him to wait there for the next one to Pittsburgh; he said it would come along in thirty minutes. The guy said he didn't get to Pittsburgh. He said he spent the night at the Bellevue Police Department. He was what they called a 'lodger.' We checked that out, and a patrolman down there named Gibbs said, yeah, he remembered that guy. They fed him and gave him a cot for the night. In those days, the police did that sort of thing. They called them bums then — today we call them homeless people. So we knew he was in Bellevue that night. [Bellevue is about thirteen miles south of Ambridge along Pennsylvania Route 65 on the northwestern fringe of Pittsburgh.] There was no record of him staying there, so we couldn't be absolutely sure. But Gibbs recalled seeing him.

"Anyway, we took the guy back to his apartment and went to see Ted Botula — to turn it over to him. We figured he'd get a warrant so we could arrest the guy and bring him in. We walked into Teddy's office with the guy's rap sheet and said, 'Hey, Teddy, this guy is worth checking out.' Botula asked, 'What case?' We say, 'The Zubryd case.' Ted shakes his head and says, 'That case is closed.' We said we knew that, but this was new information. 'Just check him out,' I said. 'That's all we ask.' Ted says, 'You guys just want me to fit him into the Zubryd case.' I says, 'No, Teddy, this guy looks like the one — we think he killed Helen Zubryd.' Well, Ted wasn't impressed. He tells us the kid did it and that our guy is crazy and that he doesn't know what he's talking about. That's when I take the crime scene photographs out of my briefcase and throw them on Botula's desk. 'Sure he's crazy,' I said. 'Who else would have done something like this? Check this guy out. This man is the sex fiend we've been looking for. This is the moon-faced guy without socks that was on the bus that night.' I could tell that Ted wasn't too excited about our guy. 'Okay,' he says, 'I'll check him out.' So Teddy took over. He and Francis Flannery went to the guy's room, picked him up, and drove him out to Barley Road. When they got up around Helen's house, they asked the guy to pick out the place where he killed the woman. When Ted and Flannery got back, they told me and Joe that our guy picked the wrong house, so they let him go. That was it. He was never arrested, charged, or anything. They put him on the lie detector, but he was too nuts for that. The guy disappeared. We never saw him again. Me and Joe talked about that guy a lot after that. Joe even had the guts to ask Eddie Boyle for a warrant. But they had the kid, so why make waves? After that, it wasn't the same between me and Teddy. Our guy murdered Helen Zubryd.

"Nobody told the kid or his relatives about our guy. Nobody told them the kid's confession wasn't any good. The case was forgotten, but I didn't forget.

"I've been racking my brain trying to remember that guy's name. It just won't come to me. I've tried before to remember, it is something that can drive you nuts.

"Let me know if you find Charlie. I'd like to tell him I'm sorry I didn't do more. I'm still trying to think of that guy's name. It would be in the file because I wrote it on a supplementary."

Joe Start and I had a long talk that day, and just before I hung up I informed him that the Zubryd file probably didn't exist. That meant I'd have to identify his suspect from scratch, unless his memory got better. I told him I was pulling for his memory.

"If it comes to me," he said, "I'll give you a call."

I thanked him, and we agreed to get together later to talk more about the case.

❑ ❑ ❑

The Zubryd case had been solved, but only a handful of cops and the D.A. knew it. They had let the boy take the rap. They had let the family think they were related to an ax murderer. They had let a killer stay free. Why? Because the D.A. didn't want to be embarrassed. Thirty years later, with the Zubryd file destroyed and Botula's memory fuzzy, the last man to know had finally gotten it off his chest. He could have taken the secret to his grave, but he didn't.

Now I had a decision to make. Should I call Chuck Duffy and tell him what I knew or wait until I had more information about the man who had killed his mother? Was this man still alive? Could he be found? Did he remember killing Helen? Had he killed again? If I couldn't come up with a name for this man, there'd be nothing more to know. I had to have a name.

I'd hold off calling Chuck. I'd see what I could find out, and if nothing came of my efforts, I'd get in touch with Chuck and tell him what I knew. I had no way of knowing how he would react. Surely he knew he hadn't killed his mother. What would I be telling him, really? Nothing. That's why I wanted to know more about Joe Start's suspect. If the guy was dead, I wanted Chuck to know that. If he was alive, we needed to know where he was. So I'd wait. What was wrong with adding a couple more weeks to a thirty-year-old secret?

13 The Moon-Faced Guy

TED BOTULA LISTENED INTENTLY AS I TOLD HIM ABOUT Joe Start's moon-faced suspect. "You know," he said, "I don't remember that. If Joe Start says it happened, I'm sure it did, but I don't remember."

He didn't remember. I believed him.

"It would be in the file, though," he said.

"The files are gone," I replied, "destroyed."

"Aw, Jesus," Botula said. "How could they do that? Are you sure? Look on the sixth floor. The files were in bins in a room that had a steel door with a padlock. You get that file and you'll know the guy."

"They got rid of them."

"That's terrible," Botula muttered.

I described Start's suspect again, hoping it would ring a bell.

"Nothing," Botula said. "I had so many."

"Joe Start doesn't think the boy did it."

"It goes back to that hatchet," Ted replied, "when the blade was embedded in her skull. Did the tissue have anything to do with freezing that blade in? Vulcanizing the blade. Did the tissue vulcanize sufficiently to create a difficult job of trying to get this ax blade out?"

"I think Start's suspect killed Helen."

"The detective's worst enemy is exhaustion," Botula said. "When you're tired, you don't follow all the leads. We had a guy — the man who put in Helen's furnace — he was a good suspect. They had him in when I was gone, and when I got back I was mad because they questioned him without me. He was from Aliquippa — an Italian. He didn't confess, so they let him go."

"So you have doubts about the boy?"

"It depends on how you would explain that hatchet."

"Thank you, Ted."

"You're welcome. Say hello to Joe Start. He was a good one."

❏ ❏ ❏

Identifying Joe Start's suspect thirty years later would not be easy. There wasn't much to go on. He was a white male who was large and probably bald and born around 1920. He'd been institutionalized at the Woodville State Hospital, arrested by the Pittsburgh police, employed at and fired by the Katherine Walker estate in Edgeworth, and was in Ambridge filing for unemployment on the day of the murder. After killing Helen, he had spent the night as a lodger in the Bellevue city lockup. He talked fast, wore shoes without socks, and sweated heavily.

I began my investigation at the unemployment office in Ambridge. The woman there was quite interested and wanted to help, but her records only went back a few years. She suggested I call the state office in Harrisburg, which I did, without result. If the suspect had filed for unemployment on November 20, 1956, the state had no record of it.

The police chief in Bellevue said his department had jail blotters going back one hundred years. He checked the entries for Tuesday, November 20, 1956, and found nothing that matched the suspect. This didn't necessarily mean that the man hadn't spent the night there as a lodger, it means that no one had made a note of it if he had.

I had been back in touch with Joe Start, who had told me more about the Zubryd case. He was trying desperately to remember the name of his moon-faced suspect. One of Joe's most vivid memories of the case had to do with Botula assigning him the job of spying on the mourners who had come to Syka's Funeral Home to pay their last respects to Helen Zubryd. Joe had tried to get out of this assignment, but Botula had insisted. Joe described his ordeal like this:

"Helen's casket was metallic gray and sat on a platform that rose two feet off the ground. Behind her, as a backdrop, there was a ceiling-to-floor pink velour drape that ran wall-to-wall across the room. In the middle of this drape, directly behind the dead woman, was a panel made of some kind of green fabric. This backdrop was usually a solid piece of cloth, but to fix it up so I could see, Mr. Syka had split the curtain on both sides of the green panel. That way I could stand behind this section and look through the splits at the people who came to see Helen Zubryd. From this place, I could see—and hear who cried and who didn't. That's one of the things Teddy wanted to know, who cried and who didn't. This peekaboo setup was okayed by Botula, who had promised Syka that I wouldn't sneeze or anything. Mr. Syka, I think, was kind of nervous about the whole thing.

"I had stood behind the curtain Thursday afternoon and that evening and all day Friday. It was one of the lousiest, most boring jobs I ever had, and it was tough on my legs. It wasn't easy on the nerves either. And when I couldn't get out to take a piss, it got downright painful. There were only two ways to get out from behind the curtain without being seen. One was through a door behind the backdrop that opened into the adjoining viewing room. The other way was parting the curtain at the panel and stepping out into Helen's room when nobody was there. Every once in a while, Mr. Syka would come up to Helen's coffin and give me a signal that it was all clear for me to come out.

"I remember that the boy's Aunt Marion and his Uncle Tom came to the funeral home to see Helen on Friday night. They had Charlie in the car, and by the time they pulled into Syka's parking lot, it was already dark. I was standing in the lobby talking to John Syka when the boy and the Stetters came through the door. Syka immediately broke away from me to greet them, and when he did I walked back into Helen's viewing room which, fortunately, was unoccupied at the time. I got myself behind the drape before Charles and the Stetters entered the room. I wouldn't have bothered doing this except Teddy had been really hot to know how the boy would react when he saw his mother's corpse.

"I remember the boy walking into the room. He had taken off his overcoat and was by himself. His hair looked darker than I remembered it because someone had slicked it down with something that smelled a lot like Brylcream — you know, that 'little-dab'll-do-ya' stuff. I guess someone had put more than a dab on the boy's head. Charlie looked nice, though, in his red bow tie, navy blue sweater-vest, crisp white shirt, and gray dress slacks.

"Because the coffin was up on the platform, the top of it came to Charlie's chin. Right away it was obvious to me he wasn't going to look at his mother's face. He was very careful not to do that; instead, he focused on her hand, the one closest to him. He wasn't crying, and it didn't look like he was going to. He stood there for a while with a blank face, then he suddenly reached in and touched her hand: then, just as quickly, he took it back, gasping. I guess the feel of it — it being so cold — must have shocked the kid 'cause his face was all twisted up like he was afraid and sort of disgusted. Still, there were no tears, and after a moment or two, he pulled himself together, turned, and walked out of the room.

"I knew I just saw something I wasn't supposed to see, somethin' that I wish I hadn't seen. I suddenly felt a little sick, and my legs got weak. There were times, you know, when it wasn't that great being a detective."

❑ ❑ ❑

Joe Start told me that day on the telephone that he had also been trying to identify people who had worked at the Katherine Walker estate in the 1950s. He was looking for former employees who might remember the moon-faced guy, maybe even know his name and remember something about him. The Walker estate sat on top of a hill in Edgeworth, near Sewickley, and included a big house with stained glass windows, considerable acreage, riding stables, a bunkhouse for the people who cared for the horses, flower gardens, and a huge lawn. Joe Start's moon-faced suspect had worked outside for Miss Walker as temporary help and had done something that day that had gotten him fired. Miss Walker also employed maids, cooks, housecleaners, and many casual help to work at special events, such as her annual Thanksgiving dinner for the Sewickley Fox Hunting Club.

The money behind the Walker estate had come from the Harbison-Walker Company, the world's largest manufacturer of blast furnace bricks. Miss Walker had been dead for five years, and the estate was about to become a housing development. She had been a tall, thin woman with a short, masculine hairstyle. "If you ever saw her downtown in her riding outfit," said Joe Start, "you'd never forget her."

Joe had talked to Joe Hatten, a plumber who had worked up at the estate. Mr. Hatten didn't remember the moon-faced man but had identified some of the people who had worked there at the time of Helen Zubryd's murder. Unfortunately, most of these people were now dead.

John Nee gave me the names of several ex-cops who had patrolled East Ohio Street in the 1950s. The moon-faced guy had been living in an East Ohio Street walk-up when he confessed to Start and Carmody. I called several of these old-timers and asked them if they remembered Start's men, and they all said the same thing: "Give me a name." I didn't have a name, and I was wasting my time trying to get it from ex-cops.

I asked Joe Start if he would allow himself to be hypnotized by someone who specialized in this kind of thing. I knew that people could remember long-forgotten details under hypnosis and that the police frequently used this technique as an investigative tool. Joe said he didn't think he could be hypnotized, but he was willing to give it a try. He said he felt he owed it to Charlie.

I made the arrangements to have Joe hypnotized, and a few nights later, we drove to Erie, where William J. Vorcheck of the Erie Institute of Hypnosis put Joe under. For a guy who thought he couldn't be hypnotized, Joe went under fast and, according to Vorcheck, deep.

I spent the next three hours in Vorcheck's waiting room. It was pure agony. Every once in a while, I could pick up bits and pieces of conversation coming from Vorcheck's office, and every so often I would put my ear against his door and listen in. (What the hell — I was paying for it.) It seemed Joe and the hypnotist were in that inner office forever. When they finally came out, I was a nervous wreck. Joe, on the other hand, looked perfectly relaxed and rested. "Did you get anything?" I asked Vorcheck before the two men had a chance to sit down on the sofa.

"We're making progress," Vorcheck replied. "He remembered the name Al."

"I heard Carmody calling the moon-faced guy Al," Joe said. "We were up in the guy's room. He was in boxer shorts because we had rousted him out of bed. His shorts were filthy, and he had this enormous beer belly. We had entered the place through the backdoor —

off the alley. I remembered George Puff was with us. I'd forgotten about George Puff. 'Puffy' was a county detective. We had taken him along because Puff had worked for the city police and had patrolled that neighborhood. We wanted him to see this guy. We figured Puff might remember the guy."

"Did he?"

"No. But I'll be damned, I'd forgotten about George Puff."

"Then we've made some progress," Vorcheck said.

"Is this guy Puff alive?" I asked.

"Oh, gee, I don't know. He'd be pretty old," Joe replied.

"Are you sure then that the suspect's first name is Al?" I asked.

"I can't be sure," Joe replied. "I might be confusing the moon-faced guy with someone I knew in the army who he reminded me of."

"Yes, but the name popped right out," Vorcheck said. "Joe was very sure."

"I don't know if the guy's name was Albert or Alfred," Joe said. "I might be confused about that."

"What about the last name?" I asked.

"I think the last name begins with the letter *T*," Joe said. "It was a German name; I remember that. I don't know. God, I'd give anything to remember that name."

"I gave Joe a posthypnotic suggestion," Vorcheck said. "There's a chance the name will come to him when he least expects it. It could happen anytime."

"What about the guy's rap sheet?" I asked. "You said the moon-faced guy had an arrest record. Do you remember anything about that rap sheet?"

"He did have a rap sheet," Joe replied. "I remember that me and Carmody were talking about the guy and that we had found out he had busts in Pittsburgh, and now I remember something about Heidelberg. That guy had been arrested for A & B with intent to ravish, B & E, and loitering. The guy had been in and out of Woodville, the nuthouse."

"Did you remember anything about the guy's confession? Do you remember what he said about Helen Zubryd?"

"Yes. He said the woman handed him the egg sandwich from the stairs. Then he said he was thirsty, and she pointed to the drinking glass that was sitting on the laundry tub. He said he went over there to the tub and drank some water. Then he got fussing with her and, the next thing, he's chasing her with the hatchet. This guy was goofy. He was crazy."

Joe Start and I left William Vorcheck's office that night at nine-thirty. We hadn't eaten, so we stopped at a restaurant before heading back to Pittsburgh. Joe was obviously disappointed, and so was I, but I tried to cheer him up.

"We learned more about your man," I said. "You also remembered George Puff."

"Yeah, but Puff is probably dead."

"Maybe the posthypnotic suggestion will work. You could wake up tomorrow with this guy's name on your tongue."

Joe refused to be cheered up. "Why can't I remember that guy's name?" he said. "For some reason I just can't remember it. This is crazy."

❑ ❑ ❑

The next morning, I called John Nee and asked if he knew anyone in Pittsburgh who could make a crime records check at the Pittsburgh and Heidelberg Police Departments.

"Sure," John said, "give me the name."

"It's Al, with a last name that begins with the letter *T*."

"That's all you've got?"

"That's it."

"I don't think that's enough."

"Maybe we could start at Heidelberg — it's a small police department — someone could go through their files on people with last names that begin with *T* pulling the jackets of white males born around 1920 who have the first name Al. That should narrow it down. If we find a guy whose rap sheet matches Start's suspect, we have our man. Then we run his name through the Pittsburgh files."

"I don't know," Nee said. "This is gonna take a detective. I'll get back to you."

"When?"

"I'll let you know today."

John kept his word, but when he called back, the news wasn't good. "Forget Heidelberg," he said. "Their records don't go back that far."

"What about Pittsburgh?"

"I got a detective who's interested," John said. "He's John Casciato, a great guy. He says Pittsburgh's got too many *T*'s they got a thousand Thomases alone — but at least the whole thing is on a computer."

"Can this guy help us?"

"Maybe. It's up to Ron Shaulis, the commander in charge of the Allegheny County Identification Center. I knew Ron when I was on the job," John said. "I was his boss for a while. I'll let you know Monday what he says."

Over the weekend, while things were hanging in Pittsburgh, Joe Start called and said he'd identified a few more people who had worked at the Walker estate. One of these people, a woman named Marie, had cared for the horses. Joe said he didn't know her last name, but he was working on that. I asked Joe if George Puff, the county detective he and Carmody had taken to East Ohio Street to meet their suspect, had lived on Perrysville Avenue. "Yes, he did. How did you know that?" Joe asked.

"There is a George Puff living there now," I said. "He was in the book."

"That must be him. I'll be damned — the son of a bitch is still alive."

❏ ❏ ❏

I called George Puff's number, and his wife answered the phone. I identified myself as a friend of Joe Start's and asked if this was the Mr. Puff who had been a county detective.

"He's the one," she said.

"Could I speak with him?"

"It wouldn't do any good," she replied. "He's ninety-two, and he hasn't been feeling good. He doesn't remember much anymore. I guess you want to know about the shooting."

"No — "

"George shot that man because he was robbing the gas station."

"Oh. Actually, I'd — "

"That guy shot George's partner in the hand."

"Thank you Mrs. Puff."

"George was a fine officer."

"Yes, ma'am. I hope I didn't disturb you. Good-bye."

George Puff was alive, but I was a little late. That can happen when you try to work a thirty-two-year-old murder case.

On Monday morning, I called John Nee, who said he had good news.

"What?"

"Commander Shaulis is interested in the case. He says he'll pull the file of every Al T. he's got. Then we can narrow it down to white males born around 1920. Ron will have us a printout this afternoon. He says he's at our disposal. When can we get down to Pittsburgh?"

"Tomorrow."

14 A Complete Reversal

T HE NEXT MORNING JOHN NEE AND I WERE SEATED IN Commander Ron Shaulis' office at the Pittsburgh Police Department looking at a computer printout list of 120 arrestees with the first names Alan, Albert, Alex, Alfonso, Alfred, Allen, and Alvin. All of these men had last names that began with the letter *T.* I was impressed with the results of Commander Shaulis' efforts and told him so. Unlike most of my fellow professors at Edinboro, I didn't own a computer — or even use one — but I liked what they could do.

Commander Shaulis, a solidly built man in his early forties, had the look and the demeanor of a man who took his work seriously. In his dark blue suit, white shirt, conservative tie, and fastidious hairstyle, he reminded me of an FBI executive. His small, sparse office was nothing more than a cubicle set in the corner of a large room that contained a waist-high service counter, a cluster of desks supporting computer terminals, a handful of clerks, and a dozen or so motorized, rotating shelves that held a couple hundred thousand criminal-history files containing data accessed by the computer.

John Nee and I sat in the two guest chairs facing Commander Shaulis' desk. It was obvious he had high regard for John, his former boss at the Pittsburgh Police Department. The only reason

Commander Shaulis was at my service, eager to exhibit the impressive abilities of his computerized crime records files, was John Nee: he had introduced me as his close friend and colleague. Otherwise, as a private citizen, I wouldn't have gotten past the clerk at the service counter, and I certainly wouldn't have had access to this kind of information. That's why I was a little nervous and also appreciative. This might be, I felt, my only chance to identify Helen Zubryd's killer, and if we didn't make a hit, I wasn't sure how many times I could come back and avail myself of this special service.

I took the list Commander Shaulis had handed me and quickly crossed off the names of the sixty-five men who weren't white, then I eliminated another fifty-one because of age. That left only four. I handed the list back to Commander Shaulis, and he punched the four names into the computer. We then walked into the big room where Commander Shaulis pulled the four criminal-history jackets out of the rotating file containers and handed them to me. I hurriedly paged through each file folder and found nothing that even remotely matched the arrest record and physical description of Joe Start's suspect.

I was crestfallen, a little embarrassed, and didn't look forward to telling Joe Start that we had been chasing the wrong guy. We were back to where we had started. I knew that Joe would be disappointed too. He had hoped that, after all of this time, he'd be able to put a name to his moon-faced killer. It seemed I'd hauled him to the hypnotist's office up in Erie for nothing.

"Hey, that's the way it goes," John Nee said. "Start was a detective – he knows how it is."

"When you come up with the right name," Commander Shaulis said, "we'll run it. How come he's not in the case file?"

"There is no police file," I said. "They destroyed all of the old records."

"Well, I'm getting you the coroner's file on the case," Shaulis replied.

"That's gone too," I said. "The coroner's office got rid of everything before 1966."

"I know," Shaulis replied. "But in 1982, the county sent those old files over to the University of Pittsburgh. They keep them in the Hillman Library. I called John Thompson, the archivist, and he said he's got the Zubryd case. Those cases are filed by date of inquest."

"I can't believe it."

"Yeah. I sent an officer over to pick up a copy of the file. You'll have it in a few minutes."

I was still trying to adjust to the idea that I would finally be able to see some solid documentation of the murder when a uniformed police officer walked into the office and handed Ron Shaulis a large brown envelope. Ron opened the package and pulled out a sheaf of papers, which he handed to me. "What do we have here?" he asked.

I eagerly leafed through the documents. "There's an autopsy report, the preliminary report from the Allegheny County Crime Lab, a list of the evidence they analyzed, some miscellaneous papers pertaining to the coroner's inquest, and several old newspaper clippings from the *Pittsburgh Sun-Telegraph.*"

"Let me see the newspaper articles," Ron said.

While John Nee and Commander Shaulis read the news clippings, I started reading the Allegheny County Crime Lab report. About halfway down the second page, I came to the part that described the condition of Helen's blue jeans. I had no idea they had been so violently ripped: "The left leg of the blue denim trousers was found to be torn lengthwise downward terminating 23 inches from the waist." I stopped reading for a moment and let that sink in. How could Charlie Zubryd have managed this? What I read next sat me straight up in my chair: They had found semen on Helen Zubryd's blue jeans! There it was, in black and white: "An area of fluorescent staining (under ultraviolet light) was observed on the left leg outer surfaces in the approximate area of the knee. It was chemically examined for the presence of seminal staining with positive results."

There had been no mention of the semen in the newspapers, and none of the people I had talked to, including Joe Start, had said anything about that. This meant that Ted Botula, when the boy was brought in to be questioned, knew about this evidence. Yet he went ahead with the confession, knowing full well that a prepubescent boy couldn't have produced semen. It occurred to me that Ted Botula had taken quite a risk. One of his detectives could have blown the whistle, or a relative could have found out. Apparently the detectives had kept silent, and Charlie's relatives were kept in the dark. I wondered if Eddie Boyle knew about the semen. Botula's boss, Henry Pieper must have known, and Teddy's partner, Francis

Flannery would probably have known as well. All of these detectives had been at the crime scene that night. I thought about Joe Start and wondered why he hadn't mentioned the semen.

Ted Botula had gotten away with illegally obtaining Charlie Zubryd's confession, a confession no one would have believed had they known about the semen. Botula had gotten away with it, and now, thirty years later, I had found a document that revealed his secret. This was a document that would have been destroyed had it not been for the archives at the University of Pittsburgh.

Botula had told the media that Charlie had "disarranged" his mother's clothing to fool the police. In reality, Ted had disarranged the evidence to fool everybody. I hated to admit it, but he had fooled me as well.

I looked up from the report. "I just found concrete proof that Charlie didn't do it," I said. "Usually you can't prove a negative, but in this case we can."

"What is it?" Commander Shaulis asked.

"There was semen on Helen Zubryd's blue jeans. It's right there, clear as a bell."

"Jesus Christ," John said. "Let me see."

"There's more. Helen had traces of the killer's blood and tissue under her nails, and they found a pubic hair at the scene that wasn't hers; and according to the crime lab report, this hair follicle didn't belong to either of the Skiles brothers."

"And it sure wasn't Charlie's," John Nee said. "She must have put up a fight, she must have scratched the attacker."

"This is hard to believe," I muttered. "The semen, the pubic hair, the blood under her nails, her ripped blue jeans — and the kid ends up taking the rap. The media and Helen's relatives swallowed it because they didn't know about the evidence."

"Ted got away with it," John said.

"If the boy had confessed in 1956, I don't think anyone would have believed it," I said. "But, by 1959, after reading about Starkweather and the other young murderers, people were starting to accept the fact that kids could kill."

"Yeah, I guess."

"People also believed what the police told them. Today everybody's skeptical, the police would have a hard time getting away with something like this."

"I don't know, people can be pretty stupid."

"I can't imagine being *that* stupid," I said.

"What do you think Charlie will say asked John.

"I don't know. It's hard to imagine what his attitude will be. I'm not sure how he'll react to me or the information. He might say, 'Go to hell—I don't want to go through this again.' He might not care one way or the other. It just depends who he is and what his life has been like."

"Where was his lawyer?" John asked. "Where was Lou Glasso, the great defense attorney?"

"That's a good question," I replied. "The coroner's file was right under Glasso's nose. If he had found the crime lab report we are looking at now, he could have nailed Ted Botula right then and there. Teddy would have been on the hook, not the kid, and it would have changed everything. Charlie would have been exonerated, and there would have been no reason for his family to throw him out."

"What does the autopsy say?" Ron asked.

I started reading the report. "The first part is about her head wounds—there's a lot of medical talk here, and it's a little confusing, but the top part of her head had been bashed in, exposing a circular area of bone that was shattered. The brain beneath this area was depressed and lacerated. There were five distinct lacerations on the left side of her head, plus the wound on her forehead caused by the hatchet blade. She had been hit at least six times."

Dr. Theodore Helmbold's description of the wound on Helen's face left by the hatchet blade was written out in great detail:

> The skin of the forehead at a point 1/2 inch to the right of the mid-line and 1 1/4 inches above the level of the supra-orbital ridge showed a contused, slightly swollen, bluish-red area of discoloration which measured 1 1/4 inches in its diameter. The skin of the anterior [front] surface of the nose at the level of the inner corner of the eyes showed a ragged, transverse laceration which crossed the mid-line and measured 1/4 inch in length. This laceration passed through the skin and soft tissues to the underlying bone of the bridge of the nose but the bone here was intact.

I looked up from the autopsy report and said, "This woman had been attacked by a madman." As I read through the five-page autopsy report, I came across important points of evidence that had not been disseminated to the media or to Charlie's relatives. There had been bruises on Helen's thighs, and her panties had been ripped: "They were torn down the left side to the hem of the left leg and then across the front of the leg just above the hem." And there was a bruise on Helen's left hand, probably a defensive wound. Dr. Helmbold had prepared three slides of vaginal smears that, according to his report, "were examined for the presence of seminal staining. None was found." The doctor also noted that Helen's "vagina was empty." He had concluded that Helen had not been penetrated and therefore not raped.

Something else in the autopsy report caught my attention. When the killer had ripped off Helen's blue jeans and panties, he had gouged the flesh at her waist, leaving deep scratches and two flaps of hanging skin: "The superficial layer of skin had been separated from the deep skin over this area and was hanging from a small tag on the lower anterior margin. At a point 5/8 inch directly above the uppermost portion of this area there was an identical type area."

After Joe Start had told me that Helen had given the moon-faced man a fried-egg sandwich, I had wondered what she and the boy had eaten that night. According to the autopsy, of the digested food in Helen's stomach, the only thing recognizable was a piece of noodle or spaghetti. This neither confirmed nor disproved the suspect's story.

According to the Receipt for Exhibits log attached to the crime lab report, several items of clothing belonging to Mr. Skiles and his two retarded sons were examined at the lab for traces of Helen. Nothing was found on these items that connected them to the crime scene or to the murder. The crime lab scientists had also examined the clothing Helen had been wearing at the time of her murder— blue jeans, a green woolen sweater, a pair of dark brown loafers, a pair of white socks, a white cotton bra, and a pair of pink panties— and had found no traces, such as hair, blood, or tissue, from her attacker.

I finished reading the report and said, "The coroner told reporters that Helen had not been 'sexually molested.' He should have said she had been sexually attacked— and *possibly* raped."

Commander Shaulis, John Nee, and I discussed the case for another hour or so, then John and I got up to leave. We thanked Ron Shaulis for locating the coroner's file, and he said he was pleased to have helped; and he reminded me that he would be willing to check any name that I might come up with against his files. Commander Shaulis was obviously interested in the Zubryd case, shocked by what Ted Botula had done to the boy, and eager to help us solve the case with his computerized collection of criminal histories.

As John and I drove north out of Pittsburgh that afternoon, I thought about the physical evidence and how it might have been used against Joe Start's suspect, the moon-faced killer. If the blood under Helen's fingernails had been typed (and there was no indication in the crime lab report that it had been) it could have been compared with the suspect's blood group. Helen's blood type was AB, the rarest group, applying to only about 5 percent of the population. It was therefore unlikely that the suspect's blood would have matched hers. Apparently there had also been no blood group typing of the semen on her blue jeans. Most people — 80 percent — are classified as "secretors," which means their blood type appears in their other bodily fluids, including semen. It would have also been important to know if the pubic hair found near Helen's body matched up microscopically with the suspect's. There was no way to know now if that hair follicle had anything to do with the crime.

The coroner's file had produced other information that was helpful. I had noticed, for example, in the inventory of the evidence seized and examined, the name Nick Schifino, a county detective I had not heard of. Nick had been at the murder scene that night, and I wondered what he would remember — assuming, of course, he was still alive.

When I got home from Pittsburgh, I called Joe Start and gave him the bad news about Al T.

"I figured it was too good to be true," Joe said. "I must be remembering that fellow I knew in the army who the moon-faced guy reminded me of. I think *his* name was Al. I don't know, I'm confused. This is really frustrating."

"I have the coroner's file on the case," I said.

"On the Zubryd case?"

"Yes, Ron Shaulis located it in the library down at Pitt."

"I can't believe it," Joe said. "Did you get any of the crime scene photographs?"

"No, but I got the autopsy and the crime lab reports, and they prove that the boy couldn't have done it."

"How's that?"

"They found traces of semen on Helen's blue jeans."

"Goddamn," Joe said. "Okay, I'm gonna tell you something—I already knew that."

"Why didn't you tell me? It means the kid was actually framed."

"I didn't want to say that because I couldn't prove it was there if Botula denied it. It would come down to my word against his."

"Did the other county detectives know about the crime scene semen?"

"Yeah, they all did."

"Why didn't somebody say something?"

"After Teddy got the kid to confess, me and him damn near came to blows over it. I said to him, 'Me and Joe Carmody worked damn hard on that case; you owe us an explanation!' Teddy looks at me and says, 'The kid came in and confessed—it's all over.' That's when I asked him about the semen. He says, 'You're just mad because you weren't here for the close. Forget it; the case is wrapped up.' I was really angry because I knew the kid didn't do it. 'What do you mean he confessed?' I says. He says, 'The kid and his mom got into a spat—the boy wanted to bake cookies to take to his aunt's house for Thanksgiving, and Helen said they didn't have time for that. So she takes him down to the cellar to spank him with the army belt, and that's when he hit her with the hatchet.' I says—'That's bullshit, and you know it.'" Joe paused a few seconds and said, "Funny, I just remembered that stuff about the cookies."

"The old cookie motive," I said. "It's right up there with love triangles and Mafia hits."

Joe Start laughed. "Yeah. I'm starting to feel guilty again," he said. "I should have done more."

"What about the district attorney, Eddie Boyle? Did he know about the semen?" I asked.

"Eddie Boyle didn't know his shit from apple butter. He knew what Teddy told him. The son of a bitch was drunk half the time."

"What if Boyle had known?"

"I don't know," Joe said. "He may have found out later. Joe Carmody may have told him."

"Maybe that's why Boyle didn't prosecute the kid," I said.

"Could be. Have you told Botula about finding the coroner's file?" Joe asked.

"No, but I'm going to," I said. "Helen had scratched the guy. They found skin and blood under her nails."

"Jesus," Joe said. "My suspect, when he got on the bus that night, had scratches on his face."

"Helen's blue jeans and panties had been grabbed and ripped so violently she had gouge marks on each side of her waist. Botula must have known Charlie couldn't have done that. There was also a stray pubic hair at the scene. It didn't match the samples the had gotten from the Skiles brothers."

"Those boys didn't do it, either," Joe said. "I was there when Teddy grilled them. It was pathetic—they were so retarded they didn't know if it was raining or sunny. They were scared shitless. Was there anything in the file about our guy?"

"No. Did they put the moon-faced man on the lie detector?" I asked, though I thought he had told me already.

"Yeah," Joe said. "But it didn't work because he was so crazy."

"I'm surprised his polygraph report wasn't in the coroner's file along with the crime lab stuff," I said.

"Were other lie detector reports in there?"

"No."

"That's odd," Joe said, "because Charlie McInerney, our polygraph man, tested about seventy-five people."

"In the file I came across the name of a county detective I'd never heard of," I said.

"Who's that?"

"Nick Schifino. Do you remember him?"

"Hell, yes, he worked on the Zubryd case."

"Is he still around?"

"I think so. He was a good detective and a nice guy. Nick was one of the few men down there who knew what he was doing. I bet he's up in his eighties now."

"I'll see if I can find him," I said. "Then I'll call Ted."

"You know, I'm not sure our guy's name was Al. I don't know why I can't remember."

"Maybe you're trying too hard."

"Yeah. Jesus, I'm glad you got that file. But it makes me feel lousy. Let me know what Teddy says."

❏ ❏ ❏

Nick Schifino was easy to find and eager to talk about the Zubryd murder case. "They were crazy for going after the boy," he said.

"Do you remember much about Helen Zubryd's body?" I asked.

"The guy had ripped off her pants, and there was semen on her denims. I think old man Skiles killed her. After he had his heart attack, I took his clothes over to the crime lab. They found semen on his underwear. I talked to his wife, and she said, 'Oh — Elmer and me had intercourse three days ago.' That was bull because I talked to Elmer's doctor — I can't remember who that was — and the doctor said, 'If that man had sex with his wife, he would have died on top of her.' Old man Skiles had a real bad heart, see. I always thought Elmer Skiles killed her. He was always talking about Helen and what a wonderful woman she was and all. I think he had a thing for her. He went over there — and she said no, and he killed her. The boy — Charlie — he couldn't have done it; Helen Zubryd was too strong. They had just put in a gas line to her house, and she had dug the ditch herself."

"Do you remember much about Detective Botula?" I asked.

"Sure, I remember Teddy. He was an okay guy; me and him were partners for three years. Teddy really liked to dress; he always wore fancy clothes, and he scored with the ladies — if you know what I mean. But Teddy shouldn't have done that to the kid. Yeah, I remember that case. I'm gonna be eighty-four next month. Wadaya think about that?"

❏ ❏ ❏

After talking to Joe Start, I had done a little research on Charles McInerney, the polygraph man who had tested the moon-faced man, as well as Helen Zubryd's neighbors and some of her relatives, including Mike Zubryd. Unfortunately, Charles McInerney was dead.

By 1956, McInerney was considered one of the best polygraph examiners in the United States. After graduating from Duquesne University in Pittsburgh, McInerney worked as a reporter for the *Pittsburgh Press*. In 1948, the year he became an Allegheny County detective, the D.A., a man named William S. Rahauser, proposed a crime lab that would be a joint enterprise of the county and the Pittsburgh Police Department. The laboratory, under the directorship of Joe D. Nicol, serving a community of 1.5 million, opened its doors in January 1951. Nicol had worked in Chicago on the staff of that police department's crime laboratory; and shortly after taking up his position in Allegheny County, he asked Detective McInerney if he'd like to join his staff as a polygraph examiner. McInerney said yes and was sent to Chicago to study scientific lie detection for four months at John Reid & Associates, the best polygraph school in the country. In November 1951, Nicol resigned his position with the Allegheny Crime Lab for political reasons, and McInerney took over as director.

❑ ❑ ❑

I didn't relish the idea of hitting Ted Botula with evidence that he had gotten a confession out of a boy he knew was innocent. I didn't know how he would respond, but I figured he had four options — claim the crime lab was wrong about the semen; say he'd forgotten about the crime scene evidence by the time he'd gotten around to questioning Charlie; admit he had done a bad thing; or remain detached, objective, and fuzzy about this aspect of the case.

I didn't want to badger him or try to coach him into a confession of some kind, but I wanted him to know what I had found, and I wanted his response. The Ted Botula I had come to know was a nice old man — not a young, aggressive homicide detective who had orchestrated a confession he must have known was false. Confronting a person with evidence of something done thirty years before was unusual and awkward — and I didn't know how to go about it. I had come to a standstill in my effort to identify the moon-faced killer, and I wondered if I'd ever solve the murder. Getting Joe Start hypnotized had been my most promising lead, and that hadn't worked out. Now I had proof that Charlie Zubryd, a.k.a. Chuck Duffy, was innocent and couldn't wait to find him to give him the news. Although identifying Joe Start's suspect was important, it wasn't necessary to clear Chuck's name. The coroner's file had done that.

I would inform Ted Botula of what I had learned, get back to Marge Zubryd to make sure she hadn't known about the semen, take another stab at identifying the moon-faced guy, then go looking for Chuck. I figured the moon-faced man, if he were alive, would be about eighty. Chuck would be forty-one. I couldn't decide if I wanted to find Helen's killer dead or alive and had been struggling with morbid thoughts of Chuck Duffy having died believing he had killed his mother. The possibility that he had killed himself kept creeping into my mind, and although I kept telling myself I had no evidence of such a thing, I couldn't get completely clear of the idea. Ted Botula had Charlie Zubryd living out in Los Angeles singing true-crime ballads, and I had him in his grave. I hoped we were both wrong.

15 The Walker Estate

I CALLED TED BOTULA AND, AS I HAD BEFORE, CAUGHT him at home in his easy chair next to the telephone. Like always, he sounded happy to hear from me. I told Ted how Commander Ron Shaulis had gotten me copies of the coroner's file on the Zubryd case from the archives at the University of Pittsburgh, and he seemed genuinely interested and pleased. "What did you find?" he asked.

"Before I get into that," I said, "I want to know if it's all right if I tape this call."

"Sure," Ted replied. He laughed, "I knew you were taping our conversations."

"Only this one," I said. "The others weren't recorded."

"Well, it's okay with me," Ted replied. "What did you find out?"

"Let me read you something from the crime lab report," I said, then read,

> "The left leg of the blue denim trousers was found to be torn lengthwise downward terminating 23 inches from the waist. Apparent blood staining was observed on the inside surface of this trouser leg. An area of fluorescent staining (under ultraviolet light) was observed on the left leg outer surfaces in the approximate area of the knee. It was chemically examined for

the presence of seminal staining with positive results."

I paused to let the information sink in, then I asked, "What do you make of that?"

"That's interesting," Ted said.

"There was semen on her. How could Charlie be a suspect?" Ted didn't respond, so I asked, "Does this change your mind about Charlie?"

"That sways my opinion when you come up with that laboratory report," Ted replied. "That kid was in no physical condition to expel any semen. But the thing that sticks out in my mind was that furnace repairman. Did you come across that in the file?"

"No."

"He was interviewed in my absence. That guy was a good suspect."

"What went through your mind when Charlie confessed?" I asked. "How did you account for the semen?"

"That's startling information. Maybe because of the time that elapsed, and then you come up with it. It sort of sways my opinion in this thing."

"Why did you interrogate Charlie when you knew there was semen on Helen's blue jeans? Can you help me with that?"

"No, not really. Tell me about the autopsy. Was there a penetration?"

"Apparently not. After his confession, you told reporters Charlie had disarranged his mother's clothing to throw off the police. You didn't mention that her panties and blue jeans had been torn. Could Charlie have done that?"

"That sways my opinion about this boy. Somewhere, in the back of my mind, I just couldn't conceive the idea that this kid was physically able to do that. But the guy that was outstanding in my mind was that furnace repairman from Aliquippa."

"Do you remember Joe Start's suspect — the guy from Woodville who didn't wear socks? He confessed to Start and Carmody. He said that he had killed Helen."

"It's not registering now," Ted said. "On the furnace we found a mark from a checkered shirt. Is that in the report?"

"There's nothing in the report itself, but on the crime lab Receipts for Exhibits log, item number eight is this: 'One lift of possible fabric impression found on side of heater next to body.'"

"That's it."

"You told me that impression matched Charlie's shirt. There's nothing in the crime lab report about that," I said.

"We have to think about the furnace man from Aliquippa. I think our direction is justly away from Charlie. In the back of my mind, I was never completely convinced, and now that you have developed that report from the crime lab and the semen and all of that—that changes the picture entirely."

Ted and I talked a little more about the Zubryd case, and when he started telling me about some of his other investigations, I told him I had to go, and the conversation ended the way it had begun, amicably.

My news about the semen hadn't affected Ted in any of the ways I had expected. He didn't deny it, but he didn't admit anything, either. I wasn't sure, but it seemed that Ted had forgotten what he had done to the boy. Perhaps he didn't think his actions were all that bad; or maybe I was just another victim of the old Botula charm. I couldn't make up my mind, and I wasn't sure how I felt about him. If Ted Botula had forgotten what he had done and now remembered, did he feel guilty? If he did, he didn't say so. It would never be the same between us. I didn't want to be conned or pretend that I didn't find what he had done repulsive. I wondered if we'd ever talk again.

❑ ❑ ❑

I was out of ideas on the moon-faced guy when I received a lead from an unexpected source—Elaine Asperger. Elaine called and said that her sister had heard Joe Start was asking people if they knew anyone who had worked up at the Walker estate back in the fifties. Elaine's sister knew a woman who had worked and lived on the Walker estate. Her name was Marie Passmore, and she had taken care of the Walker horses. Her husband, Earl, had been Miss Walker's gardener. The Passmores had started their jobs in December 1957 and had worked on the estate for seventeen years.

Although Marie and Earl Passmore had started work at the estate after Joe Start's suspect had been fired, they might have heard stories about this man. They probably wouldn't remember his name, but maybe they knew someone who would.

I called Marie Passmore, and she said she didn't remember anyone like our suspect. She said she'd check with a woman who had worked for Miss Walker as a cleaning lady. This woman had worked on the estate for many years and would have been there in 1956 when the moon-faced man was fired. Marie would also get in touch with Earl, now her ex-husband, and find out what he remembered. Miss Walker was dead, and so were her brother and two sisters. Her nephew and niece, who had spent a great deal of time at the estate, were also dead. A man named George, the chauffeur, the one who did most of Miss Walker's hiring, had passed away several years ago, as had the cook, the two gardeners, and the horseman who had worked there before Marie. The old cleaning lady was the only survivor from that era. Since she had worked inside, it was unlikely that she would have known this man, particularly if he'd been temporary. Miss Walker liked to hire transient workers, including people who had been institutionalized at Woodville and Dixmont. These helpers were usually paid in cash, so their names would not appear in any payroll records.

After talking to Marie, I wasn't very optimistic. Unfortunately, she was my best lead.

The next day, Marie called and had talked with Mary Colades, the cleaning woman who had worked at the Walker estate. Mary remembered an "outside man" named Frank who had been fired about the time Helen Zubryd had been murdered. He had shouted at Miss Walker and had even threatened her. This man Frank was later found dead under the Sewickley Bridge, which crossed the Ohio River about a mile south of the Walker estate. He had either been murdered with a gun or had shot himself. Since Frank was a DP (displaced person), with no family and no home, Miss Walker paid for his burial in the pauper's section of the Sewickley Cemetery. Mary couldn't recall Frank's last name, but she thought it began with the letter *G*.

Mary told Marie that she had a vivid memory of Helen Zubryd's murder, and after the killing, several detectives had come to the estate to interview the Walker employees. When Miss Walker died, an examination of her financial records revealed that over the years she had given a lot of money to the Skiles family on Barley Road. Mary informed Marie of Mr. Skiles's heart attack on the night of the murder and said she has always believed he was the one who had killed Helen.

Since I was more interested in Mary's Frank G. than in Elmer
Skiles, I asked Marie if Mary had described this man. Marie replied
that Mary had no idea what Frank G. looked like. All she knew was
that he had gotten into some kind of trouble at the estate, had been
fired, then turned up dead under the bridge.

Before Marie hung up, she said she would talk to her ex-husband,
Earl, then get back to me. "Find out what Earl knows about Frank
G.," I said. "I hope he can remember his last name."

❏ ❏ ❏

I called Joe Start and asked if the name Frank G. rang a bell. It
didn't.

"Did you talk to Ted?" Joe asked.

"Yeah. He mentioned a furnace repairman from Aliquippa."

"For Christ's sake," Joe said. "That guy had no more to do with
Helen's murder than you or me. He was one of hundreds we
pulled in."

"What about the fabric impression on the furnace?"

"Hell — that could have been anything. We didn't even know
how long it had been there. That's just like Ted — you ask him about
the semen, and he tells you about that guy from Aliquippa." Joe
laughed. "Listen," he said, "I'll see what I can turn up on Frank G."

"Mary says this guy ended up dead under the Sewickley Bridge."

"When?"

"I don't know."

"I don't remember anything like that," Joe said. "Are you sure?"

"No. We're relying on the memory of an old woman. I'm not
even sure Frank G. is the moon-faced guy."

"I'll check around," Joe said.

❏ ❏ ❏

There was something about the Frank G. business that didn't
feel right. I couldn't help thinking we were on the wrong trail, moving away from, not closer to, the moon-faced guy. To learn more
about the man under the bridge, I needed the date of his death. But
without a name, I had nowhere to start.

Out of desperation, I called Dorothy Moore, the archivist for the
Sewickley Valley Historical Society. I told her about Frank G. and
the way he had died. Dorothy could not recall any bodies under the

Sewickley Bridge but said she'd check her obituary files and see what she could find.

Joe Start called and said the former chiefs of police of Edgeworth and Sewickley did not remember any bodies found near or under the Sewickley Bridge. He had also checked the burial records at the Sewickley Cemetery and had found nothing that matched up with the name Frank G.

Although I hated to do it, I called Commander Ron Shaulis at the Pittsburgh Police Department and asked him to run another incomplete name through his files. That afternoon, Ron gave me a list of nine white Franks, born around 1920, with a last name beginning with the letter *G*. Once again, their backgrounds did not even come close to matching the moon-faced guy's description.

When I got back to Marie Passmore, I found out why he had struck out with Frank G. She had talked to Earl, and according to him, Frank G. was a little fellow from South America who spoke broken English. It was true that Frank G. had been fired from the Walker estate and later got into trouble with the police, but he said he didn't know where Mary had gotten that stuff about the body under the bridge: it had nothing to do with Frank G.

So Frank G. wasn't the moon-faced guy. I was back where I had started.

I called Joe Start and gave him the news. I didn't want him wasting his time on Frank G. "I didn't think his name was Frank," Joe said. "But I'm not sure it was Al, either. I know one thing, though — I'm gonna find out who that son of a bitch was. I don't care how long it takes."

❑ ❑ ❑

I had been thinking about Marge Zubryd, wondering what she would say when I told her about the coroner's file, so I called her. She could talk because Mike wasn't home.

The police had told Marge that Helen had fled to a basement window to call for help, but because the window was closed, no one had heard her screams. There was blood on the wall near the window; and splashes of blood were on the side of the furnace next to the place the killer had dragged her body for the final blow. That's where he had slammed the hatchet all the way into her forehead. Marge knew that Helen's blue jeans had been *pulled* to her knees and that her *panties* had been ripped. But no one, she said, had mentioned the semen, the blood under Helen's nails, the bruises on her upper legs, the torn blue jeans, or the finger gouges on her waist where the killer had grabbed her jeans. Marge had seen crime scene photographs of Helen's body, but the pictures didn't reveal this evidence.

"I did not feel that Charlie was guilty," Marge said, "until he told his story to Mike and me in front of the police. Had I known about this evidence, we wouldn't have taken him in to be questioned. Botula kept after us, putting doubts in our minds. Then he hit us with Charlie's confession. We believed it — then we didn't — then we did. Did Charlie do it? Didn't Charlie do it? We didn't know. It's not impossible for a kid to bury a hatchet into someone's head — if you're angry enough. We knew Charlie could be nice, but he always had to have his own way. Before his dad died, Charlie made a lot of trouble for his parents. He pitted one against the other. He was foxy. He caused arguments. Then Joe became ill. Charlie's mom spent a lot of time with Joe. The boy didn't get much attention. After the confession, McCabe and Glasso said adoption was the best thing. We let him go because of public opinion and that. Charlie said he wished he didn't have to live with us. He wanted to change his name. We felt it was best for Charlie. If he hadn't confessed, I never would have thought he killed Helen. But he was so convincing. They should have told us about the semen and that. This never should have happened."

I believed her. Had she known of the semen and the other evidence, she would have kept Botula at bay. I also believed Marge's account of how she and Mike had come to take Charlie to Botula's interrogation room on that Saturday in March 1959. They had taken the boy in because Botula had asked them to. Botula's "get this monster out of here" was ringing less and less true; it was too self-serving and convenient.

Mike Zubryd's problems with Charlie predated Helen's murder, making him putty in Botula's hands. Had he known of the semen, he would have known that Charlie couldn't have done it.

Initially, Botula had accused Mike of murdering Helen. I think that, when Botula lowered the boom of Charlie, he took the onus off Mike; and, because of this and the way Mike felt about the boy, Mike was incapable of being objective about Charlie's guilt or innocence. For Botula, Mike Zubryd had been easy game.

❑ ❑ ❑

In a last-ditch effort to identify Joe Start's suspect, I got in touch with the superintendent's office at the Woodville State Hospital near Bridgeville, a few miles southwest of Pittsburgh. I was told I'd have to speak with the man in charge of records, which I did. On the assumption that Joe Start's hypnotically induced recollection of Al was correct, I asked if there was any chance this man could be further identified by checking the names of patients admitted into the institution between 1950 and 1955. There was no chance. There were too many names and too few people to make such a search. And even if I had this man's full identification, I couldn't have access to his medical records without a court order. This was confidential stuff.

I tried the Allegheny County Behavior Clinic to find out if the court had ordered a psychiatric evaluation of this man before sending him to Woodville. I learned that these records only went back to 1960, and even if they did exist, I wouldn't be allowed to see them — the only person who could look at a defendant's file was the judge who had presided at his or her hearing.

I had run out of ideas. Nothing had worked — not the hypnosis, not the police record checks, not the leads at the Walker estate, not all of the help from local historians, not my inquiries at Woodville and the behavior clinic. I felt the same kind of frustration Botula must have felt when he couldn't make headway on the Zubryd case.

But maybe there was hope. Maybe Joe Start would wake up some morning with this man's name ringing in his ears. Otherwise, this nameless confessor would be nothing more than a haunting memory in an ex-cop's head.

I felt good about one thing: if Joe Start had not agreed to undergo hypnosis, we would not have pursued the lead that led us to the coroner's file — the evidence that proved Charlie's innocence. That was the main thing.

It was now time for Charlie.

16 "You Didn't Kill Your Mother"

O N SATURDAY MORNING, THE DAY BEFORE EASTER, I
picked up the phone and dialed the number I had for j. Duffy's
in Columbus. It was March 25, 1989, thirty years and eleven days
from the afternoon Charlie Zubryd confessed to murdering his
mother with a hatchet. I was nervous and not sure what I would say
if Chuck himself answered the phone. I had no idea what to expect.
The phone rang a couple of times, then a man picked up and said,
"Hello."

"Could I speak to Mr. Duffy?"

"I'm sorry, he's not here," the man replied. "May I take a message?"

I groped frantically for the right thing to say. "No, it's personal."
This wasn't very original, but it was safe.

"Oh. If you give me your name and number, I'll see that he gets it."

I gave the man my name and my home phone number. After a
brief pause, the man said, "Thank you, I'll make sure Mr. Duffy gets
this."

"Does Mr. Duffy own the store?" I asked, trying to sound casual
and friendly.

"He owns a third of it," the man replied. "He does the buying
and manages the place."

"Oh."

"There was another j. Duffy's store in Dayton. It's closed now."

"Out of business?"

"Yes."

"Are you one of the owners?"

"No, I just work here. Actually, we're not open today—I just
happened to come in for something. This store will be closing in
four days."

"For good?"

"Yes, out of business."

"I'm sorry."

"We've been having our going-out-of-business sale. It's been on for a month. There's not much left in the store. Apparently you have never been here."

"No, I haven't. Do you mind telling me what kind of store it is — or was?"

"It's what we call a high-style accessory store. Table-top accessories; you know, things like glassware, flatware, china, placemats, and service pieces. We sell other merchandise too — clockware, candles, clip-on lights, and things like that. Do you get the picture?"

"Yes. Thanks. Will the store be reopening somewhere else?"

"No, that's it."

"It's been nice talking to you," I said. "Please tell Mr. Duffy I have something important to speak to him about. It's not an emergency, though."

"I'll tell him — Mr. Fisher. I have your number. You wouldn't be calling from Pittsburgh, would you?"

"Not from Pittsburgh itself — but not far from there."

"I thought so. I recognized the area code. I used to live in western Pennsylvania. I'd be happy to take a message."

"I'm sorry, but it's a bit personal. You could tell Mr. Duffy that it has to do with something that happened a long time ago."

"In Pittsburgh?"

"Yes. He was just a child."

"Can I tell him who you are? In case he asks."

"Tell him I'm a college professor — I teach criminal justice courses at Edinboro University here in Pennsylvania. Have you heard of it?"

"Yes. It's up near Erie."

"That's right. I'm also a writer."

"I see. What do you write?"

"Books, mostly."

"What kind of books?"

"Nonfiction crime, what they call true crime. I wrote a book on the Lindbergh case."

"The kidnapping?"

"Yes."

"This event — involving Mr. Duffy — does it have anything to do with his mother?"

"Yes, it does."

"About her death?"

"Yes."

The man didn't respond. "Are you still there?" I asked, knowing that he was because I could hear breathing.

"I'm here," the man whispered. There was a long pause, then he said, his voice shaking, "I'm Chuck Duffy. Tell me what it is."

"I know something about your mother's murder."

"My God, that was over thirty years ago. What is it that you want?"

"I would like to talk to you, tell you what I know."

"What is your interest in this?"

"I'm interested in the case. I've been investigating the murder."

"Why? What for?"

"I've been trying to find out who killed your mother."

"Are you doing this for a book?"

"Yes — in part."

"Then you know about me."

"I know that you confessed."

"Did Ted Botula tell you that?"

"Yes, and it was in the papers."

"Ted Botula is still alive?"

"Yes."

"What did he tell you about me?"

"Botula doesn't remember much about the case or your confession. But he still believes you did it."

"I confessed to it. They said I killed her with a hatchet. I was only eight years old. They — the detectives — were very nice to me. Botula said he was my friend. He was very friendly. I was scared to death. I told them I didn't remember doing it. They said I must have done it because they had evidence. My fingerprints were on the hatchet. I can't remember what else they said. But they knew that it was me. They said I must have blacked out. That explained why I didn't remember. I didn't confess right away; they kept coming at me. They said nothing would happen to me. I would be protected. They said they had to get on with other things, and they needed to get this case summed up. Why didn't I just tell them I had done it and what I had done. I kept saying I didn't do it. I wasn't even in the house when it happened. I kept fighting; I kept saying, 'I didn't do it.' Finally, they convinced me that I had done it. I told them I had killed her, and Botula said, 'Now don't you feel better?' I did feel better! I know that sounds funny, but it's true. Do you know what happened to me after I confessed?"

"You mean the adoption?"

"Yes. Do you know about Lou Glasso and my stay at the hospital."

"Yes."

"Lou Glasso saved my life. The people at the hospital were kind. The doctors tested me and said I didn't do it."

"I know."

"I've lived thirty years wondering, in the back of my mind, if I did kill my mother. I'd wake up in the middle of the night and ask myself that question — the answer would always be no — but I always had to ask — a thousand times. I've never been *absolutely* sure. What do *you* think?"

"You didn't kill your mother. I'm sure you didn't."

"What makes you so sure?"

"I've studied the case. I have evidence. The police took advantage of you. They used you."

"Have you spoken with my relatives — the Zubryds?"

"Yes, some of them."

"Mike and Marge?"

"Marge. Mike won't talk to me."

"I'm not surprised," Chuck said. "Listen, I'm feeling a little queasy. This is like a dream. Am I dreaming this?" Chuck burst into a nervous laugh.

"It's not a dream."

"I didn't think I would hear anyone say to me what you just said. Honestly, I didn't think this day would ever come. I have dreams about what happened, but they're always bad dreams. This feels like a dream. What did Marge say?"

"She told me about the confession and about how hard it was on Mike."

"I haven't been in touch with my family in years; they went on without me. I've had to live without them. They believe I killed my mother. I'm getting shaky," Chuck said, his voice cracking.

"Are you in the store by yourself?" I asked.

"No. I'm with a friend. You just happened to catch me. We stopped by to pick up dinner service for a party tomorrow at my apartment. He's around here someplace."

"Are you married?"

"No."

"Have you ever been?"

"No."

"Does your friend know anything about this?"

"His name is Bob. No. None of my friends do. They wouldn't believe any of this. Sometimes I don't believe it." Chuck laughed. "Really, I can't believe this is happening. This call is unreal. How did you find out where I am?"

"Janice Todd."

"Janice. Oh, my God. How is she?"

"She's fine."

"Is she still a bundle of nerves over this?"

"Yes. I think she feels guilty."

"I wish she'd quit that," Chuck said. "My life has been the tragedy, and she's living it." Chuck's voice broke, and I thought he was going to cry.

"I know this has been one hell of a shock."

"That's putting it mildly."

"I'm gonna hang up so you can collect yourself. You have my number; when you've collected yourself, you can ring me back. I'll wait here for your call."

"The problem with Janice is she's hung up on the family name thing. The scandal. I'm an embarrassment."

"I told Janice that you didn't do it," I said. "I told her I could prove that."

"Did you tell Marge?"

"Yes."

"And?"

"It's hard to say. At the time, they thought you did it. It's hard to change your mind about something you've believed in for so long. I'm not sure what they think now. Janice wants to believe you didn't."

"It's not their fault. There have been times, many times, when *I* wasn't sure." Chuck began to cry. A minute passed, and he said, "I've got to get off the phone."

"Be sure to call me back," I said.

"I will."

"When?"

"In a few minutes. I'll be all right in a few minutes."

"I'll be here."

"Bye," Chuck said, then he hung up.

The moment he hung up, I realized I had let him get away without telling him what I had uncovered in my investigation. I hadn't told him about the crime scene evidence or about Joe Start's moon-faced guy. He didn't know about Ted Botula's phony fingerprints. As I sat at my desk thinking about the phone call, I realized that Botula had planted the seeds of guilt so deeply that Chuck still had doubts about his own innocence. I could almost feel his sense of shame and guilt.

I decided to sit at my desk and wait for his call. I knew that if he decided not to call back, I would have no way to get back to him: I didn't know where he lived, his home phone number was unlisted, and his store would be closed in four days. He had sounded awfully upset when he hung up. Maybe calling him like that had been a mistake. Now I would have to wait and wonder.

I had been at my desk thirty minutes and Chuck hadn't called. He had been at his store with a friend, and I realized I had forgotten to get Bob's last name. I was about to pick up my phone and call back when it rang — it was Chuck. He said he was still at the store with his friend Bob, Bob Liggett. Chuck said he was sorry for the delay, but Bob had been worried that I was some kind of nut. They had called their public library to see if anyone had heard of my book. They didn't know the title but had my name and knew it had something to do with the Lindbergh case. The woman at the library said they had the book, but it was out, so Chuck had called a local bookstore, and the salesclerk found a copy and read what it said about me on the dust jacket. Chuck seemed proud of his own investigative skills and said he felt better about talking to me about himself and his mother.

"You said you had found evidence," he said.

"Yes, evidence that proves you couldn't have killed your mother. I have information that shows — at least to my satisfaction — that Ted Botula knew all along that you were innocent."

"What kind of evidence?"

"Physical evidence — crime scene evidence — the very best kind."

"Like what?"

"For one thing, semen."

"What semen?"

"They found traces of it on your mother's blue jeans. It definitely didn't come from you."

"Are you sure of this?"

"That it wasn't yours?"

"No," Chuck replied, "that it was there!"

"I am positive."

"Did Ted Botula know this?"

"Yes, I believe he did. I don't know how he could not have known it; he was in charge of the case."

"This is shocking."

"The killer had strong hands," I said. "He tore off your mother's blue jeans. It was a brutal crime. The police found a pubic hair near her body. It wasn't hers, and it certainly wasn't yours."

"My legs feel like rubber. Have you told this to any of my relatives?"

"Yes."

"Who?"

"Janice Todd and your Aunt Marge."

"What did they say?"

"They were also shocked."

"They didn't know?"

"No."

"What about my fingerprints on the hatchet?"

"There weren't any fingerprints on the hatchet."

"Ted Botula lied?"

"Yes."

"Why did he do this to me? Why did he do this to my family?"

"I don't know. It doesn't make any sense to me, either."

"You said you talked to Botula?"

"Many times."

"What does he say?"

"Not much. Time has separated him from the case. He doesn't seem to mind that the truth has finally come out."

"Did you ask him why he would do this?"

"He doesn't deny anything, but he doesn't explain it, either."

"Do you have a theory?"

"I can only guess. Botula was under pressure to solve the case and was probably worried about his career. You were handy, so he dumped it on you. He may have figured, What's the harm, the kid's too young to go to jail. I don't know. Ted Botula also liked the limelight."

"He did this for publicity?"

"That could have been part of it."

"I was disposable," Chuck said, "to everybody. My family couldn't deal with what I had done, so they got rid of me. They didn't know how to explain me."

"It was tough on them, too."

"I'm sure it was — they're not bad people. They did what they thought they had to do."

"Janice Todd says she wants to see you."

"I'd like to see her," Chuck said. "I'll write her a letter."

"That would be nice."

"But we can't be one happy family again — to believe that is to believe in fairy tales. It's not my responsibility to forgive them. I have too many problems of my own. [Although I didn't know it at the time, Chuck had just learned that he was HIV positive.] I'm not going to put myself in any position to be hurt again. I don't know these people anymore."

"You sound angry."

"I'm also excited and exhilarated! I've been exonerated," Chuck said. "Why won't my Uncle Mike talk to you?"

"Marge says it's because of what he went through. He's still hurt and angry because the police suspected him and put him on the lie detector."

"They put everybody on the lie detector!" Chuck said. "They put *me* on it! So what? He didn't lose *his* mother — he didn't lose his family. He wasn't brainwashed into confessing to a murder he didn't do. He left the ordeal with his life intact. Now he refuses to help you help me! I'm going to call Mike — and tell him to lighten up."

"You should know that Mike — according to Marge — isn't convinced you *didn't* do it."

"What is wrong with that man? My God. He's got to make me a killer to justify the adoption."

"He'll come around."

"Boy, that hurts."

"You like your Uncle Mike."

"I do. Does he know about the evidence you found?"

"I'm sure Marge told him."

"And he still isn't sure?"

"I don't know."

"To hell with him," Chuck snapped. "He can go to hell. I'm going to call him and tell him what I think. He's my godfather," Chuck said, under his breath. "What did Marge say?"

"Marge told me that, if she had known about the semen and the other evidence, she wouldn't have taken you to Botula that day."

"What did she think before you called?"

"Once she had a chance to think about the confession, she had doubts. She says she didn't call Botula. He called her and asked her to have you brought down to the courthouse."

"Do you believe that?"

"Yes."

"Hmm."

"Janice Todd told me she's finally decided to tell her sons-in-law about you."

"Well it's about time!" Chuck laughed. "I think this has been harder on Janice than anyone. Janice feels guilty because the family let me go, and even worse, for believing that I had killed my mother. What am I supposed to do, call her up and say – Listen, I'm not a murderer? I think Janice thinks my adopted parents were critical of her – they weren't. She's got to get over the guilt. She should quit looking back."

"Another thing," I said, "Janice has always felt bad about touching the hatchet. Everybody thought she had destroyed the fingerprints. I guess you know that she found your mother on the basement floor."

"Yes. But I didn't know about the hatchet," Chuck said.

"Everybody is a victim in this thing," I said.

"It's Botula's fault," Chuck muttered.

"I haven't told you everything," I said.

"What?" Chuck replied.

"Do you remember Detective Joe Start?"

"I don't think I do."

"He was on the case."

"I just remember Botula."

"On the day after the murder, Joe Start and his partner, Joe Carmody, heard about a guy who had gotten onto a bus that night near your house. They called him the 'moon-faced guy.' Anyway, they figured this man could have been the killer. A couple of years later, after you had confessed and the case had been closed, Start and his partner ran across the moon-faced guy, and he confessed to killing your mother."

"My God!" Chuck exclaimed. "This is astounding! How come no one told me? Did my family know about this man?"

"No."

"What about Mike and Marge?"

"They know now, because I told them."

"What did they do with the man?"

"They let him go."

"What?"

"He was released."

"Why?"

"Why do you think?"

"I feel that I'm in a dream. Where is this man?" Chuck asked. "This is frightening."

"I don't know; he's probably dead."

"Who is he? Did he know my mother?" Chuck asked.

"Joe Start remembers the confession and the man, but he can't recall his name. It's been on the tip of his tongue for years, and we've tried everything—even hypnosis. Joe is worried what you'll think of him."

"I'm not mad at him," Chuck said. "He's not the one who did this to me. I'm glad he's come forward. He didn't have to."

"Joe feels guilty about this."

"I'd like to meet him," Chuck said. "We should talk."

"I'll tell him."

"If this man had confessed," Chuck said, "why wasn't he prosecuted?"

"If the district attorney had gone forward with the case, people would have found out what they had done to you."

"Are you saying," Chuck asked, "that they let a killer go just to save face?"

"Yes."

"They couldn't take a little political embarrassment?"

"I guess not."

"What kind of people would do such a thing?"

"People who are ambitious."

"I'll never understand this," Chuck said. "What did Marge say to all of this?"

"There wasn't much she could say."

"Does Mike know about this man?"

"I imagine he does."

"And?"

"I'm not sure what he thinks."

"Mike just doesn't want to believe that I'm innocent," Chuck said. "He can't admit he was wrong."

"Mike probably feels like a victim himself," I said.

"Why doesn't he face the facts? Mike should be happy for me. I'm going to call him. You're trying to clear my name — and he should help."

"I wouldn't expect too much," I said. "Maybe you should give him some time."

"I don't know what's wrong with him," Chuck replied. "Tell me how it happened."

"The murder?"

"Yes."

"Are you sure you want to hear this?" I asked.

"I want to know. Tell me."

"The man came to the door and asked for a glass of water. Your mother sent him around to the basement. He said something to her down there, and she slapped him. That's when he grabbed the hatchet and killed her."

"That's it?" his voice husky.

"Yes," I replied.

"It's so senseless!"

"The man had been in prison for sex crimes and in and out of mental institutions. If you had been there, he would have killed you."

"I hope he's dead," Chuck said, after a pause. "I would like to think he's dead."

"He probably is. I wish we knew more about him."

"I'm not feeling well," Chuck said.

"I'll let you go. I hope we can talk again."

"Yes, definitely," Chuck said. "I don't know what to say — except thanks. How can I ever thank you for this?"

"You don't have to."

"I've waited all my life to hear someone say to me 'I know you didn't do it.' No one ever has, until now. That's why I have no self-esteem. Deep down, I've been filled with shame — and anger. I've never known who to be mad at, so I've been angry at myself — for confessing."

"It wasn't your fault — you were just a child who got manipulated by an experienced homicide detective."

"I'd like to see Ted Botula," Chuck said. "I'd like to look into his face and ask, Why? Why did you do this to me? I've never experienced a feeling of success, and I've never had a successful relationship. When the going gets tough, I walk away before I'm abandoned. I haven't lived — I've survived. I *can* survive. I'd like to tell Botula that."

"Ted Botula can't bring back your family," I said. "He can't give you your self-esteem, either."

"I realize that," Chuck said. "Let's get together soon."

"I hope very soon," I said.

"Thank you again, and good-bye — for now."

17 Chuck Duffy

ON THE LAST DAY OF MARCH 1989, SIX DAYS AFTER MY initial telephone conversation with Chuck Duffy, Sue and I drove out to Columbus to visit him. Normally it's a four-hour drive from our house to Columbus; but this time, the trip took an hour longer due to a freak spring snowstorm that hit central Ohio as we proceeded west on Interstate 80. We got into the city at noon and a few minutes later parked our car in the lot next to Chuck's high-rise apartment building on the edge of downtown Columbus.

Chuck's apartment was on the ninth floor, and when he greeted us at his door, I could tell he was nervous. So were we.

To break the ice and relieve the tension, Chuck showed us around his spacious apartment, of which he was obviously proud. With its white walls, white carpet, neon art, and modern furniture, the interior was quite chic and distinctive. This was clearly a place that had been carefully, thoughtfully, and tastefully put together.

We ended up in the living room with Chuck and my wife sitting on a pair of mauve sofas; I sat on a striped high-backed chair with my boom box at my feet. Chuck had his own tape recorder sitting next to him on the couch. When I looked out the large living room window, I could see the gray Columbus skyline.

I had seen several pictures of Chuck as a boy, and as I looked at
him now, I searched for the boy in the man. The Charlie Zubryd
still there resided in Chuck's eyes, which were green and piercing,
and in his eyebrows, which were arched, giving him a slightly
haughty look. Chuck was wearing a pair of snug blue jeans, white
sneakers, and a long-sleeved white pullover shirt made of some
kind of soft and, I guessed, expensive fabric. Of average height,
Chuck was well built but not muscular. He had a full head of thick,
sandy-brown, medium-length hair combed straight back in a rather
dramatic fashion. Little Charlie had grown into a nice-looking man.
Chuck did not come off as a "sissy" or as someone who was weak —
on the contrary, he seemed emotionally solid, strong willed, and
unafraid — but he *was* definitely effeminate in his speech and body
language, and in my mind, this, more than anything, was the char-
acteristic that linked him to his childhood.

Sue and I liked Chuck immediately, and shortly after we had
settled down to talk, Chuck was relaxed and speaking to us freely.
We talked all afternoon, and following a night in a nearby motel, my
wife and I were back in Chuck's apartment as he emotionally and
painfully laid out the story of his life.

What follows is Chuck's story, as he told it to us on those two
special days in the spring of 1989.

❏ ❏ ❏

"My father was sick as far back as I can remember; and the men
who were able to be active in my life were concerned about me being a sissy. But they never made any effort to take me to a ballgame,
to take me camping, or just to have me around when they were
doing 'guy' things. I was precocious, determined, bright — let the
women deal with him. They never made any effort to take control of
the circumstances except to perhaps discuss their concerns with my
mother.

"If nothing else, these women taught me to be a survivor; something that I expect some of them are not happy about — but that de-
termination has helped me to survive.

"I feel at times as though I never had a childhood, with my father sick as long as I can remember. What I remember is, at age six
and seven, I could iron shirts, cook simple meals, even help with
the laundry.

"After my father's death, I was frightened and probably slept with my mother every night after he died. I was four and we were living in the country. You hear strange noises at night.

"Did I wear my mother's clothing and things? Yes, I did. I wore her hats and shoes, and I had this umbrella and purse I carried around. The people who dominated my life were never men; they were women. I loved that little red purse; I wish I still had it. [Laughs.]

"As for my childhood preoccupation with menstruation and reproduction, I don't remember any of that. Elaine [Asperger] and I, I suppose, had some of those normal childhood inquisitive moments. I don't think that's abnormal.

"Yes, I remember the night my mother was murdered. I had come back from Mrs. Asperger's house and went in the front door and yelled for my mother. She didn't answer, and I went through the house looking for her. I thought, 'Well, this is weird; where is she?' Then I remembered that walking between the houses I had seen a light on in the basement and I thought, 'Well, I wonder what she's doing down there.' I started down the steps and got most of the way down — I had been talking — 'Mother, where are you? — Mother, where are you' — and I got there and it was like — oh, my God — what's happened? I can close my eyes and see her lying on the floor and I can see the pool of blood. I can see the handle sticking up out of her head. I don't know what I thought. I was too unsophisticated to believe she was dead. The thought that she was laying there in all that blood — it never occurred to me. I don't know that I realized the hatchet was completely embedded in her head. The concept was, what happened? Not that something *had* happened. I recognized the hatchet; I recognized the blood; but I was probably twenty feet away. I turned on the steps and went flying out. I went next door. It gets muddled from this point on.

"I remember this interminable period when nothing seemed to be going on, and then suddenly there were all these people around. I didn't know what was going on. 'How's my mother — is she okay?' And everybody saying, 'Well, they've taken her to the hospital,' you know.

"I don't remember calling Aunt Marion or Janice that night — but I suppose that's who I would have called.

"What bothers me, even today, is that army belt. I don't understand why she had that belt. Maybe the man who came to the door bothered her; maybe she picked it up in case she might need some kind of protection. I was spanked with that belt—it was a heavy leather strap. That belt never left the hook it hung on, except when I got spanked. And that wasn't very often.

"I remember going to my mother's funeral, but I only recall being in that funeral home one night—I believe it was Friday night. I remember looking at her in the coffin. I asked if I could touch her, and they allowed me to. That was a mistake. No little child should be allowed to do that. I touched her hand, and I didn't expect the coldness. I remember the shock from that. I don't know that I yelled, but I think that something came out of my mouth. I didn't cry. I get chills now as I think about that cold flesh. I could never touch a dead body again.

"I remember that long ride to the Westmoreland Country Cemetery behind the hearse. I was in the car with my cousin Karen, and she drove me crazy. I don't remember thinking about what was going to happen to me. Not then. My mother was gone, and it hurt.

"I'm not sure, but I remember being taken to the courthouse in Pittsburgh to take a lie detector test. This was several months after the murder but long before I confessed. I remember this man coming at me with these straps. It was like when I had a tooth extracted and got gassed. I can remember that dentist coming at me with what looked like the end of a plunger. I had that same feeling when they hooked me up to that lie detector. Nobody explained to me how it worked—or if it worked.

"I remember the day I confessed, the day that changed my life. I can recall being in a very small room. Oddly, I remember a two-way mirror—knowing that I was being watched. Two or three detectives were talking to me. I asked them why we had to do this again. The explanation, as I recall it, was—I had become rather withdrawn at school, that I had not been interacting with my friends. They said I had been spending a lot of time by myself. None of this I had ever really perceived, but supposedly my aunt and uncle had talked with the police, and they had discussed all of this and felt there was something wrong—that we should talk again.

"I spent the next couple of hours being told by a series of people that I had killed my mother. They knew I had done it. They said they had a lot of evidence that pointed to me. They said, for example, that my fingerprints were on the hatchet, and they knew that my dog didn't bark that night. It went on like that for some time.

"Nothing would happen to me, they said. I would be protected, and all of that. They said they had to get on with things and they needed to get this case summed up. Why didn't I just tell them I had done it and what I had done. I kept saying I didn't do it. I wasn't even in the house when it happened. I had gone next door to Elaine's and Mrs. Asperger's. Mother and I were getting ready to go to Pittsburgh by train. We were going to spend Thanksgiving at my Aunt Marion's. My mother was getting clothes ready and packed. I went next door, and when I came back I found her. I recounted that. I kept fighting; I kept saying, 'I didn't do it, I didn't do it.' After a while it's like, okay. They said they knew that a neighbor man — Elmer Skiles, Jr. — had been sexually abusing me. That was true. My mother had found out and was going to confront him. They said I didn't want her to do that, so I killed her. I don't know if my mother knew about it or not. I just remember being abused by this man. They suggested another motive when I didn't respond to that one — they said I was spoiled, and when my mother told me to do something I didn't want to do, I flew into a rage and killed her.

"I remember the army belt. If I was going to be spanked with it, it certainly wouldn't have been the first time. I was not abused by my parents. I was a determined child. I tended to live in my own world and think my own thoughts. I would sulk; I would pout. I was a spoiled brat. If I didn't get my own way — I knew if I pouted, I might. What's the big issue? I did throw temper tantrums — I was a kid.

"The detectives didn't physically coerce me, but they got tougher as time went on. I wasn't saying what they wanted to hear. I was traumatized. The police knew that Marge and I didn't get along and that I would go for long periods and not speak to her. In fact, it was her. I caused her displeasure, and when I did, she punished me with silence.

"Finally I told them what they wanted to hear. I confessed. Then one of the detectives asked me if I felt better. That confession changed my life, it changed the lives of the Sudik family and the Zubryd family. I guess it changed the Duffys, too.

"I realized even then that the police were just trying to clear up a case. The one person I felt was my friend was Ted Botula. He had always been very friendly. He seemed to be interested in me. He had been out to visit me many times. I had no idea what these visits were leading to. I don't remember Joe Start — at least not by name — but I remember Ted Botula. Botula was 'the friend.' He was the prominent one in my interrogation and was my friend afterwards. I never judged him for what he did. He had a job that he was attempting to do to the best of his ability. Everything he had done to that point, appearancewise, was in my best interest. I don't feel that way now. I remember him telling me my fingerprints were on the hatchet. I said to him, 'My God, we lived in the country; we chopped down limbs; we chopped down bushes.'

"To this day, I cannot pick up an ax or hatchet. I can't. I see one and I freeze. I have to go the other way if I'm in a hardware store and see one. I don't watch blood-and-gore movies either. If I do, it all comes back. I really don't like, still, going into a dark basement. Normally, when I go out in the evening, I leave the lights on. That way, when I come home, I don't have to come into the dark. I have this thing about the dark.

"After my confession, they took me out to Oakland to the Juvenile Detention Center. I was there two nights. I remember being in a lounge, and I can remember all the news coverage on TV. The newscast that night was film of us leaving the courthouse to go to Oakland. I had a hat and I held it over my face.

"I remember being in that dormitory, that lounge or recreation room at the juvenile center, with that TV on. I recall seeing myself on the news. You can imagine, there were all these kids, some of them teenagers. I was a little kid, and they were looking at me like — what's this with the kid? What do we got here? You'd get fearful. When it came on TV that I had confessed to killing my mother with a hatchet, they got fearful. [Laughs.]

"Monday morning we briefly went before a judge, and then I went straight to the hospital. There was never any lag time; everything was orchestrated.

"They took me to the hospital in East Liberty, and I had the time of my life. Number one, I didn't have to put up with my aunt. I had a TV in my room. The night-shift nurses would come in and we'd watch Johnny Carson. They spoiled me rotten.

"Dr. William McCabe was very wonderful, as was Lou Glasso. They took great care to explain to me what was happening so I could understand. I went to Dr. McCabe's office to have the EEG. I had had the lie detector test before, had been hooked up to that, and suddenly they were coming at me again with all these wires.

They were testing my brain waves to determine if I could have possibly blacked out. They didn't believe that I had.

"I can remember Dr. McCabe testing my strength, putting some kind of grasping instrument in my hand that had a meter on it. They wanted to prove I couldn't have swung the hatchet. There was a lot of testing.

"On Sunday, toward the end of my hospital stay, the family came to visit. Marge came in — I will never forget her looking at me — because there I was, sitting on the edge of the bed in the new robe Marilyn Fergason had given me. Marilyn was a newspaper reporter who was writing a story about me. Dr. McCabe had arranged it. I hadn't seen my Aunt Marge in three weeks. She had a paper bag full of my things, and she said: 'You know, that's the trouble with you. People are always spoiling you.' I have not forgotten those words. I will never forget them.

"When I was in the hospital, Lou Glasso brought Florence and Frank Duffy around to see me. They were wonderful people, and when Lou Glasso told me they wanted to adopt me and asked if that was okay with me, I said yes. I spent the summer after the hospital living with the Glassos. I loved it at their house. They — Mr. and Mrs. Glasso and their three children — lived in a big house on top of a hill in Glenshaw. I remember their daughter Yolanda; they called her 'Chi Chi.' The Duffys took me in the fall of 1959, when school started. I moved into their house on Vanadium Drive in Bridgeville. It was a modest suburban home with a nice big yard. I went to the local parish grade school and was an altar boy. I was also the teacher's pet. Easter was always a big day in the Duffy house. Frank Duffy worked for J & L Steel — he was an industrial psychologist. He had worked with Dr. McCabe at the Mayview State Mental Institution earlier in the 1950s.

"When I first went to the Duffys, one of the neighbors said to my mom, 'Isn't he the little boy who was on TV?' My mom said, 'Yes,' and that's where it stopped. I never had a problem with that. The Duffys seldom talked about the murder. When we did, it was because I had brought it up. After a while, the subject never came up. I wanted to forget.

"I do not resent or regret that I was adopted — it is undoubtedly the best thing that could have happened to me. The Zubryd family was already torn apart about how Marge and Mike were raising me.

"I was disposable — when my family couldn't decide what to do with me, when they couldn't deal with what I had done, they got rid of me. I never understood that until now. They didn't know how to explain me.

"When I was in ninth grade at Lincoln Junior High, I told a friend — Jim Wise — why I had been adopted. I told him my mother had been murdered and that I had been accused. Because of that, I'd been taken from the family. Jim was overwhelmed. He didn't believe me at first. He promised not to tell anyone.

"In high school — Chartiers Valley — I had ordinary, run-of-the-mill friends. I went to football games, went ice skating, and was active in the church. I didn't drive until I was eighteen, the year I got six thousand dollars from the trust fund, money from the sale of my mother's house on Barley Road. Once, while in high school, I stayed out too late — at a New Year's Eve party — and got in trouble with my parents. They grounded me for a while. I went to the prom, was editor of the yearbook, and graduated in 1966.

"I wanted to be a writer and majored in English at Ohio University in Athens, Ohio. I had been to Athens before, and I loved it. But there was too much pressure on me to achieve — to do well. Frank Duffy had very high standards — he expected too much from me. He always worried that I wasn't studying hard enough. I got good grades in high school, but I liked to do other things. I didn't want to study all the time. Frank Duffy was constantly on me about that.

"In my junior year at college, I was under a lot of pressure to do well, and I wasn't. I had lost my sense of direction. I didn't know what to do. My grades were getting worse, and I got so strung out, I went to a doctor who put me on Librium. I got hooked on the stuff, and it made things worse. I was also hitting the booze. Tranquilizers and beer — a bad combination. I was taking thirty milligrams of Librium a day — three pills — one to get up, one to get me through the day, and one to get me to bed. Finally I just quit school. I never graduated. This caused serious problems with my dad. We went through a bad period.

"I had always tried to please the Duffys, but finally I said, 'Whoa — this is for me; I'm doing what I want to do.' In 1970, I moved to Columbus to find a job, and every time I'd go home, the Duffys would say, 'How are you?' then, 'When are you going back to school?' They never knew how much Librium I was on.

"After I moved to Columbus, I still had problems. I felt insecure and had problems forming personal relationships. I started thinking about why I had been adopted and all of that bad publicity there had been about me. I started to wonder if maybe I was a bad person. I started to wonder if maybe I had killed my mother.

"When I first went to Columbus I didn't have a job, but I did have friends there. I couldn't go home because of all the grief about my quitting college. I took a job with a mattress company, taking orders. I then went to work for a glass company that later went out of business. Then I got a job at a furniture store, where I became the administrative secretary to the president of the company—that meant I was his flunky. We were opening a new store, and I was helping set the store up and he saw some areas I had put together and he said, 'Who did all of this?' Somebody told him I had done it. The next thing I knew, I was with the design staff. And that's how I got into design.

"I had straightened things out with my parents by now, and then, in 1974 when Frank Duffy was only fifty-two, he had a heart attack and died. He was a wonderful man, and I still miss him. He only wanted the best for me. He never got over the fact I quit college.

"I left the furniture store and went to work for a design firm on the east side. That's where I built up a good clientele. I then moved to another interior design firm—a studio. About eighteen months later, the company went broke.

"In December 1978, my Aunt Olga [née Zubryd] from Canton, Ohio, called and said that my Aunt Marion was very sick. Marion had emphysema and didn't have long to live. This was the first time in twenty years anyone from the family had spoken to me. Olga said the family had talked, and they thought it would really help Marion if she could see me. So, I went to see her that Christmas. I went by myself. She was at home in Shadyside. I was tearful. I told her I didn't blame her for anything.

"Marion was feisty; she was a little woman. She was a hard worker. She was always sick on New Year's Day, and as an adult I wonder if it wasn't a hangover. She was a kind and good woman. Marion was much stronger than Tom. When Marion died, Uncle Tom almost flipped out. He remarried and he's living on the West Coast and won't have anything to do with his family. He won't even talk to his kids. They can't get past the second wife. Tom's world crumbled, and he started drinking heavily. That's when he met this woman in a bar, and in three months they were married.

"In my family, the women were the stronger people. Tom was a gentle and kind man; Marion had a mind of her own, and I know that she and Marge had more than one fight about how I was being raised. Everyone wanted to tell Marge and Mike how to raise me — which really wasn't right.

"Marion died in January 1979; and on the twenty-seventh, I went to her funeral — alone. It was the first contact I had had with my flesh-and-blood family since my confession. I was scared to death. Uncle Tom had called, so I had been invited.

"Between calling hours at the funeral home, I was at Tom and Marion's apartment in Shadyside. The whole family was there except Mike and Marge. We had come back to the funeral home from Marion's place and were in the driveway when Marge and Mike walked in front of our car. They were on their way into the funeral home, and they didn't know I had come. Uncle Mike looked into the car and said, 'Who's that in the back seat?' Karen, my cousin, was on one side, I was in the middle, and my other cousin Paula was on the other side. The three of us, when we were kids, were always together. Uncle Tom said, 'It's Karen, Charlie, and Paula.' Well, Uncle Mike went absolutely ashen, and the two of them made a beeline in the door.

"When I walked into the funeral home, Marge came up to see me and put her arms around me and told me what a fine young man I was and how wonderful it was to see me and how they had missed me. My arms would not leave my side. I could not physically lift my arms. I couldn't return the hug. Some things you cannot forgive. There are things you cannot forget.

"I saw my grandmother, Katherine Zubryd, at the funeral — she was a tough old bird — and her first remark to me was, 'Where did you get that coat? At the Salvation Army?' I laughed. I said, 'Yeah, Gram, they had a sale.' She died two years ago, and no one bothered to tell me. They all knew I was here. Marge knew. Uncle Mike, that poor man, twenty years later, couldn't look me in the face. All he had to say was, 'I am sorry for everything that happened to you.' I could deal with that. But I can't handle a man who turns ashen and walks away. It's his problem, not mine. I have survived, I will survive.

"When I came out of the church behind Marion's coffin, I was in pretty bad shape. I said to someone near me, 'You've got to understand, this is the first time in twenty years that we have been together.' Well, we haven't been back together since.

"Marion's funeral was painful for everyone because it brought everything back.

"A year after Marion was buried, my Uncle Nick died and was laid out in the same funeral room in Ambridge that had my mother. It was tough walking into that room.

"I went to the calling hours, not to the funeral. I got to see cousins that had meant a great deal to me as a boy. I felt some uneasiness from Janice Todd. Janice had a problem, and it was difficult for her to talk to me about it. She couldn't look at me without crying. Janice always felt like she had let me down. They should get over the guilt. She should quit looking back.

"I know that Janice has problems explaining me to her daughters' husbands. My life was the tragedy—and they're living it. They weren't accused. They can live the tragedy if they want to, but I want to be exonerated. They are hung up on the family name that was destroyed. The point is—what's the real tragedy here? They can call me about funerals—why can't you invite me to weddings? I'm not so difficult to explain. They didn't have a good explanation for me. I am an embarrassment to them. That's what I picked up from Janice at the funeral. I realized there was real feeling in that family that I had done it!

"I guess I need to tell them I am not a murderer. I am none of the things I was accused of being. You can accept me as you find me. I've lived thirty years without you, I can probably go to my grave without you.

"How else can I deal with this? I can't make up their minds for them. I have earned the right for justice. I am entitled to it. It's my justice, not theirs. It has no bearing on them or their lives.

"By 1983, I had a lot of good design clients, and one of these clients—a married couple—had become close friends. We had always talked about going into business together, and so we got serious about opening a business, and that was when we put together the plan to open j. Duffy's. I gave up my apartment and moved into their house with them. I became the big brother their daughters never had. They became like family. To me, family has little to do with blood and a lot to do with mental attitude. They were the brothers and sisters I never had. One time Mother—Florence Duffy—and I had this argument. She said I only make friends with people who had money.

"The only relative I've kept in touch with is my Aunt Olga in

Canton. We exchange Christmas cards. We haven't been close. She has her life, and I have mine. After the murder, I went twenty years without seeing any of them. No letters, no phone calls, no birthday cards — nothing. I have nineteen aunts and uncles and a million cousins — and all this time they were having birthdays, graduating, getting married, and so forth. I never got invited. My aunts and uncles could have reached me anytime through my mother. But they never did. I was an embarrassment.

"Are the Sudiks and Zubryds bad people? I don't think so. They are a simple people who got caught in a quagmire that they didn't have an easy way to survive. They did what they thought they had to do. But I don't have to put myself in a position to be hurt again. I have been to too many funerals. I don't require explanation — the tragedy is reality — a part of the family history. It is not pretty, but the guilt must be uglier.

"I really don't know these people anymore, and I don't intend to judge them. However, I don't know that I want to build new relationships with all of them. There are those with whom it is easy to pick up and begin anew. They are the ones who are honest today, as I always remember. But I don't think it will ever be what it might have been.

"Ted Botula owes me an explanation. That won't take away what he did. He destroyed a family. It will not make me feel any better. He almost deprived me of having any self-respect and esteem. But I'd like to know why.

"I've lived thirty years wondering in the back of my mind if I had killed my mother. That's what he did to me.

"Right after you called, a friend called me. She said, 'What is wrong with you? You sound funny.' I said, 'I just had the most devastating news in the world. It is absolutely wonderful news.' I told her what it was all about, and she said, 'This is shocking.'

"I talked with my mother last night and she said, 'What is really the point in all of this?' All I could say to her was, 'I am entitled to be freed of this burden. I was accused in public, and I have a right to be exonerated in public.' Does it make me feel any better? Yeah, it really does. It's exhilarating. I never realized how much I had lost until you rang my phone and said, 'Guess what? You really didn't do it!'"

❏ ❏ ❏

On our way back to Pennsylvania, Sue and I talked about Chuck, about what he had told us and what he hadn't. Chuck had been open and articulate and had shocked us with the revelation that Elmer Skiles, Jr., had been sexually molesting him. I remember that Chuck — Charlie — on the day of the murder had been playing at the Skileses' house, a place someone had called "an obscene hole in the ground." No one I had talked to had mentioned anything about Charlie being sexually violated, and I wondered if this was why Botula had the Skiles brothers arrested and grilled. Helen could have found out and may have confronted the man. Maybe it was Elmer's father, Elmer, Sr., she had had words with. According to old newspaper articles, one of the Skiles boys hadn't been able to account for himself when Helen was murdered, and that's why they were suspects. It had been my theory that Botula had pulled the Skiles brothers in because they were retarded, very low class, and handy. I would ask Joe Start about this and find out if he remembered anything about Charlie being sexually molested by a Skiles brother.

I had come away from Chuck's interview convinced that he was gay. Although his sexuality wasn't relevant to the murder case, the fact that he had been a "sissy," in my mind, had a lot to do with the way he was treated by his family after his confession. Chuck didn't say he was gay, and I hadn't asked because at this point it was none of my business. But he had hinted that he was, and I felt he wanted me to know that. If we were to become friends, and I assumed that we would, the subject would eventually have to come up. If I were to write a book about the murder and Chuck's life, I'd have to know.

Janice Todd had told me that Charlie's little red purse and umbrella had more to do with his problems than his confession. I agreed and couldn't help wondering if Mike Zubryd, Charlie's uncle and legal guardian, hadn't used the confession as an excuse to unburden himself of the boy. Mike couldn't really have believed that Charlie had murdered his mother, at least not after some reflection.

Chuck, on the other hand, seemed convinced that his adoption had been prompted by the belief by Mike and others in the family that he had done it. I couldn't decide which reason to get rid of him was worse.

Chuck hadn't shown much interest in Joe Start's moon-faced confessor. He didn't seem concerned that I hadn't been able to identify this man and solve his mother's murder. He had gotten what he had wanted and needed — exoneration. Apparently it was enough for him to know for certain that he hadn't swung that hatchet and that the evidence Botula had suppressed was proof to all that he couldn't have been the killer. He had also learned that Botula had known from the beginning that he was innocent, yet Botula had gone after him anyway.

Chuck was elated, and I was happy for him. But for me it wasn't enough to know who hadn't killed Helen Zubryd. I wanted to know who had. Until I identified the moon-faced man, assuming he was the one, I couldn't be satisfied. I wanted to know if this guy was still among the living, where he lived, how he lived, what he looked like, and if he had other victims like Helen. If he was dead, I wanted to know how he had died. If this man had suffered, I wanted to know that and perhaps take comfort in his misery.

It looked as though Helen Zubryd's murder might never be solved; and I, like Joe Start, would have to live with the frustration of coming up short. It might not make a difference to the victim, but whenever a murderer slips away unidentified, his killing continues, if not in reality then at least in the mind of the investigator chasing him down.

18 Winding Down to a Stop

BEFORE GOING TO OHIO, I HAD INFORMED JOE START that I planned to visit Chuck. He asked me to let him know how the interview went. Joe thought that Chuck probably hated him because he hadn't come forward with the proof, the semen on Helen's blue jeans, that would have exonerated Chuck. I understood why Joe felt guilty, but I reminded him that Chuck — little Charlie — did have the services of an experienced defense attorney in 1959. If Lou Glasso had investigated the case, simply looked at the coroner's file, he would have nailed Botula on the spot. The lawyer certainly would have had access to the coroner's information, which was open to the public. Lou Glasso could have questioned the crime lab experts who examined the evidence. They would not have lied to protect Botula; these men were scientists; they didn't work for the D.A. And what about the news media? Pittsburgh had three newspapers and three television stations, where were the investigative journalists of the day? Why had Charlie Zubryd's confession been such an easy sell?

Joe Start felt particularly guilty because he had kept the moon-faced man under wraps. Maybe he should have told someone in Chuck's family about the confession. I reminded Joe that, by then, Chuck had already been adopted by the Duffys. The boy's relationship with his blood family had already been poisoned by his so-called convincing confession, a confession Joe Start had not had a hand in obtaining. I had also told Joe there was a strong possibility that Mike and Marge Zubryd always knew that Chuck was innocent but had simply used his confession as an excuse to dump him. Joe said he had told himself that; and even if it were true, it didn't change the fact that he had not taken the opportunity to clear the boy's name when he had the chance. Several of Chuck's relatives, Janice Todd for one, had been agonizing for thirty years over the question of Charlie's guilt or innocence. The same was true of Catherine and Elaine Asperger.

Yes, someone should have blown the whistle on Ted Botula. Several of his detectives knew of the crime scene evidence, but no one came forward, and there was nothing Joe Start could do about it now except feel guilty and worry about what Chuck was thinking. I had assured Joe that I would try to explain to Chuck that coming forward with this information would have cost Joe his job and may have meant the end of his career in law enforcement. It would have meant going up against Ted Botula, Henry Pieper, and the D.A. himself. Allegheny County detectives, in Start's day, didn't have the protection of civil service or a union and, as political appointees, had no job protection whatsoever. These detectives could be fired as quickly and easily as they had been hired.

The morning after my return from Columbus, I called Joe Start to tell him that, among other things, Chuck didn't hold him responsible for what happened. I said Chuck was grateful he had come forward because, without the investigative file on the murder, the moon-faced man's confession would never have come to light. Joe was, to say the least, relieved. But it didn't resolve his feelings of guilt: "Yeah," Joe said, when I told him of Chuck's appreciation, "I was a little late."

"Better late than never," I replied.

"I'd like to meet Chuck," Joe said. "Tell him that."

"I will."

"I'd like to tell him in person how sorry I am."

"Chuck told me that he'd like to see Botula."

"I bet he would," Joe said. "Teddy should have to answer to him."

"According to Chuck, Botula told him his fingerprints were on the hatchet."

"That was a lie. The Rug didn't get anything off the hatchet."

"Even if the boy's prints were on it, it didn't prove anything. Ted told him he didn't remember killing his mother because he had blacked out."

"Jesus," Joe said. "What kind of bullshit is that?"

"Ted told the boy his mother had chased him into the basement to beat him with his dad's old army belt. Ted told me the same thing when I first interviewed him. It was also reported that way in the papers after Charlie confessed. Funny thing, though, there was no mention of the army belt before Charlie's confession. I went back and read through all of the newspaper clippings. I found no reference to an army belt laying next to her body, or anywhere else for that matter."

"There was no army belt," Joe said. "I didn't see one near her body. That's just more of Teddy's bullshit."

"Chuck told me his dad did have an army belt, and he got spanked with it occasionally," I said.

"The army belt was in their basement all right," Joe said. "But it had nothing to do with the murder. It was sitting on a shelf with some other stuff that was stored down there. It's too bad we don't have the crime scene photographs. They would prove Teddy was lying about the belt."

"Ted was a clever guy."

"A real fox," Joe said.

"Have you been thinking about the moon-faced guy?" I asked.

"Oh, jeez, I'm about ready to give up on that. Shit, I'm driving myself nuts trying to remember his name."

"Vorcheck told you to relax, remember? He said not to try too hard."

"I don't think his name is Al T. Al T. was the guy I knew in the army. I wasted our time going up to Erie. I don't think hypnosis works too well in cases like this."

"I'm not sure," I said. "I'd like to try again."

"I'll do whatever you want; I'm just not optimistic."

"I was in Pittsburgh," I said, "and heard about two forensic hypnotists who work as a team. They're psychologists, and they bring back memories that have been long forgotten."

"How long?" Joe asked.

"Years — many years. I think it's worth a try. They're specialists and supposedly good. They don't make their living getting people off cigarettes and junk food, like the hypnotist in Erie, they work on criminal cases."

"Let's do it," Joe said. "Let me know and I'll be there, because that guy's name just isn't coming to me. I got some kind of mental block. Shit, I'll take 'truth serum.'"

"Let's stick to hypnosis," I said, realizing that Joe was only half kidding.

"If they hadn't destroyed our old files, we'd know who the guy was because [Charlie] McInerney tried to test him on the polygraph, and I wrote up a supplementary on his confession. All that stuff was in the file."

"If we don't put a name to this guy," I said, "we're finished."

"Well — at least Chuck Duffy knows the truth. I feel good about that," Joe said.

"It's too bad we can't give it to him complete. We're so close."

"Yeah."

"Chuck told me something I hadn't known," I said. "When he told me I wondered if you knew about it."

"What's that?" Joe asked.

"He said Elmer Skiles, the older brother that was retarded, was sexually molesting him."

"I didn't know that," Joe said. "I don't think any of our detectives did. This is new to me. I'll be damned."

"If Helen Zubryd had found out about this, she might have confronted him. She could have threatened to call the police or tell his father. Maybe the big guy panicked — and killed her."

"That could be," Joe said. "But I'm pretty sure none of the Skileses had anything to do with the murder. I was there when Teddy grilled the boys, and we searched that hole they lived in. The crime lab came up with nothing on their clothing. We gave the whole family a real hard look, and the evidence just wasn't there. Anyway, I'm sure it was the moon-faced guy. I'm positive."

"It was just an idea. You were there, I wasn't."

"Me and Joe Carmody placed our man in Ambridge that day; he had the mentality and the criminal record. Remember, he told us he was in her basement chasing her around with a hatchet. It had to be him. This guy was a sex maniac, and he was crazy. Me and Joe had the killer, and Teddy let him go. I don't know why I can't remember his name, but I can't. This thing is getting to me. It's too bad Joe Carmody is dead, he might have remembered."

"Try not to push it," I said. "The hypnotist said it could come to you anytime, but you can't force it."

"I don't think it will," Joe said. "I lost the name, and I'm never gonna find it."

"If you do find it, call me," I said.

"I will," Joe replied. "Let me know when you line up the two hypnotists in Pittsburgh."

❏ ❏ ❏

A day or so after my talk with Joe Start, Chuck Duffy called, and he was upset. He had phoned his Uncle Mike, and the conversation hadn't gone the way Chuck had hoped. Chuck was learning that getting back into the fold would not be easy, and in some cases not even possible. Marge Zubryd had answered the phone, and Chuck, without identifying himself, had asked to speak to Mike. According to Chuck, the conversation went something like this:

"Uncle Mike, do you know who this is?"

"No."

"It's Chuck."

"Who?"

"Charlie – Charlie Zubryd."

"Oh," Mike replied. "What do you want?"

"I think we should talk."

"There's nothing to talk about."

"I want to know why you won't cooperate with Mr. Fisher."

"I have nothing to say to him."

"He's trying to help me. Why won't you talk to him?"

"That's none of your business. I don't want anything to do with this."

"You mean you don't want anything to do with me."

"What's the point of digging it up all over again? We went through hell."

"*You* went through hell — what about me?"

Mike didn't answer.

Chuck said, "All you can do is think about yourself!"

"I don't want to talk about this. I'm giving the phone back to Marge."

"Wait," Chuck said. "I don't blame you — I don't hate you. Just tell me you're sorry about what happened to me. I can live with that."

"Leave me out of this," Mike said.

"Nobody is trying to make you the bad guy. You were a victim just like me."

Mike didn't respond.

"Mike?"

"It's me, Chuck — Marge."

"What is wrong with that man?" Chuck yelled.

"He doesn't want to go through it again," Marge said. "It's too painful."

"Too painful?"

"Yes. They put Mike through hell. They told people he had done it. They fingerprinted him, grilled him, put him on the lie detector. How do you think he felt?"

"That's not the point!" Chuck exclaimed. "I know his problem — he still thinks I did it. He thinks I killed my mother."

"He's not sure," Marge replied. "Don't forget — you did confess. You were so *convincing.*"

"My God — I was only eleven! Didn't Mr. Fisher tell you I was framed? Didn't he tell you about the evidence? Didn't you tell Mike?"

"Mike doesn't want to know — he doesn't want anything to do with this. I'm convinced you didn't do it. Mike isn't sure. He wants you and Mr. Fisher to leave him alone. The poor man has gone through enough. Please."

Chuck hung up. So much for his family, his flesh and blood.

❏ ❏ ❏

Chuck Duffy hadn't been back to western Pennsylvania for ten years. He was now a sales representative for a company that manufactured bedding supplies — sheets, bedspreads, pillowcases, and things like that. In June, while on a business trip to New York City, Chuck stopped in western Pennsylvania and drove up Barley Road to his old house. He hadn't been back to the old house in thirty years. Nothing much had changed except the house itself, which now had a garage. The placed looked small and brought back memories both sweet and painful. Mrs. Asperger's old house was still there — the little Cape Cod — and so was the Skiles' foundation which, months earlier, had been gutted by a fire. Members of the Skiles family were still living in the place at the time.

From Barley Road, Chuck drove over to Bell Acres to visit Janice and John Todd. He hadn't seen Janice since her father's funeral in Ambridge in 1980. Chuck had talked to Janice a few days earlier on the phone, so the visit wasn't a surprise.

In telling me about the visit a week or so later, Chuck revealed deep sympathy for Janice, but he was also impatient with her and a little bitter. He said Janice was quite nervous and emotional and made a big thing about having just told her two sons-in-law about Chuck and the murder of his mother. Chuck felt that, because he had been exonerated, Janice felt she could now haul him out of the closet without embarrassment. Janice was happy for Chuck, but at the same time she felt even more guilty for not believing in him when it really counted. She also felt responsible for his being adopted out of the family.

Chuck tried to make Janice feel less guilty by reminding her that the police had kept vital information from the family. He also assured her that there was nothing she could have done to keep him in the family. The plan to give him to the Duffys had been arranged by Lou Glasso with Mike Zubryd's blessing. Mike Zubryd was Chuck's legal guardian, and as such, his decision on this matter was final. The adoption decision had nothing to do with Janice or anyone else in the Sudik and Zubryd families. They had had no say in the matter.

Chuck said that Janice told him she had asked a lawyer and friend of the family if there was any chance she could adopt Chuck. The lawyer had advised against this, stating that it was in the boy's best interest to live away from his old community, under a new name. That way, the boy could get out from under the stigma of having confessed to the murder of his mother and live a relatively normal life. Chuck said that, no matter what he said to Janice, she refused to feel better, and this made him extremely uncomfortable. Following a short visit with Janice's mother, Mary Philips, in Ambridge, Chuck said good-bye and continued on his way to New York.

The experience in Bell Acres had left Chuck emotionally drained and depressed, and he wasn't sure he'd go back to Barley Road or Janice Todd. Some things, he figured, were better left alone.

Chuck had expected too much. There was no way he could resume any kind of normal relations with his family. He had grown up without them, and they had grown old trying to forget.

Ted Botula's frame-up had made Janice Todd something of a basket case and had turned Mike Zubryd into an embittered, angry, and perhaps guilt-ridden man. Chuck said that the truth could set him free, but it came too late for his family.

❏ ❏ ❏

Through the winter months, Chuck and I talked two or three times a month by phone. He stayed at our house a couple of days during Christmas, and that's when he came out and told me he was gay. Chuck had never said much to me or my wife about who his friends were and how they fit into his life, and I had never asked. My interest in his being gay lay with the effect it may have had on his life with the Duffys and whether it may have had something to do with why the Sudiks and the Zubryds had rejected him when he had returned to the two funerals.

Chuck had nothing further to say about his life as a gay man, and I didn't pry. The only friend he mentioned by name was Bob Liggett, the man who had been with him at the store when I called for the first time. Chuck referred to Bob, who was sixty-two, as his mentor and close friend. He left it at that. Chuck was still a sales representative, and he now dealt with several lines of merchandise; but business was off, and he wasn't sure that he had much of a future as a salesman.

❏ ❏ ❏

It was 1990, just over a year since I had called Chuck at the store. I had gone as far as I could on the identification of Helen Zubryd's killer, so I shelved the project. I called Chuck and told him that I had hit a dead end on the case. Although he felt bad for me, he didn't seem to mind. He was doing better as a salesman, and he had been corresponding with Janice Todd and some of his cousins. He said he was coming back to western Pennsylvania to visit Karen and

Paula, Marion's kids, the cousins he was closest to as a child. Chuck promised to spend some time with my wife and me when he returned to the area.

Fearing a summer of grass cutting and, if I wasn't careful, house painting, I decided to look into another 1950s Ted Botula murder case I had run across while researching the Zubryd murder. This case, the 1958 murder and rape of Lillian Stevick in Brackenridge, Pennsylvania, had caught my eye because it was so similar to the Zubryd murder and because, from what I had read in the papers, it looked like another frame-up of a young boy—a thirteen-year-old kid named Jerry Pacek.

I had no way of knowing it at the time, but my investigation of the Stevick murder would break the Zubryd case wide open and lead to the identity of the man who killed Helen Zubryd. Talk about luck.

19 The Murder of Lillian Stevick

A T HALF PAST NINE ON THE EVENING OF MONDAY, NOvember 17, 1958, fifty-two-year-old Lillian Stevick got off a city bus at Ninth Avenue and Morgan Street in Brackenridge, Pennsylvania, a dingy mill town on the Allegheny River about twenty miles northeast of downtown Pittsburgh. Mrs. Stevick had ridden the bus from the Allegheny Valley Hospital in neighboring Tarentum, where her husband, Robert, was a patient. From Ninth Avenue, Mrs. Stevick walked south down Morgan Street en route to her house on the north side of Fourth Avenue just west of Morgan Street. As she approached the bottom of the hill, between Seventh and Sixth Avenues, Mrs. Stevick was set upon by someone who hit her on the head with a heavy object.

At 11:45 that night, a neighborhood kid named Jerry Joseph Pacek, age thirteen, knocked on the door to the house at 926 Sixth Avenue, a house occupied by Francis DeLeonardis and his family, and said, "You better get a flashlight, there is something going on in the backyard."

Mr. DeLeonardis went back inside the house to get his coat then came out and followed Jerry Pacek into the yard, where they found the victim lying faceup in the grass, mud, and weeds alongside a set of concrete steps that ran up the hill toward Seventh Avenue. Mr. DeLeonardis described the situation to reporters: "Her face looked like a piece of hamburger. Both her eyes were black. Her one hand looked like the fingers had been torn off. Her clothing was all pushed up above her waist. The boy told me he had heard her moan and went to investigate."

At 11:55 P.M. Brackenridge police officers arrived at the scene, followed ten minutes later by the ambulance. The victim, alive but unconscious, was rushed to the Allegheny Valley Hospital where, forty-five minutes later, she died on the operating table.

Back at the murder site, Brackenridge police officers took Jerry Pacek to the local police station, where he wrote out and signed a statement regarding how he had stumbled across the woman's body while on his way home. In that statement, Jerry told of a thin young man he had seen jump up from the victim's body and run across Morgan Street into the woods. Jerry said he saw the same man again, on two separate occasions, while waiting for the police and the ambulance to arrive.

Jerry was careful not to tell the police where he'd been that night between seven and eleven o'clock. He had spent the evening watching television at his girlfriend's house on the corner of Fifth Avenue and Main Street in Tarentum, but he wasn't supposed to be there. Jerry's girlfriend, Mary Daley, was twenty, while Jerry was still thirteen. (Jerry had a rare congenital endocrine disorder called precocious puberty, which produces premature physical maturation. Many boys born with this disorder are capable of fathering children at age seven. Although short, Jerry was stocky and well muscled. He smoked a pack of cigarettes a day, shaved, and had been having sex with Mary Daley since he was eleven. Jerry didn't know it then, but on the night of Lillian Stevick's murder, when he was just about to turn fourteen, Mary Daley was two months pregnant with his child. Two years earlier, after Jerry had begun to see Mary Daley regularly, his mother, Clara Pacek, had filed a complaint with the local justice of the peace charging Mary with corrupting the morals of a minor. A warrant had been issued, and Mary had appeared at a hearing before this magistrate. The case had been dismissed on Mary's promise not to see Jerry anymore, but the promise had not been kept, and Jerry had lived in fear that his mother would find out and that Mary would go to jail.

At 1:00 A.M., early Tuesday, Jerry Pacek, after being questioned at the Brackenridge Police Station and signing a written statement telling how he had come upon the body and seen the man get up and run from the spot, was returned to the murder site. Ted Botula, the man in charge of the homicide investigation for the county detective's office, walked up Morgan Street Hill with Jerry.

"Did you do it?" Botula asked.

"No."

"Do you know who did?"

"No," Jerry answered.

At 4:00 A.M., crime scene technicians and forensic experts from the Allegheny County Crime Lab searched the immediate area around the murder site. Sometime between six and seven o'clock that morning, the experts from the lab, working in the mobile crime lab truck (a 1956 Ford van owned by the county), examined the evidence picked up at the murder scene and looked at the victim's garments and other items brought to the van from the hospital by a Brackenridge police officer.

At 7:15 A.M., Ted Botula delivered to the crime lab truck a rusty, mud-encrusted hatchet he had found in the woods on the east side of Morgan, across the street from the murder site. Late in the day, he would be told by lab personnel that this hatchet was not the murder weapon.

At 10:15 A.M., Dr. Theodore R. Helmbold performed the autopsy on the victim. Dr. Helmbold found nineteen lacerations on the victim's forehead and scalp. The ones that had been sutured in the emergency room were clean-cut and gaping. The tissue on the victim's scalp was separated from the bone, and the bones of her skull were fractured in several places. At one spot on the top of her head, Dr. Helmbold noticed a large, irregular, and jagged hole in which the bone was entirely gone, exposing her brain.

As a result of his examination, Dr. Helmbold concluded that "death was due to multiple lacerations of the scalp and compound, comminuted fractures of the skull, and lacerations of the brain." Regarding the murder weapon, Dr. Helmbold said the following to a reporter: "It appears the instrument used in the attack was something with a cutting edge but not a keen edge — possibly like a shovel or a dull hatchet."

At eleven that morning, Jerry Pacek was still being questioned at the Brackenridge Police Station. He was being held as a material witness who was "cooperating in the investigation."

At one o'clock, county detectives drove Jerry Pacek to the county detective's office on the fourth floor of the courthouse in Pittsburgh to be given a polygraph test by Charles A. McInerney. According to newspaper reports, Jerry passed.

At 5:30 P.M., November 18, the day after the murder, a county detective drove Jerry Pacek back to his parents' house in Brackenridge. He had been in police custody for seventeen hours, had been grilled without the presence of his relatives or an attorney, had stuck to his original statement, and had passed *two* lie detector tests. The police had found no physical evidence linking Jerry to the victim or to the crime site, and they had not yet identified the murder weapon. Since there was no reason for the police to believe the thirteen-year-old had committed the crime, they released him. Jerry grabbed a snack at his house, tried to take a nap but couldn't sleep, then went to visit his girlfriend in Tarentum.

At 10:45 P.M., Brackenridge Police Chief Ed Vrotney and a local constable named Ed Roenick picked Jerry up as he walked along Sixth Avenue not far from his home. Jerry had been free less than five hours.

After the officers had driven a short distance with Jerry in the car, Jerry asked, "Did you find your man?"

"Yes, we found him," Roenick said.

"Who is he?" Jerry asked.

"You," Roenick said.

"I didn't do it. I found her."

"You haven't told us the truth, Jerry."

"Yes, I have."

"If you don't tell us the truth, and we find out later you've been lying, it's going to be twice as hard on you."

"I am telling the truth."

"We have a witness, Jerry, who saw you running down Seventh Avenue after the crime. Tell us what happened on the hill."

At this point, Jerry confessed to killing Lillian Stevick. He said he'd hit her with a pipe.

"Did you talk to her?" asked Roenick.

"I said to her it was a nice evening, and she said, yes, it was. I asked her where she was going. She said she was going home."

"Did you make a pass at her?"

"Yes."

"What kind of pass?"

"I felt her breast."

"Did you push her down then hit her?"

"Yes."

"Why did you hit her with a pipe?"

"I don't know."

"Was it twelve inches long?"

"Yes."

Chief Vrotney asked, "Why don't you show us where the pipe is?"

"I can't remember."

"Where did you throw it?"

"Everything is hazy for me."

Jerry finally said, "Well, I throwed it in a sewer over at the corner of Prospect and Crescent Streets."

The officers and Jerry drove to that location, where Vrotney got out of the car. He lifted the lid to the catch basin and searched the interior with his flashlight. "There is nothing here. It's not in here, Jerry. Tell us where it is."

"No, it's not in there," Jerry replied.

"You knew it wasn't in here. Why did you tell us that? We're trying to help you."

"It's at my house," Jerry said. "I took it home and washed it off in the cellar."

The officers then drove toward Jerry's house on Nesbit Avenue, and as they came to a stop in front of the house, Jerry said, "No. I didn't do that. It's not in the house."

"Jerry, we want the pipe. Where is it?"

"I threw the pipe on the hill—in a lot over on Seventh Avenue."

As they drove to that spot, it began to rain. When they arrived, Jerry got out of the car and led the officers to the steps that ran up the hill, parallel to what was called Webster Alley. Jerry said he had disposed of the weapon here. The two policemen walked around through the weeds and underbrush looking for the pipe for twenty minutes, then they gave up the search. When they all climbed back into the car, Vrotney asked Jerry if he would sign a written confession. Jerry said he would, and they headed back to the police station. It was half past eleven; it had been twenty-four hours since Jerry had discovered Mrs. Stevick's body. Except for a catnap in the back of the county police car, Jerry hadn't slept for forty-one hours.

At the police station, Jerry was placed behind a desk and told to write down, in his own words, his confession. Chief Vrotney dictated to Jerry the opening line of the statement, and Ed Roenick would go to the desk from time to time to see what Jerry was writing. Jerry wrote out a two-page confession and signed it. In his statement, he said he had killed the woman with a pipe.

Following Jerry's confession, Chief Vrotney called the county detective's office and turned the case back over to Ted Botula. At three Wednesday morning, Jerry Pacek found himself back in Pittsburgh, again being interrogated by county detectives. When he wasn't being questioned, he was kept in a holding pen on the fourth floor of the courthouse, where the county detectives had their offices.

At four in the morning, Allegheny County Detectives James DeStout and Dennis Timpona had a stenographer record a ten-page confession given by Jerry, in which he said,

> I pushed her over and I hit her with a pipe. I drug her back to the steps, and their [sic] I lifted her dress and cut her pants with a penknife. Then I tried to put my penis into her, she grabbed me by the hair and pushed me away. I took the pipe and hit her again, and as I was hitting her she put her hands on top of her head.

At eleven in the morning, Wednesday, November 19, Ted Botula and his assistant, Francis Flannery, drove Jerry Pacek back to Brackenridge, where, in the presence of several hundred spectators, he walked through an elaborate crime scene reenactment. County Detective Uldine Large played the part of Lillian Stevick; a tree branch doubled for the murder pipe, a mattress for Mrs. Stevick's body. The police told Jerry to drag the mattress over the same ground the victim had supposedly been pulled. In his reenactment, Jerry went to the garbage can into which he said he had put the victim's paper grocery bag. A reporter for the local newspaper was at the crime scene reenactment, and he reported the spectacle as follows:

There was an audience of over 500 lining Morgan St. in Brackenridge on the hilltop overlooking the scene of the crime.

Jerry stationed himself at the top of the hill where Crescent St. meets Morgan St. Mrs. Large began towards him from the nearby bus stop where Mrs. Stevick began her fateful journey Monday night.

The boy walked down Morgan St. toward Sixth Ave. talking with Mrs. Large about Mrs. Stevick's ill husband, just as if the lady detective were the deceased woman.

He walked calmly. He knew there was a huge crowd assembled and a battery of television cameramen, photographers, and reporters, but he stepped along, oblivious to his shocked audience.

When the two reached the bottom of the hill about 10 yards from the corner, Homicide Chief Ted Botula asked him to reenact the crime.

Jerry immediately pushed Mrs. Large into the vacant lot, catching her by surprise.

He shoved her forcefully enough to knock her hat off, and cause the clasp on her pocketbook to be broken. Mrs. Large is a tall woman of more than average proportions who appeared capable of holding her own, but she was knocked flat on her back.

(Mrs. Stevick, age 53, weighing about 160 pounds, was of average height.) [In fact, she weighed 180–200 pounds.]

Jerry, for all his youth, weighs 140 pounds, stands 5′1″ and is "built like a rock." He had shaved off his mustache.

He carried a tree limb about a foot and a half long up his sleeve. The limb represented the iron pipe which he told police was the attack weapon.

Now, Jerry became the aggressor. With Mrs. Large lying flat on her back, he walked around to her head and proceeded to imitate how he whacked Mrs. Stevick on the head with the iron pipe.

He swung down once or twice, then pulled Mrs. Large by the hands. (He whispered, "Am I hurting you?")

At this point, a detective laid a cotton mattress on the ground and Jerry dragged the mattress a full 15 yards up the hilly wooded section to an abandoned concrete stairway that used to be the access to the Crescent Street trolley car at the top of the hill.

Here, he slowly and deliberately brought down the limb eight times to the head of the mattress imitating how he had bludgeoned Mrs. Stevick. . . .

Someone might have shouted now, "Cut," because the reenactment drama was over and detectives quickly took Jerry to their car and drove to Matt's Tavern opposite the Brackenridge Pump Station for lunch.

Following the crime scene reenactment, Jerry and several county detectives drove to a weeded lot behind the old Anchor Brewery at Webster Alley and Sixth Avenue, two and one-half blocks west of the crime scene. Jerry said this was where he had tossed the murder pipe. It was there that one of the detectives found a rusty pipe, twenty-eight inches long, with a right elbow. Jerry said he thought it was the weapon.

That afternoon, Jerry and the pipe were driven to Pittsburgh. Irving Botton, the forensic chemist, examined the pipe in the crime lab and concluded that it could not have been the murder weapon.

District Attorney Edward C. Boyle that afternoon issued a "D.A.'s detainer," which allowed the county detectives to keep Jerry in custody twenty-four hours, so that he may be investigated further. Except for a five-hour period Tuesday evening, Jerry had been in police custody for forty hours. He had not been formally placed under arrest, taken before any kind of magistrate, or given the chance to speak to a lawyer. He was booked that afternoon into the Allegheny County Jail in Pittsburgh. He was placed into Range 3 — an isolation area reserved for dope addicts, crazy people, and prisoners with venereal diseases (VD). Jerry would remain behind bars for the next ten years — to the day. That night, his crime scene reenactment in Brackenridge was aired during the news by all three Pittsburgh TV stations.

Pittsburgh attorney John V. Snee visited Jerry in jail at eight o'clock Wednesday night. The attorney had been asked by Jerry's father, Joe, to represent the boy (the Paceks had little money, so Mr. Snee would later be appointed by the court to represent Jerry.)

Jerry told Attorney Snee that he had not killed Lillian Stevick. He said he had confessed because the police refused to believe he was innocent. Eager to please, Jerry had told them what they had wanted to hear. The crime scene reenactment, Jerry said, had been orchestrated by the police to make him look guilty. He felt he had no choice but to play along. Jerry also told Mr. Snee of his alibi that night — that he had been watching TV at his girlfriend's house from seven to eleven. He hadn't mentioned this to the police because he was protecting Mary Daley and her family. Snee told Jerry that he had dug quite a hole for himself and warned him not to talk to the police anymore about this.

The following day, Ted Botula, in referring to Jerry's guilt, was quoted in the *Pittsburgh Sun-Telegraph* as follows: "There's no doubt. He's the one." All three newspapers that day reported that Jerry, at age ten, had been involved in a morals case with a six-year-old girl. This information had come from either James DeStout or Ted Botula. The police later admitted that this information was false. The case they were referring to had to do with Jerry and his twenty-year-old girlfriend, Mary Daley. But the damage had been done.

On Thursday morning, November 20, Jerry was taken to the county detective's office, where he was questioned all day by Ted Botula and others. Jerry told Ted Botula that his attorney had advised him not to speak with the police, but Botula said, "Never mind about your attorney. We just want to ask you some questions."

The most important question Botula had on his mind that morning was the murder weapon. Botula asked Jerry if he had perhaps hit the woman with a hatchet. Since the detectives had not definitely found the murder pipe and Dr. Helmbold had referred to an "edged" weapon, maybe they were looking for a hatchet. Botula got up from the table and said, "I am leaving this room for fifteen minutes, and you'd better tell me the truth when I come back." Botula walked out of the room, and when he returned he said, "What's the story? Did you use a hatchet or not?"

Jerry replied, "Yes."

At four that afternoon, after being questioned by Botula and others for five hours, Jerry was taken to Chief Detective Henry Pieper's office, where he was questioned further by Botula and Assistant District Attorney Samuel Strauss, the man who would later prosecute him. Unbeknownst to Jerry, his thirty-page confession was audiotaped and would be played for the jury at his trial.

At 5:45 P.M., Thursday, November 20, 1958, Jerry Pacek was taken before juvenile court Judge Gustav Schramm who, after conferring with Ted Botula, ordered Jerry held in the County Jail rather than the Juvenile Detention Center in Oakland. Although Jerry was only thirteen, Judge Schramm considered him too grown-up to be held with other children his age.

It had been sixty-six hours since Jerry had discovered Lillian Stevick on the ground. He had been in custody sixty-one hours, during which time he had issued one written statement, signed three confessions, participated in a crime scene reenactment, and had admitted his guilt countless times to police officers, reporters, relatives, Sam Strauss, and even a priest who had come to the Brackenridge Police Department to comfort him. He had still not been formally charged with a crime. Jerry Pacek told his lawyer, however, that he had not killed Lillian Stevick. The next morning, the *Pittsburgh Post-Gazette* ran an article about Jerry under the headline "2 STRIKES ON BOY SLAYER." The article began this way:

> The twin elements that at age 13 brought Jerry Pacek to commit murder, as he has admitted, may very well have been a background of poverty and strange, glandular disturbances that racked his short, thickset body.

The author of this piece, a reporter named Alvin Rosensweet, having established himself as a sociologist-physiologist with criminological expertise continued,

> The family background was difficult — 7 children living with their parents in crowded squalor. And Jerry was a hard boy to catalogue — he was polite, courteous, "always a gentleman," said a teacher. Yet he was without question biologically precocious, carrying with him the de-

> moniacal desire to impose his sexual urges
> upon a woman four times his age.

Rosensweet was referring, of course, to Lillian Stevick. The caption under a picture of Jerry, standing with his hands in his pockets looking morosely into the camera, read, "Stirred by dark urges." And, Rosensweet wrote, "Only a week before the murder, seventh and eighth-grade girls carried tales to their teachers about Jerry. 'I'm guilty,' he told a school interviewer." Rosensweet didn't reveal what Jerry had said he was guilty of, leaving this part to the imagination of the reader: sexual demon that he was, it must, of course, have been something horrible.

> There had been devastating signs earlier. At 10,
> there had been trouble with a girl of 12. Also at
> that early age, County Detectives learned, he
> had molested a girl 6 years old.
>   "At 9 years, Jerry Pacek was not a boy," said a
> man who knew him well. "He was a small man."

Rosensweet wound up his piece,

> "If it (the murder) had happened a hundred
> years ago," somebody commented, "they would
> have said Jerry was possessed by devils. Now we
> know that, if he was guilty of this terrible crime,
> his sense of right and wrong went astray."
>   The answer may lie in the dark recesses of
> heredity and environment, glands and body
> chemistry.

Ted Botula seemed to be thinly veiled behind Rosensweet's story. According to Friday morning's *Sun-Telegraph*, Botula had begun to compile a "detailed picture of Jerry's background from the age of 7 to the present. This complete history will include his school record and accounts of his companions and behavior in all situations up to the night of the slaying admitted by the ninth-grader." This *Sun-Telegraph* piece quoted Botula as saying, "We're satisfied he's the one. There's no doubt."

(Later, Friday afternoon, Brackenridge Chief of Police Ed Vrotney, in the local newspaper, said he knew of no previous sex crime involving Jerry Pacek and a young girl. He wanted to set the record straight on that point. The business about Jerry and some young girl never surfaced again.)

At ten o'clock Friday morning, six county detectives and a handful of helpers from the Brackenridge Police Department roamed the hilly lots, backyards, and alleyways in the general vicinity of the murder site looking for the fatal hatchet. They combed the area for two hours and then called it quits.

An hour later, Jerry Pacek was taken from his jail cell to Coroner William McClelland's office. Once again, Jerry confessed, this time to the coroner and those in his office. "Do you ever think what might happen to you now?" McClelland asked.

"No," Jerry replied. "I figure what's the use of worrying. What they give me, I'm going to take."

On Monday, November 24, at 10:30 A.M., Detective Francis Flannery and county photographer Ed Cavitt drove Jerry Pacek back to Brackenridge, where Jerry was to tell them where he had found the hatchet he had used to kill Lillian Stevick. They were met in Brackenridge by Chief Ed Vrotney. Jerry was also going to show the officers where he had washed his hands after the attack. The group proceeded to a fire hydrant on Sixth Avenue at Morgan Street, where Jerry said he had cleaned up after the beating. He said he had washed his hands in a puddle along the curb. Next he led the police officers to a house on Sixth Avenue, one-half block west of the murder scene, where he said he had found the hatchet in a bucket behind the house among some garbage cans. (Ed Cavitt took photographs of Jerry finding the hatchet in the bucket behind the house. This was the hatchet Botula had found in the woods along Morgan Street on the morning after the crime. That same day, the crime lab told Botula this was not the murder weapon.)

Later that afternoon, Jerry was driven back to Pittsburgh and taken to Henry Pieper's courthouse office, where Jerry was told that his parents and his Uncle Anthony Pacek were waiting to see him. When Clara and Joe and his uncle walked into the room, they were accompanied by Assistant District Attorney Sam Strauss. Clara turned to Strauss and said, "Jerry couldn't do that." Turning to Jerry she asked, "You didn't do that, Jerry?"

"Yes, I did, Mother," Jerry replied.

Strauss said, "Now, I want you, Jerry, in front of your parents, to tell us the truth. Tell them what you have told us. Did you kill Lillian Stevick?"

"Yes, I did," Jerry replied.

"Why you couldn't pull that woman," Mrs. Pacek said.

"Yes I could, Mum, but they wouldn't let me." (Jerry was referring to him not dragging Detective Uldine Large at the crime scene reenactment.)

Strauss and Pieper walked out of the office, leaving Jerry alone with his parents. This was the first time he had been alone with his folks since the crime. The moment the authorities were out of the office, Mrs. Pacek said, "Jerry, did you do this?"

"No, Mum, I didn't, but they wouldn't believe my first story." Jerry went on to tell his mother how frightened he was and how all of the detectives had kept coming at him with questions until he had finally broken down and told them what they had wanted to hear.

Jerry spent Thanksgiving in jail and felt all the more isolated, alone, and depressed. He still occupied a cell on Range 3, a second-story tier of cells along a U-shaped catwalk. During the day, the inmates on Range 3 had common access to the catwalk, which ran a hundred feet down both sides of the U and was only three feet wide. At night, they were locked into their cells. Prisoners on Range 3 were never taken out to the yard and did not mix with the other inmates. As stated earlier, they were held in isolation because they were sick or crazy, had VD, or were withdrawing from drugs. Jerry was on Range 3 because he was a teenager. One of the heroin addicts on the Range spent all day on the catwalk in front of Jerry's cell rolled up in a ball screaming.

The coroner's inquest into Lillian Stevick's murder was held on the morning of December 11, 1958. Coroner William McClelland presided over a jury of six men who would determine, first, if Mrs. Stevick had been murdered, and second, if enough evidence existed to hold Jerry Pacek for the grand jury. The inquest was supposed to be a procedural safeguard designed to protect arrestees from heavy-handed prosecutors; but in practice, it was nothing more than an opportunity for the prosecution to trot out their case: in effect, a dry run for the grand jury and trial. McClelland, who had heard Jerry Pacek confess with his own ears, could be counted on to lead the jury to the right verdict. He had no doubt that the boy was guilty and was just doing his job.

At two o'clock, following lunch and an hour-long deliberation, the coroner's jury returned its verdict: "We find that Lillian Stevick's death was caused by multiple lacerations of the scalp and compound fractures of the skull and lacerations of the brain. We recommend that Jerry Pacek be held to await the action of the Grand Jury upon a charge of murder."

To reporters, Coroner McClelland said, "This is the first time in my experience as Coroner that a boy so young has been held for such a serious charge."

In the hall outside the hearing room, Jerry's attorney, John Snee, was surrounded by reporters, newspaper photographers, and TV cameramen when he announced that Jerry had repudiated all of his confessions. Jerry's confessions, he said, were the product of police coercion and brainwashing. Moreover, the so-called admissions, by virtue of the unconstitutional way in which the police had obtained them, would not be admissible at trial (assuming he'd be indicted). Snee pointed out that the police had no physical evidence linking Jerry to the crime; indeed, they didn't even know what it was that had killed the woman. First they had Jerry say it was a pipe; then, when they learned that her head wounds had been caused by something sharper, they had him say it was a hatchet. So where was the hatchet? Snee asked. Where was the murder weapon? Jerry, Snee said, happened to be at the wrong place at the wrong time, and because of this, he'd become the patsy for the police who should be out there right now looking for the real killer. This was outrageous, and if Snee had anything to do with it, the police would not get away with it.

The confusion over the two murder weapons — the pipe and the hatchet — was reflected in an article that appeared the next day in Tarentum's *Valley Daily News:*

> Two weapons — a rusty hatchet and a 28-inch pipe — were introduced as evidence at the inquest. No bloodstains had been found on either.
>
> According to county detectives, Jerry admitted striking Mrs. Stevick with both weapons when she resisted his advances.

Though the article said he admitted it, Jerry had probably not hit the woman with the pipe *and* the hatchet, yet *both* had been introduced into evidence as the murder weapon. It appeared that Botula, notwithstanding Jerry's confessions and crime scene reenactment, didn't have the slightest idea what Jerry had used to kill Lillian Stevick. Botula must have considered this hole in his case one hell of a problem.

On January 13, 1959, Assistant District Attorney Sam Strauss presented his evidence, his case against Jerry Pacek, to the grand jury. The nine witnesses who had testified a month earlier at the coroner's inquest now appeared before this group of jurors, twenty-four in all. Strauss merely had to convince the grand jury that he had enough evidence to bring Jerry to trial on a charge of murder. He did not have to prove him guilty, not yet. The evidence against Jerry, his numerous confessions, left unchallenged because neither Jerry nor his attorney were present in the grand jury room, was so incriminating that the jury voted unanimously and swiftly for a true bill, making Jerry Pacek the youngest person in Allegheny County history to be indicted for murder. Like most grand jury proceedings, the outcome of this one was a foregone conclusion, a mere formality.

Jerry Pacek went to trial on Monday, April 6, 1959. He was represented by John Snee and prosecuted by Samuel Strauss. The judge was Henry X. O'Brien. The jury was empaneled on the morning of the second day of the trial, and that afternoon they were taken by bus to the scene of the crime. The court adjourned that day at 9:30 P.M. after eight witnesses had testified for the prosecution. The next day, Strauss put on thirteen witnesses, including Ed Vrotney, who told the jury about Jerry's first confession in the police car. Ted Botula took the stand on the fourth day of the trial, at which time the jury heard the tape-recorded confession Jerry had given to Botula and Strauss. Detective Dennis Timpona followed Botula to the stand and testified that he had obtained a confession from Jerry during the early morning hours of November 19, 1958, in the county detective's office. Fifteen prosecution witnesses followed Timpona, including Irving Botton from the crime lab, whose testimony sounded impressive and incriminating — even though he said nothing that connected Jerry Pacek to the crime. The hatchet Botula had found on the morning after the crime was introduced into evidence as the murder weapon, even though there was no expert testimony identifying it as such. Under the circumstances, John Snee's cross-examination of Irving Botton must have been extremely weak and ineffective, I thought. The court did not adjourn until 9:45 that night.

The prosecution would up its case on April 10, the fifth day of the trial. The defense led off with three witnesses who had seen, on the night of the murder, a suspicious man on the corner of Ninth

Avenue and Morgan Street. Next came Jerry's alibi witnesses — Ethel Daley and her two daughters, Helen and Mary. Judge O'Brien made it clear that he did not want the jury to know that Mary Daley was pregnant with Jerry's child. Strauss got the message to the jury anyway by continually asking Mary Daley why she insisted on wearing her coat in the hot courtroom. "You would be more comfortable without it," he kept saying. Mary couldn't remove her coat because she was more than six months pregnant, and the jury now knew it.

The following day, a Saturday, the sixth day of the trial, Jerry Pacek took the stand. During his testimony, Snee made several attempts to get Jerry's polygraph test results before the jury. The judge would not allow it. Prosecutor Strauss, on cross-examination, kept Jerry on the stand the rest of the day, tearing him to shreds. The seventh day of the trial opened with more cross-examination of Jerry; then, following two additional witnesses, the defense rested its case.

The state, on April 13, put on seven rebuttal witnesses. The defense had no surrebuttal, and on this day, a Monday, the court went into another night session at which time both attorneys summed up their cases. In his closing remarks, Strauss told the jury that alibi testimony is usually "pregnant" with falsehood, a not terribly subtle reference to Mary Daley, Jerry's chief alibi witness. Following a long sidebar, the court adjourned at 10:20 P.M.

On Tuesday, April 14, Judge O'Brien charged the jury, and at 11:25 A.M., the jury retired to consider its verdict.

On this day, after the jury had retired, the *Pittsburgh Sun-Telegraph* broke a story that created quite a fuss. A reporter had gotten his or her hands on a confidential psychiatric report that contained the opinions of the doctors who had examined Jerry at the Allegheny County Behavior Clinic. These findings were highly confidential — intended for a judge's eyes only. These reports helped them determine the most appropriate sentence in the event a defendant was found guilty. When Jerry's clinic report appeared in the newspaper, all hell broke loose. The report, under the headline "JERRY NO MURDERER, ONLY A PEEPING TOM," read:

> Jerry Pacek was a conscience-stricken peeping tom, but not a murderer, according to the Allegheny County Behavioral Clinic report. . . . [T]his report described Jerry as a short, stocky, dwarf-like boy of 14, who was of average intelli-

gence and exhibits no evidence of emotional or
mental illness.

Further backgrounding Jerry's emotional
and physical development, the report stated: "A
rare congenital endocrine disturbance produced a premature biological and physical maturation. By age 7, the subject had all of the sec-
ondary sexual characteristics, and by 10 he was
shaving."

The report brought out earlier descriptions
of Jerry as a boy with the body of a man. The report said his early maturing caused an in-
tensification of desire, fantasies, and attending
guilt which normally occurs in a pre-adolescent
boy. Working this into the youth's accounts of
the crime, the report continued: "From one
month prior to his arrest, he (Jerry) had been
indulging in frequent peeping tom activities
near the site of the offense. When interrogated
as a likely suspect, he was extremely frightened,
unusually guilty, and fearful of disclosing his
peeping behavior. Finally, after prolonged interrogation, which he alleges was conducted
without sleep for forty-one hours and without
food for twenty-one hours, he falsely confessed
to committing the homicide. After a few days'
rest, he related a true explanation of what transpired and has consistently held to this."

The report concluded: "From our intensive
psychiatric, psychological, and sociological
studies, we conclude that he (Jerry) is a normal
boy with the biological and physiological maturation of an adult. While he must be judged by
the evidence, there is nothing in our examination to indicate that he would be capable of
committing such an offense, and we are in-
clined to believe this was a false confession."

That night, at 7:50, the jury returned and announced that they
had found Jerry Pacek guilty of murder in the second degree. He
would be sentenced fourteen months later. John Snee filed a motion for a new trial, and on June 10, 1960, Judge O'Brien, the man
who had presided over Jerry's trial, and two other lower-court

judges, denied this motion. Jerry was sentenced on June 23, 1960, to "not less than ten, nor more than twenty years." His sentence would be measured from November 19, 1958, the day he had entered the Allegheny County Jail.

The denial of Snee's motion for a new trial was customary and routine; Snee's next step would have involved taking the case to a higher court, an appeals court. But he didn't do that. It seemed to me that Jerry may have had a good chance at appeal. Even in 1958, detectives weren't allowed to grill a juvenile without the knowledge of an attorney. Ted Botula and Prosecutor Strauss had, in my opinion, deprived Jerry Pacek of his rights under the Sixth and Fourteenth Amendments. That meant the confession used to convict him should not have been admitted into evidence. Without that confession, Jerry may not have been found guilty.

Following Jerry's sentencing on June 23, 1960, the Pacek case dropped out of the news. I had no idea where Jerry had served his time, how long he had spent in prison, or what had become of him. Coming to the end of his story so abruptly was like being dragged out of a theatre in the middle of a movie.

As hard as it was to believe, Ted Botula seemed to have been involved in two cases in which young boys falsely confessed to murder. I couldn't help thinking that Jerry Pacek was innocent, but in all of my years as an investigator and criminal justice professor, I had never personally known of a case where a defendant convicted of murder was actually innocent.

I had either lost my objectivity or had stumbled upon another case involving an outrageous injustice, and I didn't know whether to feel lucky or just plain angry. In time, I'd feel both.

20 The Evidence

I WANTED TO BE ABSOLUTELY SURE I HAD THE PACEK CASE figured correctly because, in my experience, innocent people did not get convicted of murder, even in the 1950s. So I gave Jerry's case a great deal of thought, and no matter how I analyzed it, he came up innocent.

The Stevick murder-rape was a bloody, messy crime that included semen, blood, soil, and plenty of botanical debris. It was a crime that required close bodily contact between the victim and the offender. According to the crime lab experts, there were no traces of the victim's blood, hair, or textile fibers on Jerry's shoes, underwear, jacket, shirt, or trousers. Moreover, his clothing did not contain any crime scene soil or botanical debris. The crime lab scientists did not find any traces of Jerry — hair, blood, semen, or textile fibers — on Mrs. Stevick. If Jerry's confessions were to be believed, he had somehow raped and murdered the woman without getting anything of her onto him or anything from him onto her. In my view, that was virtually impossible.

Jerry had first confessed to killing Lillian Stevick with a pipe but was unable to tell how or show where he had disposed of it. No murder pipe was ever found. A few days after he confessed to killing her with a pipe, Jerry said he had killed her with a hatchet. This weapon was never identified, nor did Jerry know where the hatchet was. If Jerry had been so eager to confess, why hadn't he been able to produce the murder weapon? The county detectives and the local officers had worn Jerry down by the time he confessed in the police car. Once he had confessed, Jerry couldn't take it back, at least not to the police. Botula saw to it that Jerry confessed to anyone who would listen, and by the time his attorney entered the case, it was much too late. The damage had been done.

Charles McInerney had given Jerry two lie detector tests. Jerry passed them, and the county detectives released him. Jerry's attorney was unable to get the results of these tests into evidence at his trial.

Doctors at the Allegheny County Behavior Clinic had concluded that Jerry was a normal kid — mentally and emotionally — incapable of committing such a brutal crime. In their professional opinions, Jerry's confessions were false. Why hadn't Jerry's attorney called these experts to testify on his behalf?

Jerry had taken back his confessions the moment he was no longer under the control of the police. At his trial, three witnesses testified that before the crime, they had seen a suspicious-acting man loitering in the neighborhood. In Jerry's initial statement, he had described a thin young man who had jumped up from where Mrs. Stevick was laying and had run off as Jerry approached the scene.

At the trial, three alibi witnesses testified that from seven to eleven on the night of the crime, Jerry had been at their house a half mile away watching television. The victim had been attacked at 9:40 P.M. The jury obviously didn't believe these witnesses. It didn't help Jerry that his chief alibi witness was his pregnant twenty-year-old girlfriend whom he had not mentioned when first questioned by detectives.

The most damaging evidence against Jerry had been the taped confession obtained by Prosecutor Sam Strauss and Ted Botula. This interrogation had been conducted without the knowledge of Jerry's attorney, yet the judge had allowed it into evidence. Jerry had, in my opinion, a winnable appeal on this basis; however, I had to that point found nothing in the newspapers regarding Snee's appeal to a higher state court.

In a nutshell, the evidence against Jerry Pacek came down to his confessions, oral and written, and his crime scene reenactments. There were no eyewitnesses to the crime, no physical evidence linking Jerry to the murder or the rape, no motive, and nothing in Jerry's background or mental makeup to even remotely suggest he was capable of such a savage sex crime, the kind of killing committed by psychotic serial rapists and murderers.

I called Joe Start and asked him if he remembered Jerry Pacek and the Stevick murder case. He did. "I didn't work on that case," Joe said, "but I can tell you this — that kid was guilty as hell. He was only thirteen, but he was built like a brick shit house. He killed that woman up in Brackenridge, and he raped her."

I asked Joe Start about Sam Strauss, the prosecutor, and he said, "Sam was the best they ever had down there. They called him 'Singeing Sam' because he sent so many killers to the electric chair. He later became a judge, but he's retired now."

"What about Pacek's attorney, John Snee?"

"He wasn't any good. When he took the Pacek case, he was running for D.A.: he wanted the publicity. He was running against Eddie Boyle. He lost the case and the election."

"Besides Botula, who else would have worked the Pacek case?" I asked.

"Dennis Timpona and 'Chippie' DeStout had the case," Joe said. "But they're dead. Nick Schifino may remember it, and you might try Art Sabulsky — he's a district magistrate now — over in Springdale."

"Thanks."

"Any luck on the Zubryd case?"

"No," I said.

"Do you still keep in touch with Chuck?"

"Oh, yeah, we talk on the phone a lot. If I can line up the Pittsburgh hypnotists," I said, "are you still game?"

"Whatever you want," Joe said. "I'll do anything. Say hello to Chuck for me."

❑ ❑ ❑

Nick Schifino, formerly a county detective, remembered Jerry Pacek as a "short, little husky guy" who had convinced everyone with his crime scene reenactment that he was guilty. "He knew too much," Nick said.

I next talked to Art Sabulsky, who said he'd been Dennis Timpona's junior partner. Sabulsky remembered the Pacek case very well and assured me that Jerry Pacek was guilty. Referring to Jerry's crime scene reenactment, Sabulsky said, "He enjoyed the spotlight." Sabulsky said he had attended Jerry's trial and remembered that Judge O'Brien had let Sam Strauss, the prosecutor, get away with things that would have gotten other prosecutors into trouble. I asked Mr. Sabulsky if he remembered Jerry Pacek's parents, and he said, "They lived in a place not fit for a pig. They didn't care if it rained or shined."

Even my friend John Nee, the Mercyhurst College criminal justice professor who had helped me on the Zubryd case, found it hard to believe that Jerry Pacek could be innocent. "I remember that kid," John said. "He did it."

I hadn't talked to Ted Botula since I confronted him with the crime scene evidence in the Zubryd case. It had been a friendly conversation, but I wasn't sure how he'd react if I called and started raising questions about another of his cases. But when Ted answered the phone, he greeted me like a long-lost friend. Yes, he remembered the Pacek case, generally. He couldn't recall the details, but he knew for a fact the boy had murdered that woman after she got off the bus that night in Brackenridge. I asked Ted about Jerry's attorney, John Snee, and Ted replied that Snee was dead. The judge, Henry O'Brien, was also gone. "He was a tremendous judge," Ted said, "a swell man."

"What kind of boy was Jerry?" I asked.

"A nice kid, very polite," Ted replied. "He was short-legged, with big shoulders."

"Why did he do it?" I asked.

"I don't know. I guess he wanted some, and she said no."

"What happened to him after the conviction?"

"I don't know, but I remember, years later, running into Jerry while visiting the state penitentiary at Camp Hill. Jerry was working in the shop. He said, 'Hi, Mr. Botula.' He was very polite."

"How come you were never able to identify the murder weapon?" I asked.

"It was a hatchet," Ted replied. "We found it in the woods across the street from the body."

"Are you sure about that?"

"Oh, yes, it was a hatchet."

Changing the subject abruptly, I said, "I've talked with Chuck Duffy."

"Who?"

"Charlie Zubryd."

"Oh? What does he say?"

"He says he didn't do it, and you told him he did, and that he didn't remember killing her because he had blacked out."

"Yes, the boy said, 'If I killed my mother, I must have blacked out.'"

"You said his fingerprints were on the hatchet."

"He used that hatchet to chop trees," Ted replied. "Did you find if he's queer?"

"He's gay," I said.

"I'm not surprised. What's he do for a living?"

"He was part owner of a store, now he's a salesman. He's not singing crime ballads."

Botula laughed, then said, "I thought that guy who called me from L.A. was Charlie. What's Jerry Pacek doing now?"

"All I know about Jerry is what I read in the newspaper."

"He was no Charlie Zubryd. He was no ordinary kid — he was a little man. I got along with him very well."

"Do you remember interrogating him with Sam Strauss and taping his confession?"

"No."

"That tape was played to the jury."

"I don't remember."

"Do you remember the crime scene reenactment in Brackenridge?"

"Yes. Jerry walked us through the crime — half the town was there. I don't think you'll have much luck with that case."

"Thanks, Ted."

"And good luck."

❏ ❏ ❏

I could see that Jerry Pacek, unlike Charlie Zubryd, was going to be a hard sell. Moreover, I respected the opinions of Joe Start and John Nee, and I was starting to have doubts about my take on the Pacek case. Everything I knew I had gotten from the newspapers, hardly a reliably factual, solid base. I needed to verify several key points, and to do this, I needed documentation. I knew that police files that far back didn't exist (from my experience with the Zubryd case), but thanks to Commander Ron Shaulis, I knew about the archives at the University of Pittsburgh that housed all of the old coroner's files. This was where I found the smoking gun in the Zubryd frame-up, and I hoped it was where I'd find the evidence I needed to determine if the same thing had happened to Jerry Pacek.

I called John Thompson, the associate curator of the Archives of Industrial Society at the University of Pittsburgh, and asked him to check and see if he had the coroner's file on the Stevick case. I gave him the date of the inquest, December 11, 1958, and he said he'd see if he had it. I waited while he looked, and a few minutes later he gave me the good news — it was there. John said that it wasn't necessary for me to go to him, he'd copy everything and mail it to me. I'd have it in a few days.

The copies arrived, and I found the eight-page autopsy report on Lillian Stevick by Dr. Helmbold, the same physician who had performed the autopsy on Helen Zubryd. There was a five-page Allegheny County Crime Lab report, signed by Irving Botton, forensic chemist; Charles A. McInerney's polygraph report; photographs of Mrs. Stevick laid out in the morgue; miscellaneous reports filed by the emergency room physician who had worked on Mrs. Stevick; and several photographs of Jerry Pacek taken on November 24, 1958, in which he is finding the so-called murder hatchet and washing his hands in the puddle along the curb on Sixth Avenue in Brackenridge.

I was interested in the hatchet, the one found by Ted Botula on the morning after the crime in the woods along Morgan Street, not far from the scene of the murder. On page six of Irving Botton's report, he stated:

> A hatchet found at the scene and turned over to the Crime Laboratory personnel was examined for traces of blood, hairs, fibers, and tissue with negative results. The hatchet had a light coat of rust on the metal surfaces and a thin layer of mud on the cutting edge. The rust and mud did not appear to be disturbed.

Pat "The Rug" McCormick, the fingerprint man, one of the men who had pulled the hatchet out of Helen Zubryd's head as she lay dead on her basement floor, examined Botula's hatchet for Jerry Pacek's fingerprints. He found nothing.

The implications of these negative findings were staggering. Ted Botula, when he arranged to have Jerry Pacek photographed "finding" the hatchet Jerry had supposedly used to kill Lillian Stevick, had been told and knew that hatchet was not the murder weapon. These photographs, five in all, depicted an event Botula knew had not occurred.

Irving Botton had this to say about Jerry's clothing:

> A paper bag labeled "Jerry Pacek Clothing" was found to contain a pair of khaki trousers, a greenish-gray sports shirt, and a pair of shorts.
>
> The trousers were devoid of any mud or botanical stains. Several small human bloodstains were found above the left cuff. These stains originated from the inner surface of the trousers. Blood grouping studies were complicated by the presence of an interfering substance. The stains were indicative of blood group "A." (The victim's blood type was "B.")
>
> No bloodstaining found present on the shirt.
>
> A pair of jockey-type shorts were found to manifest signs of having been worn for an extended period of time without being washed. Chemical tests for the presence of seminal material were essentially negative. Microscopic searches for the presence of spermatozoa were inconclusive because of the interfering debris present on the shorts. Attempts to obtain seminal samples from Jerry Pacek were unsuccessful.
>
> A pair of brown suede shoes taken from Jerry Pacek were not found to be bloodstained.
>
> A blue corduroy jacket having metal studs and belonging to Jerry Pacek was examined for the presence of blood with negative results.

The victim's clothing was not as clean: "The outer rear panel of the skirt bore dirt and botanical residues similar to the tomatoes found growing in the field where the attack occurred. The clothes were extensively blood soaked."

According to the Allegheny County Crime Lab report, there was absolutely no physical evidence linking Jerry Pacek to the victim. And that wasn't all—the report contained information that, in my mind, actually exonerated him:

> An envelope bearing hair samples reportedly
> found on the victim's hands was found to con-
> tain several hairs, three human scalp hairs and
> one human body hair probably pubic in origin.
> A hair comparison effected between hair sam-
> ples taken from Jerry Pacek resulted in findings
> which indicated that the hairs could not have
> come from Jerry Pacek. The scalp hairs found
> were within the hair range of the victim and
> could possibly be from her own scalp.
>
> In a small envelope labeled "Right Hand"
> and "Dirt on Nails" several very thin accordion-
> ated strips of tissue were found. The gross ap-
> pearance was typical of skin that has been
> scratched off and collected under fingernails.

To me, that last paragraph meant that Lillian Stevick had scratched
her attacker. To my knowledge, no report indicated that Jerry Pacek
had scratches on him that night.

In his confessions, Jerry said he had hit the woman on the head
as she walked down Morgan Street. He then, according to his confessions, *dragged* her unconscious body fifty-five feet off the sidewalk into the DeLeonardis backyard, where he hit her some more
then raped her. When he reenacted the crime, Botula had Jerry
drag a mattress through the grass and underbrush to where the
rape and further beatings had occurred. Botula had used this dem-
onstration to prove that Jerry, only five feet tall, was strong enough
to pull a nearly 200 pound woman up the hill through the underbrush. However, according to the lab report, it couldn't have happened that way; she had to have been carried some of that distance:

> No gross signs were noted in the field to indi-
> cate that the victim was dragged or pulled along
> the ground for any appreciable part of the total
> distance between the point of the initial assault
> and where the body was found.

According to Charles McInerney's polygraph report, Jerry Pacek had been tested on the lie detector *four* times. The first two
tests, given on November 18, the day after the crime, were adminis-
tered before Jerry had started confessing. After passing these two
tests, Jerry was released.

I knew that Ted Botula had great faith in Charles McInerney and the polygraph. He had used the lie box to break dozens of cases. I also knew that most detectives would accept polygraph results when they confirmed a suspect's guilt and would ignore them when they didn't. Botula, having such respect for McInerney, must have wanted to reconcile Jerry's subsequent confessions with McInerney's findings. That was probably the reason for the second series of tests given on December 3, two weeks after all of Jerry's confessions. According to McInerney's report, he asked Jerry this: "Are you connected in any way with the killing of the woman in Brackenridge?" Jerry had been told to answer "yes" in an effort to determine if his confessions were lies.

McInerney surely would have told Botula that Jerry's "yes" response to the same question he had responded "no" to when he had passed the test would not produce a chart McInerney would be able to interpret as either truthful or deceptive. Because of Jerry's confessions, the "yes" answer would not show up as a clear lie because Jerry was no longer a suitable subject for the polygraph. But Jerry was tested anyway, and the results were predictably inconclusive. In his report, McInerney wrote:

> On Wednesday, December 3, the subject was re-examined for the purpose of determining whether he was telling the truth in admitting that he killed Mrs. Stevick. The results of the re-examination were not conclusive because of the inconsistency of his responses.

This meant, to me, that Jerry Pacek had passed *four* lie detector tests given by the head of the Allegheny County Crime Lab. When he was told to say he had confessed to killing the woman, the polygraph didn't buy it, and I was certain Charles McInerney didn't buy it either.

Jerry Pacek had been framed; and now I knew it, just like Botula knew it, Mary Daley knew it, the real killer knew it, and Jerry Pacek knew it. I hoped that someday, everybody would know it.

It was hard to believe that Jerry Pacek had actually been convicted. I wanted to see how that had happened, so I spent the next week knocking around Pittsburgh looking for the thirty-one-year-old transcript of his trial. I started at the Allegheny County Clerk's Office, where I was told I had to go somewhere else to get the trial number. I got the trial number (OT 50), returned to the clerk's office, and was told they didn't have the transcript. There was no guarantee, the clerk said, that Pacek's transcript was ever typed up. If his attorney hadn't appealed the case to a higher court, it might not have been. The clerk sent me across the street to the court reporter's office, where a nice woman there said they didn't have it, but she asked me where Jerry had served his time. I wasn't sure, but Botula had said he'd seen Jerry at the Camp Hill State Correctional Institution, located in Camp Hill, a small town near Harrisburg. The clerk said the prison may have a copy of Jerry's trial transcript. I returned to the county clerk's office to see if they had any record of Jerry's murder conviction and incarceration, and to my surprise, they didn't.

Someone in the clerk's office suggested I call the state Parole Board in Harrisburg. The Parole Board was known to keep trial transcripts. I called, and the man who answered said they only kept trial transcripts seven years after a conviction, unless the defendant had been sentenced to life, then transcripts were saved for thirty years. I was told to try the Harrisburg Records Center, where all of the prison records from Camp Hill were maintained. I called, and the person there informed me that a particular trial transcript, if not taken out by the prisoner upon his or her release, was destroyed four years after the prisoner's maximum sentence was served. I asked if they still had a record of Jerry Pacek at Camp Hill. The clerk said no. A prisoner's file was also destroyed ten years after his or her maximum sentence ran out. Jerry's maximum sentence had been twenty years and would have run out in 1969. Ten years later, in 1979, all of his prison records would have been destroyed. The clerk said the only information they still had on Jerry Pacek was his old inmate number — C 5734.

I had started out looking for a trial transcript and had wound up with a number. I was desperate. I decided to call District Attorney Bob Colville. It had been slightly more than a year since John Nee and I had been in Colville's office asking him to look for the county detective's file on the Zubryd case. Colville hadn't found it, but he had tried. I hoped he'd remember me; and at the risk of being a pest, I called and asked if he would try to locate the transcript of Jerry Pacek's trial.

Colville said that, if the transcript existed, he knew where it would be, but he wasn't optimistic because much of the old stuff had been destroyed. He said he had a vague recollection of the Stevick murder and asked why I was so interested in the case. I told Colville that I thought Jerry Pacek had been framed. Colville was skeptical and wondered if my experience with the Zubryd case had thrown my bullshit sensor out of whack. Jerry Pacek, after all, had been convicted by a jury after confessing many times. I assured the D.A. that I had not turned into one of those phony do-gooders who never met a defendant they didn't love or a cop they didn't hate.

"What does John Nee think about the case?" Colville asked.

"John thinks that Jerry Pacek did it," I replied.

"Well, if the transcript is still around, I'll give you a call." Colville then hung up.

The D.A. wasn't optimistic, and after talking to him, neither was I.

Four days later, at nine in the morning, Bob Colville called me at home. "Guess what? We've found the transcript. It's a thousand pages. We've made a copy for you — it's bound into four volumes." Colville sounded excited. "It's here in the office."

"Thank you," I said. "I'll be down to get it today."

"I've read it,' Colville said. "They had nothing on the kid but his confession. They didn't even have the murder weapon! Sam Strauss introduced a hatchet into evidence that his own crime lab people said wasn't the weapon. The judge let it in anyway. Incredible. The kid's attorney and the judge just sat there and let the prosecutor have his way. I've never seen anything like it. The confession shouldn't have been admitted, either. Everything you told me about the case is true! If I went to court with a case like that, the judge would throw the whole thing out the door. I've never seen anything like it."

"Then you agree the Stevick murder is unsolved?" I asked.

"Yes."

"Since there is no statute of limitations on murder, would you consider reopening the investigation?"

"I don't know," Colville replied. "The killer might not even be alive. The investigation would cost a lot of money, and my detectives are already busy with current cases."

"It would be good for Jerry," I said. "It would show that you and your detectives believe he didn't do it."

"That's true, but what are the chances we can solve a thirty-two-year-old murder?"

"The case has never been investigated; someone ought to give it a try. You owe that to Mrs. Stevick."

"We don't even know if Botula's file on the case is still around."

"I'll give you what I've dug up."

"Which is?"

"Mrs. Stevick's autopsy, Jerry's polygraph results, and a county crime lab report. I also have the old newspaper clippings."

"I'll talk to my chief investigator," Colville said. "He's going to be skeptical. I don't know."

"Thanks for the trial transcript," I said. "I'll leave copies of my stuff when I come down to get the transcript. I hope you decide to reopen the case."

"I've never seen anything like it," Colville said again. "Maybe we can help. Say hello to Johnny Nee."

21 Jerry Pacek

THE PACEK TRIAL TRANSCRIPT CONTAINED 996 PAGES, and I spent four days reading it and taking notes. It was clear that the prosecutor, Samuel Strauss, dominated the courtroom. He overwhelmed Jerry's attorney, John Snee, manipulated the jury, and controlled the judge.

Strauss knew that the crime lab had ruled out the hatchet that Ted Botula had found on the morning after the crime; nevertheless, he managed to get it into evidence. He also knew that Jerry's clothing and the victim's contained nothing that incriminated Jerry, yet he had each garment placed into evidence as an exhibit. He put Pat McCormick on the stand, even though there was no fingerprint evidence linking Jerry to the murder. McCormick testified that simply because Jerry's fingerprints were *not* on the bloody grocery bag the victim had been carrying that night did not mean that he hadn't touched it. (The killer had taken this bag and thrown it into a trash can behind a house not far from the crime scene.) McCormick described how latent fingerprints can be smudged and why fingerprints are often not picked up on paper and, as such, leave no evidence that an object has been touched. McCormick also testified that he had found no fingerprints on Botula's hatchet. McCormick was asked about that by Jerry's attorney on cross-examination: "Had there been any fingerprints on the handle of that axe, is the wood in the handle such that a print could be discerned if there were one there?"

"Yes," McCormick answered. "We would very likely be able to develop a print on this type of wood."

On redirect, Strauss asked, "But if there was movement . . . ?"

"Yes, any movement such as the throwing of something or pushing it aside, may cause a smudge."

"It would destroy it, it is that fragile a thing?" Strauss asked.

"That's right."

This was incredible. The prosecutor and his expert witness were talking about a phantom fingerprint on a hatchet they both knew wasn't the murder weapon. Jerry's attorney, of course, objected to all of this, but to no avail. Judge O'Brien was apparently loath to interfere with Strauss's magnificent courtroom performance.

Jerry Pacek did have a defense and a fairly good one. Three witnesses took the stand and said they had seen a suspicious-acting man at the corner of Ninth and Morgan, at the gas station that night. This man met the general description of the person Jerry had seen jump up from Lillian Stevick and run into the woods on the other side of Morgan Street. Three alibi witnesses testified that Jerry was half a mile from the murder scene watching television when Lillian Stevick was attacked. He also had several character witnesses and took the stand himself and tried to explain how the police had worn him down until he had confessed. He told the jury that he had figured the police would eventually catch the killer then let him go. What Jerry didn't realize was this: once the police had him, they would stop looking.

Apparently the jury didn't believe Jerry or his witnesses. They had decided he was guilty at the close of the prosecution's case. Snee's defense was too little, too late.

Ted Botula took the stand to introduce the tape of he and Strauss interrogating Jerry, an interrogation Jerry's attorney didn't know about until it was over. Strauss asked Botula how Jerry was treated during the interrogation, and Botula said: "I would say very kindly, as a child."

Jerry Pacek was presumed guilty, a presumption his attorney was never able to rebut.

❏ ❏ ❏

After studying the trial transcript, I was certain that Jerry Pacek was innocent. Whoever killed Lillian Stevick had gotten away with it. I was also struck by the similarities between the Stevick and Zubryd cases. Besides being murders handled by Ted Botula in the late 1950s, the cases had many other things in common.

The victims, middle-aged women, had been struck in the head several times with a hatchet or similar object.

The victims had been attacked sexually, as evidenced by the position of their clothing and the presence of semen.

Both crimes had occurred on November nights.

Young boys without criminal or violent backgrounds had been questioned by the police until they had confessed.

Both youngsters had confessed many times in front of numerous people. Then each had sealed his confession with an elaborate crime scene reenactment.

Neither boy was connected to the victim or to the crime scene by physical evidence.

Both murders and the boys' confessions made front-page headlines in Pittsburgh newspapers and made television news.

Objective psychological and psychiatric examinations of each child had convinced the examining doctors that their confessions were probably false.

Jerry Pacek had passed four lie detector tests given by Charles McInerney. Chuck Duffy was also tested.

The two murders also had some key differences.

In the Pacek case, Ted Botula hadn't obtained the initial confession. The investigation had been handed back to Botula after the local cops had grilled Jerry in the police car.

The murder weapon was never identified in the Stevick murder case.

Jerry Pacek was tried, convicted, and sent to prison for ten years. Chuck Duffy spent two nights in the Juvenile Detention Center and three weeks in a private hospital.

At the time of Jerry's conviction, there was little doubt among the police and the public that he was a murderer. In Chuck's case, there were some who never believed he had killed his mother.

❑ ❑ ❑

In May 1990, I told Chuck Duffy what had happened to Jerry Pacek.

"Was Ted Botula involved?" he asked.

"Yes."

"I'm not surprised," he said.

"Jerry was tried in April 1959, a month after Botula had coaxed the confession out of you."

"Ted was on a roll," Chuck said. "Where is Jerry now?"

"I don't know. Jerry's mother and several of his brothers still live in the Brackenridge-Tarentum area, but he's not listed in the phone book."

"Are you going to find him?"

"I'm going to try," I said.

"And when you find him, then what?"

"I'll call him, like I did you."

"And tell him that he didn't do it."

"Yes, but he already knows that," I said.

"He knows it, sure, but he's probably going to be damn glad to hear someone like you — someone he doesn't know — tell him that he's not a murderer."

"I hope so. I don't know anything about him. I don't even know if he's still alive. He'd be forty-six now. There's a chance he'll be very unhappy about me digging around into his past. He may not want the whole thing brought up again. He might be keeping his past a secret."

"He might, but take it from me, someone who had to live under the same cloud, he's going to be relieved and very happy to hear what you have to tell him."

"I'm still nervous about it."

"He'll be nervous too, but it will be worth it. Look what you've done for me."

"I hate to say it, Chuck, but I still don't know who killed your mother."

"So? You did your best."

"I won't be able to finish the book, either."

"I know those things are important to you," Chuck said. "But they're not big items with me."

"It's a shame Joe Start can't remember that guy's name. If we just had the name."

"I hate the man who killed my mother," Chuck said. "But the bad guy in my life is Ted Botula. And now the truth is out — about what he did to me and what he did to Jerry Pacek."

"If Jerry Pacek doesn't object," I said, "I'm going to reinvestigate Lillian Stevick's murder. It's a long shot, but there's a chance the same guy killed your mother. Of course, there's no guarantee I'll do any better with the Stevick case than I did with your mother's."

"Do what you have to do; but please, don't feel that you have to do it for me."

"I understand."

"Good luck, and let me know what happens," Chuck said.

❑ ❑ ❑

When Lillian Stevick was murdered, Jerry Pacek lived with his parents on Nesbit Avenue in Brackenridge. His father, Joe, a heavy-drinking, unskilled mill worker, had been ill and out of work for several months. Jerry, the oldest child, had three brothers and three sisters. According to some of the old newspaper articles about Jerry, he had been a popular, happy-go-lucky kid, who spent a lot of time on the street when he wasn't in school.

I had checked the greater Pittsburgh phone book, and Clara Pacek, Jerry's mother, still lived on Nesbit Avenue. Brackenridge, the home of the giant Allegheny Ludlum Steel Mill, is a small industrial town on the Allegheny River, twenty-five miles northeast of downtown Pittsburgh, sandwiched between Tarentum to the west and Natrona to the east. I had never been to that area and was curious to see the town, Jerry's old neighborhood, and the site of the murder.

On May 5, a Saturday, Sue and I drove down to Brackenridge. The trip took about one and one-half hours, and when we got to Sixth Avenue and Morgan Street, not far from the murder scene and the Pacek house, I could see that very little had changed in this neighborhood since the murder.

Nesbit Avenue was really an unpaved dead-end alley that ran below a row of large deteriorating houses that were built against the hill and faced the valley and (in the distance) the Allegheny River. I wanted to see where Jerry had lived, so we drove along Nesbit looking up at the houses and the long flights of wooden stairs that ran up the hill to each place. Because the alley was lined with cars on both sides, it was slow going. The Pacek house was the last one on the street. I'd gotten the car turned around, and we were looking at the dilapidated house, when Sue suggested that we go up to the house and introduce ourselves to Mrs. Pacek. This had not been the plan, and I wasn't sure I was ready for that. I didn't know a thing about her or about Jerry and was worried about what kind of reception we'd get from her. After arguing with myself for a few moments, my curiosity overwhelmed my sense of caution. We parked the car, climbed the stairs to the Pacek front porch, and knocked.

A short, thin, white-haired woman with a weathered face and wearing a shapeless, loose-fitting print dress came to the door. I asked her if she was Mrs. Clara Pacek, and when she said that she was, I identified myself as a college professor who had been studying her son's case. That brought Mrs. Pacek out onto the porch. I then introduced my wife and said straight out that I was convinced Jerry had not murdered Lillian Stevick.

Mrs. Pacek was wary, and I had the feeling that she thought I was some cop or governmental official looking for her son. She obviously didn't want to reveal too much about Jerry's whereabouts, but as we talked, she opened up and began discussing Jerry's ordeal, including his arrest, his conviction, and what it had been like for the Paceks. Jerry had served ten years in prison at Camp Hill and was now living with his new wife, Peg, his eighteen-year-old son from his previous marriage, and his two-and-one-half-year-old daughter, Jennifer. They lived near a little village called Slate Lick not far from Kittanning, Pennsylvania, where Jerry worked as a carpet installer and was doing just fine. I had been to Kittanning, a small town in Armstrong County twenty-five miles up the Allegheny River from Brackenridge. It's the county seat, and if I drove east from my house, I'd get there in about ninety minutes.

There came a point in our conversation when I sensed that Mrs. Pacek felt she had said too much. Before leaving, I asked her if she thought Jerry would mind talking to me. She wasn't sure how he would take to the idea. I asked Mrs. Pacek if his new wife knew about his past. Yes, Peg knew everything. But Jerry's family — his brothers and sisters — never spoke of it, and most of Jerry's nieces and nephews didn't know what had happened to him. Suddenly concerned, Mrs. Pacek said she hoped I wasn't going to put any of this into the newspaper. I assured Mrs. Pacek that I was not a newspaper reporter. She said she didn't want the Pacek name dragged through the mud again. "His father," she said, "never got over it."

"Is Mr. Pacek still alive?" I asked.

"He fell down those very steps," she said, "two years ago. Broke his neck and died right there."

Just before my wife and I carefully started down those steps, I handed Mrs. Pacek a piece of paper containing my name and phone number. "Would you give this to Jerry?" I asked. She said she would, then to my surprise she gave me Jerry's home phone number. As we drove away from the house on Nesbit Avenue that day, I wasn't sure I had done the right thing.

I waited a few days for Jerry to call me, and when he didn't, I called him. Over the next two days, I dialed his number twenty times and got a busy signal each time. Jerry, I figured, had taken his phone off the hook. I wouldn't call him again or try to contact him in any other way. The last thing I wanted was to harass a man who had served ten years in prison for a crime he didn't commit. I would go no further on the Stevick murder case.

❑ ❑ ❑

On the Tuesday following my talk with Mrs. Pacek, at seven in the evening, one of my daughters, Leslie, walked into the living room and said that Jerry Pacek was on the telephone.

"I'm Jerry Pacek," he said. "I'd like to know why you were in Brackenridge talking to my mother."

I told Jerry who I was, how I'd gotten interested in his case, and then I said, "I found evidence that convinces me you were innocent."

For a moment there was silence, then Jerry said, "You're the first person in thirty-two years to say that to me. I've known it all along, but I never heard it from anyone else."

I laid out exactly why I thought he had been railroaded, and when I finished Jerry said, "You're telling me things I didn't know."

I told Jerry about Chuck Duffy and my work in the Zubryd case. When I mentioned Ted Botula, Jerry said, "That son of a bitch put the screws on me. What did he tell you?"

"He says he doesn't remember much about either case. He's old."

"If you don't mind me asking, what's in it for you?"

"Nothing, except maybe a book or two. But that's down the road a bit and iffy."

"I don't know if I'd want that," Jerry said. "I've lived in this community eighteen years, and most people don't know about me. If my boss found out, I might lose my job."

"You're innocent; you've nothing to hide. You have nothing to be ashamed of."

"I was accused; I confessed; I was convicted. People *think* I did it, so it doesn't matter if I know I didn't. You still feel the shame because you know what people think."

"Don't worry about any book, if you don't want me to write one, I won't. The book isn't the main thing. I'd still like to meet you and talk more about this. I'd like to bring my wife."

"I guess that would be all right," Jerry said.

"How about a week from tonight?"

"All right."

"I'll send you some material about myself, including a book I wrote. If you change your mind, give me a call."

Jerry gave me detailed directions to his house. "I'll see you and your wife next Tuesday," he said, then hung up.

❏ ❏ ❏

Jerry and his family lived in a small well-kept house on a large plot of land on top of a wooded hill. To get there, we drove for a quarter of a mile up his rutted gravel driveway. Jerry was waiting for us in his front yard. He had a full, neatly trimmed, graying beard, thinning brown hair, and glasses. He looked like a friendly man and had a quick smile, an infectious deep-throated laugh, and a voice that reminded me of the actor Martin Sheen. Jerry's most striking feature, however, had to do with his height — or lack of it. Jerry stood only five feet, and not being a tall man myself, I was not used to towering over another man. In his newspaper photographs, particularly when he was dressed up for court in his suit and tie, Jerry looked like a barrel-chested cross between Marlon Brando in *On the Waterfront* and a young Jimmy Hoffa. I wondered if his tough-guy good looks had been a blessing or problem in prison. As an adult, he had just the opposite look. It was hard to believe that this man had done time for murder.

My wife and I liked Jerry immediately, and I knew we were going to become good friends.

Sue and I exchanged pleasantries with Jerry and his wife, Peg, out in the yard, and when it came time to get down to some serious talk, we took seats around Jerry's kitchen table. Jerry said he remembered Ted Botula very well. Shortly after the ambulance had come to take Mrs. Stevick to the hospital, Botula had walked Jerry up the Morgan Street Hill. Botula wanted to know if Jerry had attacked the woman, and Jerry told him he hadn't. One night later, after the local cops got Jerry to confess in the police car, the real nightmare began. Jerry said he confessed so many times, to so many people, his memory of what happened that week is just a blur. He did recall the Botula-orchestrated crime scene reenactment in which he dragged a mattress from the sidewalk to the spot in the yard where the victim had been beaten and raped. I asked Jerry how he felt performing as a killer in front of his neighbors, schoolmates, and members of his own family. He said, "I was numb."

"Did you hate Botula for making you do it?"

"No, not really. I figured he was just doing his job. He was making a mistake. I thought, when they catch the real guy they're going to be sorry for what they did to me."

"They didn't, though."

Jerry laughed. "That's right. Tell me about it."

"You must hate the man who killed her and let you go to prison."

"I hate that son of a bitch, but the anger can tear you up. I learned that a long time ago. I had to get on with my life."

"Do you remember being questioned by Botula and Sam Strauss?"

"I remember he came to see me with Strauss. They didn't tell me they were taping it. I had a lawyer then, and he had told me not to talk to any more cops. Shit, I'd already confessed a thousand times, what was I supposed to do?"

"Did John Snee know they were questioning you?"

"Hell, no."

"Was he any good?"

"Who?"

"Snee, your lawyer."

"Are you kidding? All he wanted was the publicity. I remember thinking—at the trial—why isn't he asking the witness this question or that question. It was frustrating. He was no match for Strauss—nobody was." Jerry laughed. "That guy was vicious."

"Do you think Snee believed you were innocent?"

"I think he did. He was all I had. I remember when he came to see me in the jail. He told me not to worry; I remember his fingernails—I couldn't get over how clean they were." Jerry laughed. "Funny what you remember."

"Did you get much support from your family?"

"There wasn't anything they could do. My mother had all the kids at home—my old man—well, ya know. They had no way to get down to Pittsburgh to see me."

"You were thirteen years old, charged with murder, and on your own."

"That's right. One time, out in the hall, before we went into the courtroom, Mr. Snee gave me a hug. That was the first time anyone—*anyone*—showed me any affection." Jerry's face suddenly turned red, and he broke into tears. The rest of us sat there in silence, looking on, as Jerry, his hands covering his face, sobbed uncontrollably. Jerry took off his glasses and wiped his eyes.

"Are you okay, Jerry?" Peg asked.

Jerry laughed. "I'm fine—there's a lot more where that came from."

"We can stop," I said.

"No, let's go on. I needed that. That felt good."

"Did John Snee tell you he was appealing your conviction?"

"Yes, the court ruled against me," Jerry said.

"That's not true," I replied.

"What do you mean?"

"After Judge O'Brien and the other two trial judges denied the motion for a new trial, Snee appealed your case to the Pennsylvania Supreme Court, and they agreed to hear it. But on September 25, 1961, Snee withdrew the appeal."

"How do you know that?"

"It's in the court papers pertaining to your case. I found them in the Allegheny County Clerk's Office. Snee withdrew your appeal when he petitioned Judge O'Brien for his legal fees."

"Why in God's name would he do that?"

"I can only guess."

"What?"

"I don't think he expected the Supreme Court to grant him a hearing. When they did, he backed out."

"Yeah, but why?"

"Appeals take a lot of work. Snee wasn't that kind of lawyer. He took your case for the publicity. There isn't any glory in filing appeals, just a lot of legal research. It's too bad because Snee could have gotten you a new trial."

"They would have just convicted me again," Jerry said.

"They wouldn't have been allowed to use your confessions in the second trial. Without the confessions, they had no evidence. There wouldn't have been a second trial. You would have gone free."

"Why didn't Snee tell me the truth? I could have gotten another lawyer!"

"I don't know why; but I know this: the system didn't work for you. What Snee did could have gotten him disbarred."

"I never would have known that," Jerry said. "Deep down, Snee must have thought I was guilty."

"Or not worth the effort," I said. "What happened to you after your conviction?"

"They took me back to the county jail. I was there a couple of months before the judge gave me my sentence. After that, I went to the Western Penitentiary at Rockview—that's near State College—to be classified. I was there five days then put on a bus with some other guys and hauled to Camp Hill. I remember getting off the bus and walking toward the prison with all the inmates standing around hollerin' at us. Makin' threats. I was wearing overalls that were too big—the crotch damn near dragged along the ground." Jerry laughed. "I was scared to death."

"How long were you behind bars?"

"Ten years, exactly. I got out November 19, 1968. They had a race riot on my last day, and I thought, 'Jesus Christ, I'm never getting out of here.' A couple of guards I knew, actually they were friends, hid me in someone's office until it was over. They said, 'Stay here until we let you out.' When it was over, they came and got me. Those guards actually threw a going-away party before I left. They never do that in prison. One of the guards—my shop teacher—gave me a set of carpet installation tools he had paid for out of his own pocket."

"So you learned how to install carpet in prison?"

"Right. I learned a lot in jail. I got my high school degree and even took some college courses. I took every shop course they had. I figured, hell, I'm in here, I might as well take advantage of it."

"I'm sure the prison administrators — the corrections people — or whatever they called themselves — took great pride in the fact they had rehabilitated you."

"Right!" Jerry said, then laughed, "I was their model prisoner!"

"You're the best kind," I said. "You're not a criminal."

Jerry laughed again. "Honestly, I never thought this day would ever come. I can hardly believe it."

"Did Mary Daley come to see you when you were in prison at Camp Hill?"

"It was tough on Mary. She had the baby — Jerry, Jr. — and it was a long bus trip. She did for a while."

"Did you correspond?"

"Yes, then that stopped too. I told her to forget about me, to go on with her own life."

"Was it hard getting started after you got out of prison?"

"Yes. I lived in Carlisle with the family who sponsored me. They were great people. I worked at night at the Burlington rug factory and in the day worked at a hamburger joint and laid carpet on the side."

"Your son was ten years old when you got out. Had you seen him?"

"No. I hadn't seen Mary since November 1965. She came to Camp Hill to tell me she was pregnant again. She didn't love the guy or anything; he was married and it was one of those things. It just happened. I didn't take it very well. She never came back. Mary had a girl, and she named her Carolyn."

"What happened to Mary and your son?"

"After I got out, I went back to Brackenridge to visit my family. It was Memorial Day, 1969. That's when I got reunited with Mary. Little Jerry was ten. We got married in October 1970. We had our second son — Sean — in 1973. I had gotten a carpet-installing job in Kittanning, so we moved back to western Pennsylvania. I got off parole in November 1978. About a year later, Jerry, Jr., was killed in a car wreck. He was twenty." Jerry hesitated for a moment to collect himself. "It was tough. Jerry and I were so close in age we were more like buddies than father and son. I missed the first ten years of his life because I was in prison."

"Have you ever applied for a pardon?" I asked.

"Several times, but I never got anywhere with it. I gave up on the idea."

"If you don't mind me asking, what happened between you and Mary?"

"Mary died in February 1987. She had a brain tumor and then had a stroke because of the drugs they were giving her. Finally she came down with pneumonia and died. The doctors kept calling me to the hospital because they thought she was going to die. That went on for months. I could hardly stand it anymore. How many death watches can a guy go through?"

It was getting late, and Jerry looked exhausted. So did Peg. I had put Jerry through the wringer. "This has been tough on you," I said.

"It has, but I feel great. Where do we go from here?" he asked.

"I'm not sure."

"I'd like to get a pardon. I'd like to clear my name. Will you help me do that?"

"Yes," I replied.

"I have to get my family together — my mother, my brothers, and my sisters. They have to be prepared."

"What do you think they will say?"

"They won't like the idea," Jerry said. "We never talk about it. It's something that has kept me away from the family."

"They know you're innocent, don't they?"

"I think they do — but I've never been sure."

"How many people around here know about you?" I asked.

"Not very many. My boss doesn't even know. If this goes public, I could lose my job."

"Are you willing to take that chance?"

"Are you kidding? I've been waiting thirty years for this day. I'll do anything to clear my name, to get out from under this."

"What amazes me, Jerry, is that after all you have been through, you can still trust someone."

"You have to trust people," Jerry replied. "When you quit doing that, you're dead. What do you think my chances are of getting a pardon?"

"I don't know anything about pardons," I said. "But I know this — we'll have to prove you didn't do it. In a thirty-two-year-old murder case, that's not going to be easy. It would help a lot if I could

prove who *did* kill Lillian Stevick. The D.A., Bob Colville, is already
interested in your case, so who knows — we might have a chance.
I'm willing to try, if you're willing."

Jerry got up from the table and took my hand. "Let's go for it,"
he said.

22 A New Investigation

IN MAY, AFTER VISITING JERRY, I INTERVIEWED FOUR OF
the Pacek trial jurors. They were men; they still lived in the Pittsburgh area; and they had remarkably similar recollections of the
trial. They remembered in great detail how they had lived for nine
days in the special dormitory at the county jail. They spoke of the
experience the way one would recall an enjoyable vacation. They
took their meals at the elegant William Penn Hotel downtown and
played poker at night. When the trial ended, the jurors had become
such good friends they planned a reunion. I couldn't help wondering to what extent such camaraderie had stifled independent thinking when it came time to decide the fate of Jerry Pacek.

In the minds of these jurors, Judge O'Brien was a saint; Sam
Strauss, a relentless but compassionate prosecutor; John Snee, a
court-appointed attorney doing his job in a losing cause; and Jerry
Pacek, a cocky, streetwise tough guy still young enough to be saved
if the proper action were taken. By finding Jerry guilty of second-
degree murder, the jury was taking that action — they were remov-
ing him from the mean streets and alleys of Brackenridge and sending him to a maximum security prison, where he would learn a
trade and perhaps straighten out.

Ted Botula had told me that Ed Vrotney and Ed Roenick, the local cops who had broken the case by getting Jerry to confess, were
both dead. He was half right; Vrotney was still living, and I gave
him a call.

Ed Vrotney did not want to talk about the case and asked me not to come to his house. He said that his wife was very ill, that he had to spend most of his time caring for her. Although Jerry Pacek was obviously guilty, Mr. Vrotney made it clear that his department had had nothing to do with Jerry's crime scene reenactment in Brackenridge. That had been Botula's doing. The local police didn't even know about it until it had happened.

My interview with Mr. Vrotney ended when he asked me not to call him again. I said I would comply.

Shortly after my summer school classes ended, I called Ted Botula to talk to him some more about the Pacek case. I read him parts of the trial transcript, including excerpts from his own testimony, to jog his memory about the so-called murder hatchet, Jerry's polygraph tests, the inconsistencies in Jerry's confessions, and the obvious lack of physical evidence tying him to the crime.

Ted stated that he couldn't say more than he already had about the case, and I got the distinct feeling that I had, as the country song goes, "worn my welcome thin." Ted had become defensive and must have sensed the change in my attitude toward him. He didn't come out and say it, but he felt I was picking on him, making him the bad guy in the Zubryd case and now in the Pacek case. Ted reminded me that *he* hadn't prosecuted the boy or ruled his taped confession admissible as evidence or dropped the ball on the defense or found Jerry Pacek guilty. After he had released the kid, Jerry had confessed to the local cops, and the case had come bouncing back to him. All of that was true, of course, but Ted had been in charge of the case, and if the evidence did not point to Jerry, it had been his responsibility to look for a more suitable suspect. If he had, he might have solved the case and brought the real killer to justice. Matters of this nature should not be left entirely to lawyers. Botula agreed that all of this was true, but in Jerry's case, they had the right man, and justice had been done.

❏ ❏ ❏

I telephoned Pittsburgh to see if District Attorney Bob Colville had made a decision about reopening the Stevick investigation. The prosecutor said he had read the autopsy, polygraph, and crime lab reports and was even more certain of Jerry's innocence. He asked me to submit a report detailing my work on the Stevick case. Then he told me that he'd ask his chief investigator, Ralph Yovetich, to read the report, review the autopsy and other documents, then study the Pacek trial transcript. Colville said Detective Yovetich would call me when he was ready to discuss the case.

That night, I called Jerry and told him that Bob Colville didn't believe he killed Lillian Stevick and is seriously considering re-opening the investigation. The news got Jerry excited. He said he couldn't believe it, then he started to cry. Then, suddenly, Jerry was angry. "The son of a bitch who killed her is going to pay for what he did!" Just as quickly, Jerry calmed himself and said, "I can't get angry, that will tear me up. I'm so goddamn happy!" he blurted, then laughed. "Thank you. I mean that, Jim, thank *you.*"

Early the next morning, Jerry called me at home, where I was in my office working on Colville's report. He said his wife, Peg, was listening on the extension phone. "I've got to see you," he said, his voice urgent. "I didn't get to bed last night until three. I couldn't sleep with all of this on my mind. It's finally sunk in — and it's mind-boggling!"

"Sure, Jerry." The urgency in Jerry's voice concerned me a little.

"Do you think the killer can really be identified? Could he be convicted?"

"I don't know, Jerry. It depends. The older a case is, the harder it is to solve. We don't have much to go on."

"But there is a chance?"

"There is always a chance."

I met with Jerry, and then a month passed. I had written up my report and had sent it off to Colville. Just when Jerry and I were starting to lose hope, John Nee called and said his old friend and colleague Ralph Yovetich had just telephoned and asked that he bring me down to Pittsburgh for a meeting. John said Yovetich didn't think Jerry Pacek had killed Lillian Stevick, and he was officially re-opening the Stevick murder investigation. He had assigned two detectives to the case full-time, and they wanted to meet me. The meeting was set for Thursday, August 23, 1990.

That evening I called Jerry and gave him the news. "Oh, Jesus," he said, laughing, "another night without sleep."

❏ ❏ ❏

The offices of the D.A.'s investigative branch are not located in the Allegheny County Courthouse; they are housed in a long, narrow, one-story building that runs from Fifteenth Street to Six-

teenth Street between Penn Avenue and Liberty Street in Pittsburgh's Strip District, a north side neighborhood dominated by
produce, poultry, and wholesale fish distributorships. As John Nee
and I drove to Pittsburgh, John warned me that Yovetich could be
rather blunt, and he didn't take to strangers quickly. So I wasn't to
take it personally if Yovetich seemed a little cool.

The meeting took place at half past ten around a conference
table in Yovetich's nicely appointed office. A pair of Colville's young
assistant D.A.s, Russ Broman and Mike Ahwesh, were present, as
were the two detectives who would actually work the case, Fred
Cooper and Jerry Fielder. John Nee introduced me to Yovetich and
Fred Cooper, then Yovetich introduced John and me to the assistant D.A.s and Jerry Fielder. At first we were all a little stiff, then as
the meeting progressed, things lightened up a bit. I knew that Bob
Colville was enthusiastic about the case, but I wasn't sure how his
detectives felt.

According to John Nee, Fred Cooper had been a top homicide
detective with the city before he retired and joined the D.A.'s staff.
A nice-looking, dark-haired man in his early sixties, Cooper seemed
the friendliest of the bunch. I figured that was because he had been
so close to John Nee. The two men had worked together for years
on the Pittsburgh Police Department. Like Yovetich, Fred Cooper
had been an honest and well-respected city cop. Jerry Fielder,
Cooper's partner on the D.A.'s squad, the man who would be in
charge of the Stevick investigation, had just been hired by Colville.
Fielder was fifty-one and had recently retired from the Pennsylvania State Police, where he had worked for twenty-seven years,
mostly as a vice investigator. Fielder was known as a "wire man" because he was an expert in the field of electronic eavesdropping. A
husky six-footer, Fielder had salt-and-pepper hair, a ruddy complexion, and a deep voice. A cigarette smoker whose eyeglasses
mostly rested on his chest from a chain around his neck, Fielder
had little to say. He had his tape recorder going and took notes as I
laid out my evidence. Like most cops, Fielder wasn't one to open up
to strangers.

After the meeting, I met privately with Yovetich. Although Yovetich must have been sixty, or close to it, he struck the figure of a
younger man and, though not tall, was big boned, muscular, and
trim. With his crew cut and military bearing, Yovetich reminded
me of a U.S. Marine drill instructor. "I'd appreciate it," he said, "if

you'd discontinue your investigation until Detective Fielder has completed his. If you have any undeveloped leads, give them to Jerry. Do you have any problems with that?"

"No," I lied.

"Good. We'd also like to meet the kid — Pacek."

"He's forty-six now," I said.

Yovetich smiled. "Right. I'm afraid he'll always be 'the kid' to me, though."

"Do you believe that he's innocent?" I asked.

"If I thought he was guilty, you wouldn't be here today," he said.

Just before John Nee and I walked out of the office, Yovetich asked, "What does Jerry think about us reopening the case?"

"He's thrilled about it," I said.

"His name might be dragged through the mud again. Some people will never believe he didn't do it."

"He's willing to take that chance," I said.

"The kid's got guts," Yovetich replied.

Three weeks later, on September 12 Detective Fielder called me to report that so far they hadn't had much luck in their investigation. Since the meeting in Yovetich's office, Fielder and I had talked on several occasions, and I was convinced he was enthusiastic about the case. He said he had spoken to Ted Botula and, although he hadn't found the county detective's file on the case, they were still hunting for it.

The fall semester at Edinboro had started, and I was back to teaching. Jerry Pacek and I had talked about his pardon, and I had looked into the matter. Going for a pardon was a long, drawn-out process; and from what I had learned, I was not optimistic. The biggest problem was this: in Pennsylvania, there had never been a pardon granted because a man or woman had been innocent and therefore wrongly convicted. Pardons had only been granted to people who admitted their crimes and asked for official forgiveness and mercy. This did not apply to Jerry. I had also learned that, in Pennsylvania, there had never been a pardon granted to a person convicted of murder. I explained all this to Jerry, and he remained optimistic.

To get a pardon, the candidate had to fill out an application and mail it, along with a check and five passport photographs, to the

Pennsylvania Board of Pardons in Harrisburg, the state capital. The
board, consisting of the lieutenant governor, the attorney general,
and three others, would review the application, then they would
vote on whether to grant the candidate a hearing. It would take two
"merit votes" to get to the hearing stage. While he was still in prison, Jerry had applied several times, but he had never been granted
a hearing.

At the pardon hearing, the candidate — or the person presenting
the candidate's case — had fifteen minutes to make the appeal. In
Jerry's situation, this would be unusual because the board did not
have the power to retry a case. Moreover, because the board was not
an appellate court, it could not officially overturn a conviction. Nevertheless, since this was the only arena we had, Jerry had no choice
but to go for it. If at least three members of the board voted for a
pardon, they would recommend clemency to the governor, who
could then grant a pardon or decline to do so. In the end, it was
strictly up to the governor.

Jerry asked me how long the pardon process would take, and I
told him the truth as I knew it — years. Getting Jerry Pacek *un*convicted of murder would require much more time and effort than it
had taken Sam Strauss and Ted Botula to get him convicted.

❑ ❑ ❑

I called Jerry Fielder on October 25 with some information he
had requested a few days earlier, and that's when he told me about
an interesting interview with Lillian Stevick's seventy-five-year-old
sister, Marjorie Kutchko. I didn't know the victim had a sister. According to Mrs. Kutchko, a man in a green sedan had tried to run
Lillian down a few days before she was murdered on the Freeport
Road near the hospital in Tarentum. Then, Lillian was walking toward the bus stop when a man followed her around on foot. Lillian
had feared that this and the incident with the green car were connected, that someone was trying to kill her. Mrs. Kutchko didn't
know who but hinted that it had something to do with Robert's girlfriend, a woman he had gotten pregnant. Lillian had angered this
woman by spending so much time at the hospital visiting Robert.
Mrs. Kutchko told Detective Fielder that Jerry Pacek didn't have
anything to do with the Stevick murder. Had detective Ted Botula
or any of his men bothered to talk to any of the victim's relatives, he
might have found the solution to the crime through Robert Ste-

vick's girlfriend. Mrs. Kutchko couldn't remember the girlfriend's name and didn't know if she had given birth to Robert Stevick's baby. When asked if she thought Robert Stevick had wanted his wife dead so he could marry the woman, Mrs. Kutchko would only say that Jerry Pacek should never have been arrested.

Fielder said the Brackenridge Police Department still had a case file on the Stevick murder, which included morgue photographs of the severe head wounds and notes regarding a police interview of her retarded thirteen-year-old son, Robert, Jr., whom everyone called "Bobby." Fielder said there had been rumors at the time that Bobby, so retarded he couldn't read, write, or even tell time, had killed his mother. There was also some loose talk that sometime prior to the killing, the boy had tried to burn down their house.

According to the material in the Brackenridge police file, Bobby had been meeting his mother at the bus stop at Ninth and Morgan to walk her home after the hospital visits. On the night of the murder, Mrs. Stevick was late, so Bobby started walking east on Ninth Avenue toward the hospital. He hadn't walked very far when the bus with his mother on it passed, going the opposite direction. Bobby said he saw his mother through the bus window, and she was wearing her blue hat. And that was it; there was nothing more in the file about Bobby or the night in question.

Fielder and I agreed that Bobby's information raised a couple of interesting questions. What ever happened to Mrs. Stevick's blue hat? What had Bobby done that night after seeing his mother on the bus? Because the victim had stopped at the store on the corner of Ninth and Morgan, Bobby would have had plenty of time to catch up to his mother to accompany her home.

I asked Fielder if he had checked up on Bobby, and the detective said that he had. Bobby was currently in his fifties and living in a group home in Pittsburgh. All of his affairs were handled through an attorney, which made Fielder's efforts to question him somewhat complicated. Fielder said he had managed to get Bobby on the phone, but all he could get out of him was, "I didn't do it; you have to talk to my lawyer."

I could tell from Fielder's voice that he had really warmed up to the investigation. There is nothing better for a detective than to be at the threshold of a case that is presenting good leads and the promise of a solution. Before we hung up, Fielder said he hoped to identify Robert Stevick's girlfriend and to arrange an interview with Bobby. "We've got leads," he said.

A few days later, on Halloween, Fielder called and said that he and Yovetich would like to meet and question Jerry. I was welcome to come, but they wanted to speak to Jerry in private. The next day, I called Jerry Pacek and set up the meeting, which would be held in Yovetich's office on Tuesday, November 6. Jerry was, to say the last, apprehensive. He couldn't help feeling that Fielder and Yovetich were going to grill him, that in essence he was being accused once again. Although he realized in his mind that they were just trying to investigate the murder, in his heart, he was afraid. I kept telling Jerry that Colville wouldn't be spending the taxpayers' money if his detectives thought for one second that he had killed Lillian Stevick. Jerry said he understood that, but it didn't make going down there any easier.

I met Jerry at a Denny's Restaurant on Pennsylvania Route 28 near the Pennsylvania Turnpike, and we drove into Pittsburgh in my car. I waited outside on the bench in the hallway as Jerry first talked to Detective Fielder then to Yovetich in Yovetich's office. At one point, Ralph came out to hand me a cup of coffee. "The kid's doing fine," he said. "He got a good look at the man who jumped up from the body. He's really got it together."

"He's solid," I replied.

"We have photographs of the victim," Ralph said. "Shots taken at the morgue."

"Where did you get those?"

"At the Brackenridge Police Department. We showed the photos to Jerry. I also asked him why he confessed, and I liked his answer." He continued, "The kid got a raw deal."

"Are you making progress on the case?"

"We are doing the best we can," Yovetich said before going back into his office.

Afterward, Jerry and I had lunch at Denny's, where we had left his car. Jerry liked the detectives, and they had treated him well, but he said he felt like the bad guy again, and he was tired of being the bad guy. Being questioned by the detectives had brought back many bad memories and all of the shame and the anger. It had been a rough morning for Jerry, and he was depressed.

❏ ❏ ❏

It was Wednesday, December 19, 1990, and Sue and I had just returned from Columbus, Ohio, where we'd been visiting Chuck Duffy. My daughter Leslie said that Ralph Yovetich had called that morning with an important message; he wanted me to call him back as soon as possible.

I reached Ralph by phone later in the evening, and he said the reason he had called was that they had gone about as far as they could in their investigation. He said that, although he couldn't tell me what they had been up to, it might help if I went public with Jerry's story and Colville's reinvestigation of the Stevick murder.

"How would that help?" I asked.

"We've been getting help from the FBI in Quantico, Virginia," he said. "One of the FBI agents on the psychological profile squad suggested that you take the story to a newspaper. The publicity might flush out a witness or maybe another victim. If the killer is still out there, the newspaper story might rattle his cage. Just a little something in the local paper."

"That would be the *Valley News Dispatch*," I said.

"Right. Be sure not to tell them *why* you're coming forward. If the paper finds out we're using them, they might not play along."

"Who should I call?"

"Call Tony Klimko. He's a good reporter."

"I've got to check with Jerry Pacek," I said.

"Sure. If Jerry doesn't want it to go public, we understand. If he doesn't want to do this, we'll think of something else. It's gonna take a lot of guts for him to come out of the closet."

It was late, but I called Jerry anyway and put the question to him.

"Let's do it," he said.

"Are you sure?"

"I'm tired of hiding," Jerry replied. "I'm tired of feeling guilty about something I didn't do, and I want to see those guys catch the son of a bitch."

"There are no guarantees, Jerry."

"I know that."

"Your family won't approve."

"I know that too," he said. "It's gonna be tough on them."

"You could lose your job."

"If I do, I do. I'll just have to take that chance."

"I'll call Yovetich and tell him it's a go," I said. "We are playing with fire here. There's no way to predict what will happen."

"What the hell," Jerry said, then laughed.

23 The Media Spread the Stories

JERRY PACEK CALLED A FAMILY MEETING AT HIS MOTHER'S house on Nesbit Avenue in Brackenridge to break the news about the upcoming newspaper article about him and the case. The get-together, attended by his three brothers, two of his sisters, and a dozen nephews and nieces, degenerated into a shouting match between Jerry and his relatives. They were shocked that he had agreed to such a thing without consulting them first. Did he have any idea what this would mean? What about the children? Everybody at school would know about their Uncle Jerry, that he was a convicted murderer. The Pacek name would be dragged through the mud all over again, and they would all suffer. Hadn't they suffered enough?

Jerry had expected a difficult time with his family but not this. He tried to explain what it was like living with the knowledge that people who knew about his conviction considered him a murderer and a rapist. He told them what it was like living in anger and shame. Yes, but think what this will do to us, they said.

The meeting went on for several hours; there were many angry words and some tears. Jerry had never been close to his family, and now he was asking for their support. Jerry said he had not been close because he was never sure about how they felt about him. As far as he knew, some of them may actually believe he *was* guilty. Jerry's brothers replied that they always knew he was innocent and had figured that he stayed away because he didn't like them. By the time the meeting broke up, everybody was exhausted, but they had gotten somewhat used to the idea of the article. They did appreciate the chance to prepare for the publicity and thanked Jerry for that. Maybe now there was better understanding in the family; maybe now the healing could begin.

It hadn't been easy, and there was a great deal of fear, but in the end, Jerry got the support he wanted from his family. They were all Paceks, and they would stick together.

❑ ❑ ❑

I talked to Tony Klimko, the *Valley News Dispatch* (formerly the *Valley Daily News*) reporter who worked out of the Armstrong County Bureau in Kittanning. He was fascinated with the case and Jerry's fight to clear his name. Klimko went out to Slate Lick and talked to Jerry.

Jerry called me on Thursday, December 27, and said he was depressed. He couldn't eat, sleep, or concentrate at work. He'd been thinking about the man who killed Lillian Stevick, how he'd gotten away with it, and it was getting him down. Jerry had also been worrying about the upcoming newspaper article. He said his interview with Klimko had gone well — the reporter seemed very sympathetic and was a nice guy — but Jerry worried that the article would turn out wrong. What if people read it and thought he *was* a murderer?

When Klimko's article came out, on Saturday, December 29, in the weekend edition of the *Valley News Dispatch*, it was carried on the front page under the headlines "32-YEAR-OLD MURDER CASE RE-OPENED" and "EX-FBI AGENT STUDIED BRACKENRIDGE CASE." The article was long, well organized, factually correct, and beautifully written. As for the content, I couldn't have hoped for a better job. I called Jerry, and he was ecstatic. He had read the article and liked it as much as I did. His family approved as well. "Now people are going to know I didn't do it," he said.

On New Year's Eve Day, Jerry called to report how people had been reacting to him and to Klimko's article. He was a hero at work: Jerry's boss had called him into his office and had praised him for his courage. He also offered to run full-page ads in the *Pittsburgh Press* and the *Post-Gazette* proclaiming his pride in having Jerry as an employee. Jerry told his boss that wasn't necessary, but he thanked him for the thought. Wherever Jerry went, people would come up to him to shake his hand; and at church, his pastor said some very nice things. Everyone said they were outraged over what had happened to Jerry, and they couldn't believe the jury had convicted him.

Jerry said that he would be celebrating the new year that night with his brothers and sisters. Now that everything was out in the open, he was getting closer to his family. As I listened to Jerry, I couldn't help thinking about Chuck Duffy and how different it had been for him. When the truth finally came out about Chuck, most of his family took cover. I realized that comparing the two cases was perhaps unfair to the Zubryds, but I couldn't help noting the contrast. After talking to Jerry, I called Chuck to wish him a happy New Year. Instead, I got his answering machine.

Jerry Fielder called on January 2, 1991. "I had no idea," he said, "we'd get this much publicity. We got more than we'd bargained for."

Fielder was right. Jerry's story was not just in the papers, it had been on the radio and featured on Pittsburgh's three television stations.

Fielder had been back in touch with the psychological profiler with the FBI and had talked to a local criminal psychologist who did similar work, and they both said the same thing — keep the heat on — someone might come forward.

❏ ❏ ❏

The Pacek case caught the attention of a feature writer for the *Pittsburgh Press Sunday Magazine,* Dave Templeton, who wanted to do a story about Jerry. He changed his mind after I told him about the Zubryd murder and Chuck Duffy. Dave asked if I thought Chuck would agree to an interview, and I said he probably would. I wasn't sure about Joe Start, and I didn't think Janice Todd or Marge Zubryd would cooperate. Ted Botula had talked to Tony Klimko about Jerry Pacek; therefore, I figured he'd talk to Dave Templeton about Chuck Duffy.

Dave said he was captivated by Chuck Duffy's story and liked it all the better because it hadn't been told. If Joe Start and the others would talk to him, the article — a cover story — would come out in the spring.

❏ ❏ ❏

Steve Oppenheim, a field producer for the nationally syndicated television program *Inside Edition,* called on January 3 to say he'd seen the Associated Press article on the Pacek case. Steve said he wanted to do a show on Jerry and wondered if he would be interested. I said I would check with Jerry and let him know.

On Monday, January 7, Dave Templeton from the *Pittsburgh Press Sunday Magazine* called to let me know he had spoken to Chuck Duffy, Joe Start, Marge Zubryd, and Janice Todd, and they had all agreed to an interview. Dave said he had called Ted Botula's number and a man with a deep, golden voice had said Mr. Botula was not at home and would not be commenting on the case. I was amazed that Marge Zubryd and Janice Todd had agreed to be interviewed and wondered if Ted Botula regretted talking to Tony Klimko.

I called Chuck Duffy to get his reaction to being the subject of a cover story, and he was pleased and excited. He had spoken to his mother about it, but Florence Duffy was less than enthusiastic. Chuck was also surprised that his Aunt Marge and Janice Todd had agreed to be interviewed. Chuck said Dave Templeton was coming out to Columbus with a photographer the following week. "I read the article about Jerry Pacek," Chuck said. "I'm so happy for him. Are they going to get the man who did it?"

"They're trying, but at this late date it's hard to solve the murder."

"I don't imagine you've made any headway with our man."

"Nothing. I'm sorry."

"I understand; I just thought I'd ask."

"I'm hoping the magazine article about you will bring someone out of the woodwork, maybe someone who knew the moon-faced guy."

"I didn't think of that," Chuck said.

"It's a long shot, but it's all we got."

"Tell Joe Start I appreciate what he's doing. When the story comes out, he's going to be criticized."

"That's a price he's willing to pay," I said.

"Say hello to Jerry Pacek."

❏ ❏ ❏

Lisa Zompa, an on-air newsperson with WSEE-TV, the CBS affiliate in Erie, was producing a thirty-minute documentary on the

Pacek case. She had arranged to film Jerry at his house on Wednesday, January 9. Jerry and I were going to meet Ms. Zompa and her crew at the McDonald's on Pennsylvania Route 422 in West Kittanning, four miles from Jerry's house. The roads were bad that morning; Lisa and her crew were late, and Jerry was nervous. When the TV people did arrive, they followed us back to his house.

Lisa had jet-black hair and was young, petite, and pretty. Jerry and Lisa hit it off immediately. Still, Jerry wasn't sure he was doing the right thing. When Lisa asked him on camera if he had killed Lillian Stevick, Jerry looked her straight in the eye and said, "No." Although Lisa was a sympathetic interviewer, it was not easy for Jerry. He felt he was being accused, once again. I realized that if Jerry was going to get through this phase of being a public person, he'd have to get used to the idea of being interrogated.

The next morning, Jerry and I were in Brackenridge with producer Steve Oppenheim from *Inside Edition*. Jerry had been back to the old neighborhood many times to visit his mother, but on this occasion, with the camera rolling, he walked to the spot next to the concrete steps where he had found Lillian Stevick. I could tell Jerry was trying hard not to show his discomfort, and this was making me uneasy.

Oppenheim was a big, friendly New Yorker inside an oversized army coat bulging with soda cans, bags of assorted junk food, and recently purchased comic books. Although Steve looked like a couch potato who'd been living on the street for nine years, he knew what he was doing and radiated the kind of energy that comes off a mad scientist. When Steve wasn't draining a can of Coke or polishing off a candy bar, he was writing furiously in the little notebook he carried. Jerry and I liked him the moment we met him and considered him some kind of creative genius.

That afternoon, Steve and his crew filmed Jerry sitting at his dining room table responding to Steve's off-camera questions. Seeing Jerry there reminded me of our first talk, at that table, eight months earlier. Things went smoothly until Steve asked Jerry how he felt about me. Jerry tried to find the words but couldn't, and that's when he broke down. The camera kept rolling, and we all looked on silently as Jerry pulled himself together. "People have no idea of what it is like to be thought of as a murderer," he said. "Nobody knows my pain, nobody."

The interview ended and Steve got up from the table. "Do you think Ted Botula will talk to me?" he asked. I noticed that Steve's eyes were red.

"I don't know," I replied. "The last time a reporter called him he answered the phone and told the reporter that Ted Botula was out of town on vacation."

"Would you call him for me?"

I didn't relish the idea of calling Ted, but I did it.

"I didn't like that TV woman from Erie," Botula said. I assumed he was referring to Lisa Zompa.

"I'm with a guy from *Inside Edition*," I said. "You know, the TV show."

"I know the program," Botula replied.

"He'd like to have a word with you."

"Tell him no. I've got nothing more to say about those cases."

"I guess you're mad at me."

"No, not at you. I don't like those people. I didn't like the way she talked to me."

Ted and I said good-bye; as it turned out, we wouldn't be speaking to each other again. I wondered what Jerry was thinking as I used his phone to talk to the man who had helped send him to prison.

❑ ❑ ❑

That night, I got home late and found a message that Jerry Fielder had called. I telephoned him at home, and he said, "We're spinning our wheels on this end. All that publicity, and no one has come forward."

"So what's that mean?" I asked. "You're not closing the case?"

"Hell, no, we still got leads, but it doesn't look too good."

"So what's next?"

"Ralph and I were talking," Fielder said, "and we got an idea."

"What?"

"Forensic hypnosis."

"On who?"

"On Jerry Pacek."

"I don't know about that," I said. "I don't think he'll go for it. What's the idea?"

"To get a better description of the guy he saw at the crime scene. The hypnotists can take Jerry back to that night, then we can get someone from the state police to do an Identi-Kit drawing based on what Jerry remembers." He continued, "Maybe Jerry will remember something that could help us. No one back then took him seriously as an eyewitness. Maybe they missed something we can pick up."

Jerry was home when I called the next morning. He wasn't going to work that day because he was spending the afternoon with Steve Oppenheim and the *Inside Edition* crew. I asked him about the forensic hypnosis and was surprised by his positive and quick response.

"Why not?" he said. "I saw that guy three times and got a pretty good look at him. Go ahead and set it up."

That evening, late, Jerry Pacek called. He'd been in Brackenridge with Steve Oppenheim and his crew. Steve had wanted to interview Jerry's mother, Clara, and she had agreed, so they had lugged all of the TV gear up the steps to her house, set the stuff up, then proceeded with the interview. When it was over and they were packing up to leave, Jerry overheard Steve tell the sound man they couldn't use any of it.

"Why not?" I said. "Technical problems?"

"No, it was my mother—what she said and how she said it. It wasn't what they wanted."

"What did she say?"

"I can't remember," Jerry said. He sounded exhausted and at the end of his rope. "She just whined about how hard it had been on *her*."

"I'm sorry, Jerry."

"Nobody understands what it's like for me—they only think of themselves. I'm tired." Then Jerry said he had decided not to undergo hypnosis.

"That's fine, Jerry. It's up to you."

"It always comes back on me. Why don't they hypnotize the fucker who killed her. That son of a bitch isn't affected by any of this. It always comes back to me, it's always on my shoulders. I'm tired of it."

"Ted Botula and Sam Strauss put it on your shoulders, and Jerry Fielder is trying to get it off—and he needs your help. If you were there, you saw the man, and there's nothing we can do to change that."

"It always comes back to me. I shouldn't have to prove anything.

I didn't do it. I was a kid—an innocent *boy*—and I'm still being tested. I can't trust anyone. I'm angry—and I don't know how to deal with it."

When I gave Jerry Fielder the news, he was disappointed—not in Jerry Pacek but in his decision not to be hypnotized. Fielder had already lined up the two psychologists for February 25. "Maybe Jerry will change his mind," he said.

"I doubt it."

"I won't cancel the hypnotists for a few days, in case he does."

"If Jerry changes his mind, I'll let you know," I said.

The second article about the Pacek case by Tony Klimko appeared on Saturday, January 12, in the weekend edition of the *Valley News Dispatch*. The piece began,

> Nationwide attention has been focused on the reopening of a 32-year-old murder case here.
>
> Inside Edition, a nationally syndicated TV show, has spent the last several days filming the story of Jerry Pacek, 46, who served 10 years in prison for the November 17, 1958, murder of Mrs. Lillian Stevick, 52, of Brackenridge. . . .
>
> Steve Oppenheim, field producer of the New York City–based program, said Friday he heard about the case from wire service stories based on the original story which appeared December 29 in the *Valley News Dispatch*.
>
> "When we saw it we knew it was a story crying to be told," Oppenheim said. "Here is this guy who was railroaded. He said he was innocent all these years and nobody believed him."

I felt a little better after reading Steve Oppenheim's quote, and I called Jerry Pacek to see if he had seen the article. He had and was in a much better mood. "I'm ready for the hypnosis," he said.

"Are you sure?"

"I'm willing to give it a try."

I waited until Monday before calling Jerry Fielder to give Jerry Pacek an opportunity to change his mind over the weekend. He didn't, and so on Monday I gave Fielder the news. "We're already set for Monday, February 25," he said.

"Any progress in the investigation?"

"We're still trying to question Bobby Stevick. His attorney wants a criminal lawyer there when we do it. I said to this guy, 'What's wrong with you people? We're not accusing him of anything—we just want to talk to him about his mother.' So it's taking some time setting it up."

"What about the rumor that he set fire to his house?"

"We haven't been able to nail that down. There are a lot of rumors."

"Like what?"

"Someone told us that after the murder Bobby ran to a relative's house in Tarentum where they washed his bloody clothes."

"How does this person know that?"

"They just heard it somewhere."

"Where in Tarentum?"

"They don't know. We keep running into walls in this case."

"What about Mr. Stevick and the girlfriend?"

"We've interviewed the old guy. He's eighty-three and married to a sixty-two-year-old woman. She drove him down to the office."

"What did Mr. Stevick say about his old girlfriend?"

"Nothing. It was obvious he didn't want to discuss any of that in front of his wife. But we know he did have a girlfriend. People told us he'd take the girl into his bedroom, and they'd have sex with Mrs. Stevick in the house."

"Have you identified this woman?"

"No."

"How old was she?"

"I don't know. She was younger."

"Where did she live?"

"In Brackenridge somewhere. People called her 'Little Red Riding Hood' because she had this red coat she always wore."

"I wonder where she is now."

"We think she's dead. Someone said she died in a car wreck with her husband."

"When?"

"Sometime in the 1960s. That's all we know."

"The murder could have been an ordinary triangle killing," I said.

"Sure. We know that Mrs. Stevick was afraid of someone because she had gone to the Brackenridge Police Department four times asking for protection."

"I guess she didn't get it."

"I guess not."

"Can you prove she went to the police?"

"With documents?"

"Yes."

"No."

"Anything else?"

"Yes. Mr. Stevick told us some guy tried to rape Mrs. Stevick a few days before she was murdered. He said it was the man who delivered milk and eggs to the house. She fought him off and ran screaming across the street."

"Did Mrs. Stevick report this to the police?"

"No, she told Mr. Stevick."

"What did he do?"

"We asked him that," Fielder said. "You know what he told us?"

"What?"

Fielder laughed. "You won't believe this — he said, 'We canceled the buttermilk.'"

"That's it?"

"That's it."

"What's the eggman's name?"

"We don't know. That's what we call him — the 'Eggman.' If Mr. Stevick knows, he won't say."

"I wonder if Mr. Stevick had anything to do with the Egg-man and the attempted rape?" I said, "Maybe it was an attempted murder. Maybe he was the guy who tried to run her down in the green car."

"Yeah. I've thought about that too. We're gonna question him again — but this time we're gonna do it without the wife. He won't say anything in front of her."

"Does he have any kind of criminal record?"

"We can't find anything. But people tell us he was pretty rough with his wife and kid. That's the trouble with this case, it's so old you can't document anything. Too many people are dead."

"Ted Botula had suspects coming out of his ears," I said. "He had Bobby, Mr. Stevick, Little Red Riding Hood, and the god-damned Eggman."

"Right. The girlfriend had brothers, maybe one of them did it."

"Botula stopped the investigation with Jerry. He could have solved the case. They would have found the bloody clothes and the murder weapon. Jesus, there was so much physical evidence, and they had a good witness in Jerry Pacek. Jerry got a good look at the killer that night. Ninth and Morgan was a busy corner back then; we're trying to find Jerry's defense witnesses, the three people who saw the suspicious man lurking around the Esso station. One of the witnesses is living in Arizona somewhere."

"What else was on that corner?"

"Schied's Drug Store, Joe Sini's Groceries, and a dairy store. Those places are long gone." After a moment, he said, "Let me know if there's any problem with the twenty-fifty for Jerry."

❏ ❏ ❏

There had been a time when I thought Lillian Stevick and Helen Zubryd had been murdered by the same man. They were middle-aged, lower middle class mill-town women who'd been sexually attacked and bludgeoned to death on November nights. But Joe Start's moon-faced man didn't look anything like the man Jerry had seen that night, and he didn't match the description of the shadowy man seen lurking around the corner of Ninth and Morgan by the three witnesses who had testified for the defense at Jerry's trial. Moreover, Helen Zubryd had lived on the other side of Pittsburgh, forty miles from Brackenridge.

I had by now told Jerry Fielder about the Zubryd case and what Ted Botula had done to Chuck, but he hadn't shown much investigative interest, so we didn't discuss it in any detail. There was no need: the murders were apparently unrelated.

As I saw it, the Stevick investigation was a long-shot proposition, and the Zubryd case, already dead and buried, wasn't coming back to life.

24 Hypnosis

THE CBS AFFILIATE IN ERIE, WSEE-TV, AIRED LISA ZOM-
pa's thirty-minute documentary on Saturday, January 26. It was
called *Justice Delayed: The Vindication of Jerry Pacek.* I thought it was
well-done, and Jerry liked it too. The various media had treated
Jerry sympathetically, and that was how people were responding to
him. The airing of the Zompa documentary would mark a turning
point in Jerry's attitude toward the media and the detectives who
were working on the Stevick case. From that point on, he gained
more confidence, was more trusting, and became less prone to
bouts of depression.

I had been in touch with producer Steve Oppenheim regarding
the airing of the *Inside Edition* segment. Steve didn't know exactly
when Jerry's show would air but thought it would be sometime during the summer months.

On Monday, February 25, Jerry Pacek and I were in Pittsburgh
at eight in the morning for Jerry's first session with Dr. Kay Thompson and Dr. Russell Scott, the forensic hypnotists. Jerry was nervous. "Everything's jumping around inside," he said.

Jerry Fielder met us in the grand jury room and introduced us
to the psychologists, who were seated at the conference table. The
doctors greeted Jerry warmly, and I could tell he liked them right
away. Dr. Kay Thompson was a tall, thin woman in her fifties. She
wore glasses, had long brown hair, and was wearing a pair of purple
slacks. Dr. Russell Scott, a stocky man in his sixties, had a full head
of white hair and a beard to match. He wore a rumpled blue sports
coat, a pair of darker blue trousers, a blue tie, and a white shirt that
needed pressing. Dr. Scott was sucking on a piece of candy and
spoke with a gravelly voice.

I left Jerry at the conference table and took a seat in the small
office adjacent to the grand jury room. There, I would watch the

session on a TV monitor with Jerry Fielder and Fred Cooper. As I watched Jerry and the two doctors make small talk at the conference table, I couldn't believe they would be able to hypnotize him in such an unlikely setting.

Dr. Scott asked Jerry what it had been like in prison, and Jerry told him about the race riot that occurred on his last day there. Jerry said that things had been tough at first, but as time went on the guards treated him better, that they threw him the going-away party.

"If this is going to help the investigation," Jerry said, "I want to do it."

"It's not going to be easy," said Dr. Scott.

"We don't know what to expect," Dr. Thompson added.

"We're here to help you," Dr. Scott said.

"I feel like I'm finally getting my turn," Jerry said. "And I feel guilty about this because most people don't get the chance. They live that way all their life. Ya know, abused wives, kids — why me? I feel guilty about that. I didn't think I'd ever get my turn."

"Many others are cheering for you, Jerry," Dr. Scott said. "Maybe their turn is coming up. It took guts; you took a risk; take advantage of it."

I could see that Jerry was relaxing. Sometimes the doctors would speak at the same time, in soothing voices about running water, the sky, the wind, and moving back into time. Dreaming and letting go. "How much different do you feel now?" asked Dr. Scott.

"I'm not sure."

"You can ask questions anytime. You can close your eyes. You're feeling more comfortable. Let it go — apprehension. Freedom of knowing. Understanding. It is your turn. Sinking, secure, aware, aware, and that's nice. Deeper and deeper in a way that helps you know everything you need to know. Deeper and deeper. What you've experienced — move back through time — a day at a time, year at a time. Little steps, big steps. That's neat. Deeper, and further, and further. Feeling a power, peacefully, calmly. Let's move back to that time — because you are the one who was there. You are the key. . . . Deeper and further back. What are you experiencing, Jerry?"

"My head feels huge; my lips feel heavy. There is a blank."

"We can move through that void. You know so much. You remember so much. Your head has to be big to take in everything —

for you to explore it. Let your body tell you a great deal. . . . And now, Jerry, how do you feel?"

Jerry didn't respond.

"Take your time. I'm going to ask you to remember your thirteenth birthday. What is that like? Is that okay with you?"

"I see a blank, twilight sky. It changes different shapes," Jerry said. He seemed to be talking in his sleep.

"Let it happen. What will those shapes turn into? It's your turn. Deeper, slowly moving around inside those shapes. What's happening now?"

"I don't see anything happening — it's just blank. It's dark."

"Picture yourself at thirteen. Let me know when he's there."

"I remember buck shoes I used to wear. Corduroy jacket with my middle name on the back — 'Joe.' It's dark blue or black. 'Joe' is on metal studs on the back. That was the style. I used 'Joe' because 'Jerry' was too long."

"What's he like?"

"All's I see — I don't see — I just remember — standing there. I don't see it — I just feel it."

"Standing where?"

"Nowhere, just standing." Jerry suddenly opened his eyes. "Can I go to the bathroom?" he asked.

After Jerry left the room, Dr. Thompson said, "He's very scared."

"He's scared out of his tree," Dr. Scott replied.

Jerry returned to the table and sat down. He was smiling. "I felt myself going, and I thought, You guys got me."

Dr. Scott reached over and touched Jerry, and Jerry was under. Drs. Scott and Thompson kept the litany going until Jerry responded by speaking to himself as a thirteen-year-old. "I'm sorry I let you down, Jerry," he said. "I let my innerself down." Jerry jumped to his feet and broke down crying. The doctors got up and stood next to him, holding his hands.

In the adjacent office, Jerry Fielder looked at me and said, "I feel like a window peeper. This is tough to watch."

I felt the same way and was worried about what I had gotten Jerry into.

Out in the big room, Dr. Scott was saying: "Doesn't it feel good, really good, to know you can get in touch with that? It's the best thing you can do. It's not going to overwhelm you."

Jerry stood there and cried, his entire body shaking. I said to Fielder, "I hope they know what they're doing."

Fielder rolled his eyes and lit a cigarette. "I know what you mean," he said.

Finally, Jerry stopped crying and sat down. "I'm so afraid of that rage in me," he said. "I don't want that rage — it's not doing me any good."

"Be aware of where that rage is directed," said Dr. Scott.

"Those bastards hurt me. I didn't do anything wrong."

"Then tell them that," Dr. Thompson said.

"Feel my goddamn pain!" Jerry screamed.

"You touched the rage," Dr. Scott said.

"Yes." Jerry was much calmer now.

"It is safe to touch it. It is not going to destroy you. Now you're beyond that. You still have the rage, but you have a way to deal with it. You have power."

Jerry started crying again, and I could hear Fielder squirming in his chair. "Jesus Christ," he murmured. "I don't know if I can get used to this."

Jerry stopped crying suddenly and said, "Thank you."

"That wave of emotion," said Dr. Scott, "represented years and years of hurt. You have to be such a man to get beyond that. Look at it — you can be free of it."

"I'll never be free of it. I want to be free. That rage was put into me — it's not mine."

"What are you thinking about now?" asked Dr. Thompson.

"Ted Botula, you son of a bitch, you've sold my soul!" Jerry broke down again and was sobbing so hard I was worried he wouldn't get control of himself. Jerry was on his feet again. "It's terrible," he said. "Do you mind if I sit down? I need something to hold onto. I'm shaking." Jerry sat down and the doctors put their hands on him. Jerry suddenly laughed. "I-I felt I could have cried forever. I wanted to get it out. I'm ashamed of the rage. I don't know what to do with it. It feels good sometimes; it feels bad sometimes."

"You have a right to have it," said Dr. Scott.

"I really feel I'm starting to relax, but I feel twitches in my legs."

"Don't hurry. Don't push. Don't make anything happen. Don't push the river — it has its own flow. . . ."

After a while, Jerry's head dropped forward, and with his chin on his chest, he looked asleep. He breathed deeply. "What does Jerry do?" asked Dr. Scott. "How does he spent his time?"

"Go to school. Go home. Go to Mary's house."

"Good relationship with Mary?"

"Yeah."

"Anything special happening with Mary?"

"I'm not allowed to see her 'cause she's older than me. I want to see her anyway because I love her."

"When do you see Mary?"

"After school. She lives in Tarentum. Walk or run down — I go to her house — takes ten, fifteen minutes. Six o'clock. See her every day. Usually when news comes on, I go out her backdoor, down steps, and up Sixth Avenue."

"Is that where he was going the night things happened?"

"I can see myself leaving her house. It was cold. I'm walking up Sixth Avenue. I don't seem to be moving — I'm looking up Sixth Avenue. I see street lights, cars parked along Sixth. I'm getting a blank. I'm going to go up the street and find Mrs. Stevick. I see it coming. That's why I'm afraid, I know."

"You don't have to be afraid anymore. Go ahead."

"I'm getting little things — I seen the man get up off the ground. I just see black — like a silhouette. That's all I see, kneeling there, staring at me."

"What was he doing on the ground?"

"I don't know. That's all I see. It's like a still picture."

"How far away are you?"

"A big picture about five feet from me."

"Where are his hands?"

"One's on his knee."

"Where is his other hand?"

"No — looks like it's by his side. I can't see the other hand."

"Which one is on his knee?"

"Don't know."

"Next photograph — what's he doing in that photo? Take your time."

Jerry breathed deeply. "I seem to be getting a picture of his back — his rear end and part of his back. He's either running or walking. I see a black belt, a gray shirt, he doesn't have a hat. I see two pictures — one of him walking away and one of him standing on top of the hill. I'm seeing both at the same time. Shiny hair. I see someone standing on top of the hill, standing sideways. I see his left side — skinny and tall. It seems like he's looking down at me." Jerry paused.

"What do you feel?"

"I don't feel anything. It's blank . . . It's black."

"Deeper, Jerry. What goes on in that picture. So many pictures between now and then. What's happening now?"

"I still get that still picture. I'm frustrated I can't get any further."

"Take that deep breath, hold it until I count to five. Let that tension go. Still deeper. Second deep breath — two, three, four, five — and let it out. You know what to do now. Just let him go now." Dr. Thompson got up and stood behind Jerry with both of her hands on his shoulders. "Now it's your turn, Jerry," she said. "Take those photographs out of storage — let us share, so you don't have to bear them alone. Are you ready? We can take another look. Just let it happen."

"All I see is this light — my heart beating in front of my eyes, a light blinking in time with my heart."

"What are you feeling?"

"Nothing, it's blank."

Jerry suddenly appeared to wake up. He opened his eyes to look at Dr. Thompson, who had returned to her chair. "I feel like I'm wasting your time," he said. It was 10:45; they had been working with Jerry for more than two hours. The hypnotic session was over, but Jerry and the doctors sat at the table and talked for another hour, while Fielder and I went for coffee and asked ourselves if we were doing the right thing. "I've never seen anything like that," Fielder said.

Just before noon, Fielder and I joined Jerry and the doctors in the grand jury room. "It's not like I'm seeing it for the first time," Jerry was saying. "I thought I'd see exactly what I saw. I thought it would be like watching a movie. I feel relaxed, like I'm sleepy, like I haven't slept for three days," Jerry laughed. He looked at me and said, "You look like you've been through hell."

"Don't worry about me," I said. "What about you?"

"I feel good. That crying bit — wow. There's a lot there. There's no one person I can blame. I can't focus on the guy who did it. The anger would come out on my wife — Mary — and my kids — I overreacted a lot. I'd feel so damned bad. The anger would come out for no reason, and I'd hurt someone. I feel bad about the anger. Recently, I found a lot of peace." Jerry pointed his finger at me. "It's because of you, old buddy, and don't say it ain't!" he laughed.

"Jerry," Dr. Scott asked, "do you know why you confessed?"

"They took control of my mind and did what they wanted."

"You were in a trance — an altered state. You were vulnerable, afraid. You were thirteen. You did the only thing you could do. Dr. Thompson and I are using hypnosis to break through a previous hypnotic experience. They did a number on you."

"I wanted to please them," Jerry said. "Ted Botula befriended me — gave me a cigarette — got me something to drink. He dressed real sharp — I didn't come from that."

"You were shafted," Dr. Scott said. "It couldn't happen today. You were railroaded, that's the rage."

"I blamed my parents," Jerry said. "Also, I was different. Something told me I wasn't being brought up right. Dad drinking, mom bitching. I didn't see it in other people's homes."

"All that is in the past now," said Dr. Thompson.

Before we broke that day, Jerry agreed to have a second session with the doctors. It was scheduled for Monday, March 18, and according to Jerry, he was looking forward to it. "Maybe next time," he said, "I'll get a better look at the man. I'm sorry if I let you down."

❏ ❏ ❏

On March 8, reporter Tony Klimko wrote his third article about the Pacek case for the *Valley News Dispatch*. The headline read: "WOMAN BELIEVES KILLER STALKED SISTER IN 1958 MURDER." The article reported the attempt on Lillian Stevick's life before her murder:

> Lillian Stevick of Brackenridge was being stalked by an unknown man for a month before she was killed 32 years ago, her sister said.
>
> "She told us this green, four-door sedan would follow her when she left the hospital after visiting her husband. She had feared for her life," said her sister, Marjorie Kutchko, 75, of Allegheny Township.

Jerry had already sent off for and received his pardon application form, and I had been working on a lengthy report to supplement his appeal. I talked to the D.A., Bob Colville, about helping

Jerry with the pardon, and he said, "Jerry deserves a pardon. I'll back him all the way. I'll write a letter to the board."

❑ ❑ ❑

Jerry Pacek and I were back in Pittsburgh on March 18 for a second session with Drs. Thompson and Scott. He was in high spirits and said he had been looking forward to the session. The three of them sat down at the conference table, while Jerry Fielder and I repaired to the little office to watch them on the TV monitor. The doctors began to relax Jerry.

In the little office, as Jerry slowly went under, I asked Jerry Fielder how the Stevick investigation was proceeding. He told me that, during the past eight months, he and Fred Cooper had spent 90 percent of their time working on it. They had located one of Jerry's defense witnesses, the one living in Arizona, and learned that the police, because they had Jerry Pacek in custody, had ignored this person's information about the suspicious man seen on the corner that night just before the murder. Fielder said one witness had passed away several years ago; and the third, a local man, didn't remember much about that night.

"Have you questioned Bobby Stevick?" I asked.

"No. With his lawyers and everything, we're having a hard time arranging it."

"What about Mr. Stevick, have you gotten him alone?"

"Not yet. The guy is glued to his wife." Fielder then said, "The other day, Fred and I were up on the sixth floor of the courthouse — and guess what?"

"What?"

"We found the old county detective's file on the Stevick case."

"I thought all those old files had been destroyed."

"That's what I was beginning to think."

"Jesus. Where did you find it?"

"Up in this little room — you have to go through two doors to get into it. The place is a mess with papers all over the floor and boxes piled up on each other. We found more photographs of the victim, pictures showing Jerry's crime scene reenactment, and even the hatchet they introduced into evidence as the so-called murder weapon."

"I can't believe it."

"The file had some handwritten notes made by Botula. He had written down two names—people to check out."

"You mean suspects?"

"We think so, yes."

"Who are they? How are they connected to the murder?"

"We don't know that yet. We're checking out the names. One of the suspects, I'll call him Fred, has a record."

"For what?"

"For rape."

"Did he do time?"

"No, but he has several arrests."

"Did the guy deliver milk and eggs?"

"We're checking that out."

"Is he alive?"

"Yes, and he still lives in the area. He was last arrested in 1980."

"For rape?"

"Yes. We're still doing a background check on him."

"Does he meet the description of the man Jerry saw that night?"

"We think he does. We're gonna ask him to come down for a little talk."

"What about the other suspect?"

"He's dead. We don't know why Botula had him down. He's got no record that we can find. He lived on Ninth Street, five or six blocks from Morgan. We don't know what he looked like."

"Anything else?"

"Yes. Botula must have questioned Bobby Stevick. According to Botula's notes, the kid had said, 'Mother made me do bad things.'"

"That's all?"

"That's all that's in the file."

"There were enough leads in this case for ten murders." Then I asked, "When did he question Bobby—before or after Jerry's confession?"

"I don't know, Botula's notes aren't dated. Those guys weren't known for their paperwork."

"You said there were other files up there."

"Boxes of them—stuff going all the way back to the 1930s."

"You didn't happen to see another hatchet up there, did you?"

"No, but that doesn't mean there wasn't one. Why?"

"Do you remember me telling you about the Zubryd case?"

"Yeah, the eight-year-old kid who killed his mother with a hatchet."

"Right," I said. "Only he didn't. Another man confessed to killing Helen Zubryd. He told Joe Start he did it, but Start can't remember his name. We think his name is in the Zubryd file. If I can find that file, we might be able to identify the man who killed Helen Zubryd."

"I don't remember seeing anything up there on the Zubryd case, but we were looking for Pacek stuff. It could be up there."

"When can I go up and look?"

"Someone will have to be with you," Fielder said.

"Then when can we go?"

"We'll have to get permission from Colville."

Out in the grand jury room, the doctors had Jerry Pacek under. They had taken him back, and he was at the point where he had found Mrs. Stevick.

"I hear somebody moan — it scares me. I see the man get up and go. I can't see the person who is moaning. I holler, 'Do you need any help?' I holler again. I don't know what to do. I go to his house [Mr. DeLeonardis's house] because I know there's somebody in his backyard hurt. I hear them moan. He says, 'I'll go get my shoes on.' I'm standing there waiting for him to come out. He walks around the house. We see someone lying on the ground on the right side of the steps. He says, 'I'll go call the police.' He leaves me there, goes back down the steps to his house. I walk around front of his house and stand on the sidewalk. I see the guy on top of the hill. He walks across Morgan Street to the steps. He walks up the steps and walks away. At first I just see his shadow. When he gets on the steps, I see his head and his whole body from the back."

"What's he wearing, Jerry?" Dr. Scott asked.

"I see his face, a black-and-white picture. He's kind of skinny. He's got a high forehead, shiny hair. His face is chiseled."

"Did you see him again?"

"I keep getting pictures of steps. A man — I can only see part of him, from the waist up. I'm standing on the steps. He's facing me. He's standing there. I can't see his hands. I see him turn to his right. He walks away. I stand there. I'm scared inside. I'm still on the steps. I'm standing, waiting. It's late, it's dark. I can see because there's a streetlight. I'm waiting for the guy to come back out of the house."

Jerry paused, then took off his glasses and wiped his eyes. "Oh, man, I feel beat," he said, out of the trance. He laughed. "I couldn't get through it. I didn't want to force myself, I didn't want to make any mistakes."

"You saw a man on three occasions," said Dr. Scott. "Was it the same person?"

"I know it's the same guy," Jerry said. "He had the same build through the shoulders. The way he looked around the shoulders — they were narrow."

"Can you remember what he was wearing?"

"A gray jacket that went to the waist. It had a zipper. His forehead was shiny. The jacket was plain, and it had a collar."

"You did good, Jerry," Dr. Thompson said.

Jerry laughed. "It was too much. I felt the heartbreak of being in jail. It was like I was right there. I'm sweating. I was off in wonderland. I saw all kinds of stuff — Mom, Dad, my brothers and sisters. I saw flashes of everything. I kept seeing Morgan Street, looking up the hill. I don't know where you put me." Jerry laughed again. "My-oh-my, man-oh-man. Looking up that hill, standing on the tracks on Sixth Avenue. I saw stuff I hadn't seen for years. I saw Camp Hill — the building I worked at — looking across the street. I saw the carpenter shop, the barber shop, J-Ward. I saw myself walking into the institution the day I entered Camp Hill. I remember my mom — being heavy, wearing those ugly dresses she wore. And my dad with the work hat he wore. Holy cow. Boy, I tell ya, I feel like I was right back in the institution again. Serving time again."

"I think you've had enough for today," Dr. Scott said.

"I feel beat. Thank you for everything."

"Do you want to do this again?" asked Dr. Thompson.

"Yes," Jerry replied.

Dr. Thompson checked her date book and asked, "How's Wednesday, April 10?"

"It's fine with me," said Dr. Scott.

"I'll be here," said Jerry.

❏ ❏ ❏

On Wednesday, March 20, Jerry Pacek mailed nine copies of his pardon application along with five passport photographs and a check for twenty dollars to the Board of Pardons in Harrisburg. He had listed me as his official representative, the one who would present his case to the board if it saw fit to grant him a hearing.

25 The Threads of Two Investigations

THE RECENT PUBLICITY ABOUT JERRY PACEK AND THE Stevick murder had not produced any witnesses or information helpful to Detective Fielder and his investigation. Fielder still had hopes that something would break. Late in March 1991, two Tony Klimko articles were published in the *Valley News Dispatch* on consecutive days, keeping the story alive. The first had to do with Jerry's hypnosis sessions, the second with Jerry's pardon plea.

I had written a letter to Bob Colville for permission to look for the Zubryd file on the sixth floor of the courthouse. I called a few days later, and he said, "Dig around all you want, and wear old clothes."

On March 28, the day after Klimko's article about Jerry Pacek's application for a pardon, Jerry Fielder and I had lunch downtown then walked over to the courthouse and rode the old elevator to the top floor. I followed Fielder down the narrow, tunnel-like hallway past dozens of windowless steel doors. The sixth floor of the courthouse was a huge attic, a dimly lit catacomb of hallways, doorways, and secret rooms. It seemed like we'd walked a mile, turning down one hallway after another. Finally, he stopped at a green, paint-chipped steel door with "#18 county works" painted across it in white block letters.

"I hope I brought the right keys," Fielder said, as he started inserting keys from the large ring he had brought with him. He also had a flashlight. After several tries, the lock turned, and he opened the door and probed the darkness with his flashlight. "We gotta go through another door," he said.

I stepped into the space between the two doors and held the flashlight as Fielder inserted another key into a door marked "D.A.'s Office."

"No wonder no one can find anything up here," I said.

Fielder opened the door, switched on the light, and we stepped inside the fifteen-by-fifteen-foot room. The place was painted green and lit by a bare 100-watt lightbulb that hung from the ceiling. "I told you it was a mess," Fielder said.

He was right. Large cardboard boxes, stuffed with old case files and assorted pieces of physical evidence were piled against the walls halfway to the ceiling. Four of the free-standing metal shelves had toppled over, spilling their contents — document, pieces of bloody clothing, wigs, bullets, shell casings, burglary tools, false teeth, pieces of rope, and crime scene photographs — onto the floor. "We're gonna be here a while," I said.

"Be careful what you put your hands into," Fielder said.

We spent three hours digging through the debris. I found old county detective cases going back to 1933, dozens of 1950s cases, investigations I had read about in the old newspapers when I was looking up Ted Botula's old cases. Many of Ted's investigations were still up there. But I didn't find the Zubryd file and neither did Fielder. We rode the elevator down in silence.

I had told Joe Start that I had a good lead on the Zubryd file and had promised to let him know what was in it when we found it. The moment I got home from Pittsburgh I called Joe to tell him it wasn't there.

"That's a goddamn shame," he said. "I thought you had it."

"So did I."

"I'll never remember that fucker's name," Joe said.

"I've talked to Drs. Thompson and Scott, the hypnotists who are doing such a good job with Jerry Pacek," I said. "They think they might be able to jog your memory. They are good. What do you think?"

"Whatever you say. I'll try anything."

After I got off the phone with Joe, I called Chuck Duffy. I was feeling a little sorry for myself and told him that. "We still can't find the file."

"Something will turn up," he said. "I know it will."

On Easter Sunday, three days after Jerry Fielder and I came out of the courthouse empty-handed, Dave Templeton's article about

Chuck Duffy came out as the cover story of the *Pittsburgh Press Sunday Magazine*. The beautifully written article, called "The Defense Never Rests," portrayed Chuck Duffy sympathetically without making him look pathetic:

The 42-year-old Duffy resembled a Yuppie Jackie Cooper who exudes intelligence, class, self-assurance. He's quick to discuss his personality and eloquence: "I've always been sensitive and enjoyed artsy things," he says. "I'm fairly literate and incredibly verbal."

After his . . . confession in 1959, newspaper accounts noted how 10-year-old Charlie "could stare a hole through you." "The fact is," Duffy snaps, "he still can."

Anyone familiar with Duffy's background understands he's a survivor who's recycled the rubble of childhood tragedy into a successful life. However, his lifestyle cannot whitewash the back horror of Nov. 20, 1956, when his 41-year-old widowed mother was slain in the basement of their Sewickley Township (now Bell Acres) home. A hatchet was buried 5 inches into her forehead.

The murder of Helen Zubryd sparked the largest investigation to that date in Allegheny County history. Fifteen to 20 detectives interviewed more than 1,300 people, chased down 1,600 leads and spent 14,000 man-hours investigating the case at a cost of over $100,000. Yet, more than 2 years after the murder, police were stumped. That's when Chief Ted Botula of the Allegheny County Homicide Unit asked Charlie Zubryd's uncle and guardian, Michael Zubryd, to bring the youngster in for questioning.

According to Duffy, Botula and Detective Francis Flannery pumped him to confess. Finally, the skinny orphan — only 8 years old when the murder occurred — said he ran to the basement and grabbed the hatchet after his mother threatened to whip him with an Army belt. After having Charlie confess in front of his relatives, Botula took him to District Attorney

Edward Boyle's office where he had Charlie reenact the murder with Botula playing the role of his mother.

Had Charles been tried for the crime, he would have been the youngest murder defendant in Allegheny County history. But despite their public proclamations of Charlie's guilt, police never took the case to trial. Hiding his face with a red hunter's cap, Charlie broke into tears when Boyle told an Allegheny County Common Pleas Court judge that his relatives no longer wanted him. Months later, Charlie was adopted by Frank Duffy, an industrial psychologist, and his wife Florence, who lived in Bridgeville.

With Charlie's adoption, police closed the county's most celebrated murder case.

Charlie assumed the Duffy surname and pursued a normal lifestyle. He graduated from Chartiers Valley High School and Ohio University, then started a retail venture in Columbus before using his poise and communication skills to establish a career as a sales representative.

But doubt about his confession has haunted him. The nagging feeling of innocence was confounded by police claims that he'd erased all memory of the brutal act. It left him thinking that maybe he did black out — "I learned that I had to tune it out or else go mad," Duffy says of his torment. "But there was confusion in my mind for 30 years."

Dave Templeton had attempted to interview Ted Botula but had come up short. "A person answering the phone at Botula's home in Aspinwall said the retired detective would have no comment on the case except to say it was properly handled." Joe Start, on the other hand, had been forthright and had this to say about the moon-faced man,

"In my mind, I feel very strongly that he was the guy who committed the murder," Start says. "When we were able to put him in Ambridge that day and got his rap sheet, any doubt went out the window."

Start filed a report with the Allegheny County Homicide Division identifying the man as a murder suspect and the man was taken into custody. Start says Homicide detectives said the man couldn't identify the Zubryd house, and concluded he was "nuts."

But it didn't surprise Start that the man couldn't identify the house. New owners had added a garage where the basement door had been. Even Duffy had problems identifying the house during a recent visit.

"The fact that they said he was nuts shouldn't have had any bearing on it," Start says. "Based on what I saw in the basement that night, the person who did it had a lot of problems." . . .

Start, meanwhile, says he regrets never re-opening the Duffy case once he became Chief of the County Homicide Division in the mid-1960s. He's now cooperating with Fisher to exonerate Duffy. "Something has to be done here," Start says. "What the hell, it was wrong and I can't make it right. But if he (Duffy) has been laboring under this cloud all these years, he's entitled to know that someone else killed his mother."

Marjorie Zubryd, Charlie's aunt and former legal guardian, blasted the county detectives who had handled the case. "'This innocent child was left to suffer for all these years because three detectives (Botula, Start and Carmody) put their jobs higher. I don't think very highly of Allegheny County detectives.'"

Chuck Duffy's cousin, Janice Todd, who, in my mind, had suffered more than any of his blood relations, said, "'It's been a terrible experience for us. But this is a big relief. The doubt in our minds turned out to be true. It's good that we've lived to see proof that it wasn't Charlie.'"

The final word belonged to Chuck himself:

"This has been, and I expect it to be, a cleansing process," Duffy says. "It's one of the first times in my life where I have a little bit of self-esteem. Jim Fisher has told me something I never expected to hear."

I was curious about how Joe Start felt about the article and gave him a call. I was a little worried that the publicity, which in his case was both good and bad, might put him into a shell, leaving me high and dry on the Zubryd investigation. Joe said he liked the article except the part where Marjorie Zubryd had lumped him — and his partner Joe Carmody — with Ted Botula. He hoped the piece would bring a witness or two out of the woodwork.

"From your point of view," I said, "how are people reacting to it?"

"Oh, you know, I've gotten a few angry calls."

"From who?"

"One guy is an ex-cop who called me a traitor. The rest were from people who are angry because I didn't come forward sooner. I expected that. Let me know when you're ready for the hypnosis."

I also talked to Chuck that Sunday, and he was exhilarated. He said the article "blew him away." But Chuck also felt bad for Joe Start and was shocked that Janice Todd had virtually admitted that she and her husband, although they had doubts, had believed he had actually killed his mother. Chuck said he'd always suspected that, but there it was, in black-and-white. Regarding Joe Start, he said, "I hope he doesn't become the scapegoat."

"I wouldn't worry about that," I said.

"Tell him I appreciate what he's doing."

"I will."

"Are you still trying to identify the moon-faced man?"

"I'm still trying, but I'm not getting anywhere," I said.

"Is that important?"

"It is to me."

"Will you ever give up?"

"Eventually, yes. But I won't forget."

Monday morning I called Jerry Fielder to talk about the Pacek investigation, but he wanted to discuss the Zubryd case. He had read Dave Templeton's article, and it had set him on fire. "I wonder if the moon-faced guy is still alive?" he said.

"He could be."

"Jesus. If he is, we'll reopen that case, too. I'd like to go after that son of a bitch."

"Problem is, we don't have a name," I said.

"He was in a nuthouse, right?"

"Right, at Woodville."

"Woodville. When I was with the state police, I was assigned to the Finley Barracks for a while. They cover Woodville. The patients are always walking off the place, so they call the state police to pick them up and bring them back. It's a real pain in the ass. Anyway, I still have contacts at Finley, and those guys know a lot of people at the hospital. Give me the best description you have of the guy, and I'll call it over to the barracks. They can take it from there."

"He's a white male, born between 1915 and 1920. He lived on East Ohio Street, on the north side, worked at the Katherine Walker estate near Sewickley, and was an ordinary laborer. He'd been arrested by the city for A & B with intent to ravish, breaking and entering, and loitering. He also had a record with the Heidelberg P.D. He had a round, ruddy face, sandy-colored, thinning hair, a big belly, and wore work shoes without socks. Oh, yeah — he's crazy."

"That'll be a lot of help at Woodville," Fielder said.

"That's all I got on the guy."

"I'll see what I can do."

"Now that you're on the case," I said, "maybe there's something else you can do."

"What?"

"See if you can find the crime lab file on the Zubryd case. I've got the coroner's file, but I'm missing the crime scene photographs and Charles McInerney's polygraph reports. According to Joe Start, McInerney polygraphed the moon-faced guy."

"Do you have a file number?"

"Yeah, 6659."

"I'll take a look," Fielder said.

"Call me as soon as you know anything," I said.

He said he would; and on Tuesday, he called me at school with the good news. He had found the crime lab file on the Zubryd case; and guess what — he had the crime scene photographs, 110 of them.

"I can't see how anyone who looked at these pictures could have fingered the kid. I've never seen anything like it. Man, these photographs are *brutal!*"

I was speechless. Finally, I said, "I can't believe you found them."

"There's pictures of her with the hatchet in her head and photographs with it out. They had moved her body to another place in the basement where they'd yanked it out of her head. It's hard to believe they'd do something like that. No kid put that hatchet in there like that. People in the office down here are looking at these photographs, and they've never seen anything like this."

"Is there anything else in the file?"

"Hell, yes, all kinds of stuff. They must have polygraphed fifty people. I haven't had a chance to read anything. There's also a couple of supplementary crime lab reports and several other documents. I'm not that familiar with the case, so I'll leave it for you to sort out. When are you coming down?"

"I'm stuck up in here in Edinboro the rest of the week," I said. "Could you mail me the file?"

"I couldn't do that," Fielder replied.

"Right."

"You're still coming down for Jerry Pacek's session with the hypnotist?"

"Yeah, I wouldn't miss that."

"So, I'll see you on the tenth. I have copies of everything – even the photographs."

"I hate to wait that long."

"It's only eight days."

"All right."

"Oh, yeah, I talked to a couple of [state troopers] over at Finley, and they said they called over to Woodville, and the people over there had read the Duffy article. They're interested in the case and said they would help."

"When *I* called them over there they didn't give me the time of day," I said.

The next day, I was still basking in the good news I'd gotten on the Zubryd case when Fielder called with some news that was bad. He said there'd been a meeting at Woodville about the moon-faced man, and the director had decided they could not cooperate with us.

"Why not?" I asked.

"For one thing, they need a name. It would take too much time going back through the old files looking for a guy who fits your profile."

"Is there anyone there *now* who fits the profile?"

"They won't say."

"Why not?"

"The director is afraid of legal repercussions."

"Shit."

"And that's not all."

"What?"

"If we do come up with a name, we'll need a court order."

"Can we get one?"

"I don't know," Fielder said. "Actually, we don't use court orders anymore, we just get search warrants."

"Can you get a search warrant?"

"Jesus, Jim, this isn't even an official case!"

"Can you?"

"Get me a name, and we'll see."

"All right."

"I'll see you and Jerry Pacek next Wednesday?"

"Yeah."

"I'll have the Zubryd file for you."

"It's too bad about Woodville."

❏ ❏ ❏

At 8:15 A.M., March 18, I met Jerry Pacek at the McDonald's on Penn Avenue, just up the street from Fielder's office. It had been unseasonably warm, but this morning it was cold and windy. Jerry, wearing a pair of dark slacks, a white pullover sweater, and a blue jacket, had been there an hour drinking coffee. I had finished the report I had been working on for the Board of Pardons and gave a copy to Jerry. If it looked okay to him, I'd mail it to Harrisburg the following day. Fifteen minutes later, as Jerry and I walked down the street to Fielder's office, he said he was looking forward to another session with the forensic hypnotists.

We were greeted in the grand jury room by Jerry Fielder, who introduced us to Jack Legett, a plainclothes state policeman assigned to the Pennsylvania State Police Barracks in Washington, Pennsylvania. Legett was there to fashion a composite Identi-Kit drawing of the man Jerry had seen and described at the scene of the murder. Since the doctors hadn't arrived, Jack Legett and Jerry sat down at the conference table and got to work on the drawing. Fielder and I went into the office adjacent to the big room to go over the crime lab file on the Zubryd case.

Before I opened the envelope containing the crime scene photographs, I leafed through the other material, which included the preliminary crime lab report (which I already had) and nine supplemental reports containing the results of the polygraph tests given by Charles McInerney. There were several other crime lab reports involving examinations of known pubic hairs from various people and an examination of a piece of tissue for semen. The tissue, a piece of Kleenex, had come from Helen Zubryd's car. All of these tests had been negative. There was also a report by a questioned documents examiner that seemed unrelated to the case. Also in the file were newspaper clippings, a collection of memos, handwritten notes, and several Receipt for Exhibit log forms.

I realized I wouldn't have much time to study this material because I didn't want to miss what was going on with Jerry and the doctors, so I quickly glanced through it. McInerney had tested more than fifty people on the polygraph.

Thirty-seven of these examinees were listed, along with the results of their tests, in one two-page report dated June 6, 1957. Everyone mentioned in this report had passed the test. As I ran my eyes down the list I recognized several names. The first, Jim Flevaris, surprised me. Flevaris was the part-time township constable who had lived up the street from Helen Zubryd. McInerney had tested him on December 26, 1956, a little more than a month after the murder. I wondered why they had put him on the box. On the two occasions Flevaris and I had talked, he never mentioned it. Mike Zubryd, Charlie's uncle, had been tested on January 2, 1957, and Charlie himself had taken the polygraph on March 4 of that year.

This list also included Margaret Skiles, the wife of the man who died of a heart attack in Helen Zubryd's front yard; and Floyd Skiles, a brother of the two retarded men, Elmer, Jr., and James, who had been hauled in and grilled by Botula. According to the newspapers, Elmer, Jr., and James had been released after passing polygraph tests. But their names were not on McInerney's thirty-seven-person list. I wasn't surprised because the brothers would not have been suitable for that kind of thing. That Margaret and Floyd Skiles had passed the polygraph convinced me that no one from that family had anything to do with the murder. By not solving the case, Ted Botula had left a permanent cloud over the entire Skiles family.

None of the other names on that particular list meant anything to me. I knew that none of the names in that report belonged to the moon-faced guy because they had all been tested prior to March 22, 1957, slightly more than two years before Charlie had confessed.

That ruled out the moon-faced man because he had confessed *after* Charlie had.

In leafing through the file, I found an unsigned waiver form dated March 4, 1957. It read:

> As uncle and guardian of Charles Zubryd, I request that he be given a polygraph (lie-detector) examination to determine whether he is telling the truth in connection with the death of his mother, Helen Zubryd, on November 20, 1956.
>
> _____
> **Michael Zubryd**
>
> **Witnesses:** _____
>
> _____

This waiver surprised me for two reasons. First, I hadn't realized that anyone had doubts the boy was telling the truth, particularly so early in the case. Since the evidence showed he hadn't done it, what would he have lied about? Perhaps Botula thought Charlie was covering for someone. But Botula would have known, for example, that Charlie wasn't covering for his Uncle Mike because Mike had already passed his polygraph test. Second, it seemed more than a little inappropriate for Mike Zubryd, Charlie's guardian, to allow such a thing in the first place, particularly after having suffered the humiliation of being tested himself. Surely Mike Zubryd didn't think the boy was lying, or worse, was the murderer. I found this puzzling.

There were eight other polygraph reports in the file, but I was running out of time, so I stuck all of the documents back into the envelope. I had checked the dates on these reports, and no one had been tested beyond July 1958. That was not good news because the moon-faced guy would have been polygraphed sometime after March 1959.

Drs. Scott and Thompson had arrived, and Jerry and Jack Leggett were about finished with the composite drawing of the suspect. I still had a few minutes, so I decided to take a quick look at the photographs of Helen at the murder scene.

I had read Helen Zubryd's autopsy report many times, but I was still shocked by the crime scene photographs that showed the hatchet stuck so deeply into her skull. As I looked over the black-and-white photographs, I realized I'd pictured the scene incorrectly in my mind. I'd been aware, of course, that Helen Zubryd's murder had been brutal. But you had to see it to believe it. Now that I was seeing what Ted Botula had looked at in person, I had a much stronger sense of the crime and was even more bewildered that the detective could have blamed such a savage murder on a child. These photographs, more than anything, told the tragedy of Charlie Zubryd and his mother.

Helen Zubryd was on her back about a foot from the furnace, with her feet almost touching a metal toolbox that sat against the basement wall beneath a window. She had apparently run to that window, jumped up on the toolbox to yell for help, then fallen straight back off the box when the killer clubbed her with the hatchet from behind. He finished her off as she lay on the floor by slamming the hatchet into her forehead, leaving the blade completely inside her skull, with the handle running diagonally across her face. Had it not been for the bridge of her nose, which had been crushed by the handle, the blade would have sunk even deeper. The killer then bared the middle section of her body by ripping down her blue jeans and panties, leaving them down around her knees, which he had spread apart.

Helen's face was turned toward the furnace, probably from the weight of the hatchet. If the killer had straddled her torso and swung the hatchet from there, he would have been right-handed, given its angle on her face. But she was so close to the furnace, he would have hit it not her. However, a left-handed man would have had room to swing and, from that position, would have left the hatchet as it was found. As others had thought, in my mind too, although it was only an educated guess, the killer was left-handed. Unfortunately, so was Charlie.

The side of the furnace was splattered, and a wide river of blood ran from the victim's head to the drain in the floor.

I found several photographs of Helen after they had removed the hatchet. The detectives had pulled her body to another part of the basement and had laid old newspapers under her head. The wound on her face was huge and gaping. I remembered a photograph John Syka had given me: it showed Helen in her coffin, and I suddenly had great respect for Mr. Syka's skill as a mortician.

Out in the grand jury room, Drs. Scott and Thompson had put Jerry under, so I stuffed the Zubryd file into my briefcase and turned to the TV monitor.

"I'm thirteen and I see myself at the tracks like I'm coming home from school," Jerry was saying. "It's a sunny day in the fall. I'm reaching out to myself but I can't reach my hand. I see myself at Mary's house — the kitchen, the hallway — being there. A good feeling, revisiting the past. I'm trying to convince myself that as a kid it's okay. I can't collect him with me — it's okay now — he's three steps ahead of me. I can't get his hand. I feel so bad for him. I'm going to tell him — I feel bad for you — I need you. Please let me help you. I'm here."

Jerry seemed to come out of his trance and said, "He was right there — I could grab him and kiss him, but I didn't think he's ready. I'm feeling peaceful, and confident." A few minutes later, Jerry, apparently still under, was recalling his boyhood life at home with such candor I felt a little embarrassed: "My dad left me — but I loved my dad more than my mom. I probably didn't know my dad. She bitched all the time. She was always there. He bitched . . . when he was there. He was always mean — always. We didn't spend a lot of time together. I was always afraid of him. 'Don't slump your shoulders,' he'd say when we walked to the barbershop."

The session ended at half past eleven, and Jerry said he felt great. Jack Legett had produced a composite drawing that Jerry said looked a lot like the man he'd seen that night. The doctors scheduled what would be Jerry's fourth and final session for May 13, a good day for me because by then I'd be out of school, a free man. At this point, Jerry's sessions had become more therapeutic than investigative. I mentioned this to Jerry Fielder, and he said, "As long as it's helping Jerry, they can do this as many times as they want. It's the least we can do."

Jerry Fielder offered to buy lunch that day, so Fred Cooper, Jack Legett, Jerry, and I piled into my car, and we drove out to East Liberty and had lunch at a fancy Chinese restaurant. Seeing Jerry at the table, laughing and joking with the detectives, made me wonder if he could ever have envisioned himself in this picture. I felt good for Jerry, but I had Helen Zubryd on my mind, so I felt bad for Chuck Duffy.

Before we left the restaurant that day, Fielder took me aside to tell me that they were closing the Stevick investigation. They were out of leads and had run out of ideas. They had spent so much time on the case that there was a backlog of current investigations in the office that had to be worked.

Fielder said they had questioned Robert Stevick in their office without his wife, but the interview produced nothing. Mr. Stevick was very old, in poor health, and in Fielder's opinion, perhaps a bit retarded. Although the old man didn't say anything that exonerated him, he didn't incriminate himself, either. Since he was not a suitable subject for the polygraph, Mr. Stevick's involvement in his previous wife's murder would remain unresolved.

Fielder had also questioned the man he called Fred, the suspect with the history of rape arrests, the suspect whose name had been written into the case file by Ted Botula. Fred was not at all nervous or bothered by the fact that he was being questioned as a suspect. He said that he had never delivered milk or eggs, that he had been a mechanic. Moreover, Fred denied ever knowing the Stevicks. There was no evidence whatsoever connecting this man to the crime; therefore, the matter had to be dropped right there. Thirty-two years after the murder, Fielder was in no position to crack a suspect's story by breaking an alibi or catching him in a lie.

After numerous attempts, Fielder finally got his chance to question Bobby Stevick in the presence of his attorney at the group home. Fielder said he was shocked by the severity of Bobby's mental retardation. It appeared that Bobby had been close to his mother, that he had liked doing little things for her like tying her shoes. The lawyer assured Fielder that Bobby Stevick had never been violent and was completely incapable of such a brutal and violent crime. Fielder left the interview convinced that Bobby was not Lillian's killer.

Fielder said he felt bad closing the case after all of the work they had done. The investigation had looked so promising in the beginning then had slowly fizzled out. I realized then that Fielder had truly hoped to break the case. He wanted it for Jerry. He had done his best, and Jerry's name had been cleared, at least unofficially. Jerry now had a chance for a pardon, thanks to Bob Colville, who as D.A. had shown his faith in Jerry's innocence by assigning detectives to the reinvestigation.

The identity of Mrs. Stevick's killer probably meant more to Fielder and to me than it did to Jerry Pacek. Jerry had already acquired what he never thought he would get: vindication and recognition for a life well lived under the most difficult of circumstances. Jerry Pacek was a hero, and now everybody who counted knew it.

Fielder told me that, if I decided to pick up the investigation on my own, District Attorney Colville would support me and move in if I came up with the goods on the killer. I said I was willing to do this, but Jerry and I had talked about this possibility earlier, and it was his desire, if the police couldn't make the case, to let it drop. Jerry had lived with Mrs. Stevick's murder for thirty-two years and was looking forward to the day, soon he hoped, when he could put this part of his life behind him and start fresh.

I hated to let the Stevick case go, but I realized the chance of solving the case was slim. Besides, there was nothing I could do that Detective Fielder and his partner, Fred Cooper, hadn't done. Now that the Stevick case was closed, I'd concentrate on Helen Zubryd's murder.

I had thought that I would never get my hands on the Zubryd crime scene photographs, a development that had renewed my optimism and shot new life into the investigation. Maybe Detective Fielder's involvement in the Stevick case would pay off for me in the Zubryd murder.

Later, outside the restaurant, when I told Jerry Pacek that the case was being closed, he didn't seem bothered.

"I'm going home," he said.

26 Woodville

WHEN I RETURNED HOME FROM PITTSBURGH LATE IN the afternoon March 18, I went straight to my office and began studying the crime scene photographs I'd gotten from Jerry

Fielder. I was looking at a photograph of Helen that showed her entire body in proximity to the furnace and other surroundings, when I noticed something that did not belong in the picture. It was a purse, a vinyl or leather handbag about the shape and size of a loaf of bread. It had a pair of short handles, was clamped shut, was dark in color, sat on the floor about two feet from Helen's head, and showed up in at least a dozen photographs. Whose was it? Why was it there?

I had read nothing about the purse in the old newspaper articles and had seen no reference to it in the coroner's file. Moreover, no one I had talked to had said anything about a purse. Surely this was something that would have to have been explained. If it belonged to Helen, why had she carried it into the basement? The only plausible explanation I could think of was that the moon-faced man had come to the door and asked for money. But still, why would Helen have taken her *purse* with her into the basement? She would have just taken the money. And Joe Start hadn't mentioned anything like this when he related the details of the man's confession.

That purse must have belonged to someone else. Two women had been in the basement that night before the police got there — Catherine Asperger and Janice Todd. I'd have to check with them.

I looked at several close-ups of the furnace and saw what appeared to be a group of palm prints left in the dust. These prints could have belonged to anyone and were clearly not the fabric impressions Ted Botula had talked about. I sifted through the photographs and didn't find any additional shots of the furnace, nor did I find pictures of fabric impressions.

I spent more than two hours with the photographs, doing my best to reconstruct what had happened to Helen Zubryd that night. I was about to clear them off my desk when I realized something was missing. I looked at every shot of Helen that showed the area around her body, and sure enough, it wasn't there. The only piece of physical evidence that corroborated Charlie Zubryd's confession — the army belt — was nowhere to be seen. According to Charlie's confession, his mother had chased him into the basement to spank him with the belt. Well, where was it?

I had always assumed the detectives had actually found an army belt on the floor next to Helen's body. It hadn't been mentioned in the newspapers prior to Charlie's confession, but I thought perhaps the police were keeping that evidence secret. I quickly found my copy of the preliminary crime lab report, the one listing all of the evidence that had been taken out of the basement that night: there was no army belt. How in the hell had I missed that? No army belt!

I checked my collection of old newspaper clippings. All three newspapers in reporting Charlie's confession made reference to the army belt. In the *Pittsburgh Sun-Telegraph*, District Attorney Eddie Boyle said, "Detectives were always puzzled *by the belt found near the body*. They never felt it was an instrument to protect her . . . from an attacker" (italics mine). In the same paper, in an article the next day reporting Charlie's reenactment of the murder in the D.A.'s office, the army belt was mentioned again: "A heavy Army belt with a thick buckle lay close to Botula, *just as detectives found it close to Mrs. Zubryd*" (italics mine). In the *Post-Gazette*:

> County Detective Botula called the case a "heart-breaker particularly for any fellow who has children."
>
> The detective said that several factors convinced him and Flannery the boy was involved. They are: . . .
>
> 4. The Army belt found near the body seemed more of a weapon a woman would choose to punish a boy rather than to defend herself against an intruder.

I remembered that Joe Start had always questioned the belt, but without proof, without the crime scene photographs, he wasn't sure he remembered this correctly. Thirty-two years *is* a long time, and the mind can play tricks. As it turned out, Joe had been right. The army belt came into the picture the moment Botula decided he needed a motive to go along with the confession he had pulled out of the boy.

If I correctly interpreted the crime scene photographs, if Helen Zubryd had in fact fled to that window and jumped up onto the toolbox, there was no way Charlie could have hit her on the back of the head with the hatchet. He wouldn't have been tall enough.

Ted Botula had been right about one thing, this case *was* a heartbreaker.

I put the photographs away and turned my attention to the polygraph reports I hadn't had a chance to study when I was in Pittsburgh with Jerry Pacek and Jerry Fielder.

Charles McInerney had tested fifteen people after he'd examined the thirty-seven subjects listed on his initial report. He'd tested this later group of examinees during a one-year period from July 1957 to July 1958. I recognized two names in these reports — Catherine Asperger and Harry Zubryd, Mike's brother (both had passed).

I arranged the eight supplemental polygraph reports by date, then I studied each one until I got to the last report, the one dated July 29, 1958. Up until that point, all of the thirteen subjects in the seven reports had passed the test. When I got to the last report, dated July 29, 1958, I read that McInerney, on that date, had tested a man named James Homan. Homan had passed. In the same report, I read that McInerney, on July 22, 1958, had examined a William Spiegel. Regarding that test, McInerney had written:

> On Tuesday, July 22, 1958, William Spiegel was brought to this Laboratory for the purpose of taking a polygraph examination in connection with the murder of Helen Zubryd in Sewickley Township on November 20, 1956.
>
> This subject was totally unresponsive, and the examiner was unable to make a positive determination as to the truthfulness of his denials. *It was learned that the subject had been treated for mental illness since 1939* [italics mine].

Wait a minute. Spiegel — a German name. July — it had been summertime. A history of mental illness — Woodville. Might this have been Joe Start's man? Was William Spiegel the moon-faced killer?

I dug through the file looking for more on Spiegel and found something. According to a crime lab report dated July 18, 1958, and submitted by Irving Botton, "Pubic hair samples reportedly from the suspect, W. Spiegel, were examined and compared with the body hair found at the scene. Significant differences were found between the evidence and sample hairs." The hairs didn't match, but that meant little because in all probability the crime scene hair had nothing to do with the murder. What did matter was this: on July 9, Botula had a man in custody from whom he obtained samples of pubic hair. Nine days later, Irving Botton examined hair at the crime lab, and four days after that, McInerney tested the guy on the polygraph. It looked to me like someone had considered this man a serious suspect.

There was only one problem. Joe Start said the moon-faced guy had confessed *after* Charlie's confession. Spiegel had been the subject of police interest eight months *before* that. Of course, there was always the possibility that Joe Start, thirty-two years later, was a little mixed up on his chronology. If that were the case, then Joe, had he gone public with this man's confession, would probably have denied Botula the chance to frame Charlie, and the boy wouldn't have been adopted. Ironically, Chuck Duffy considered his adoption a godsend.

That night, I called Joe Start. I told him I thought I might have a name for the moon-faced guy. Rather than tell Joe the name outright, I started reading from a list of ten names, and when I got to Spiegel, the fifth name on the list, he said, "Spiegel, that rings a bell. What are the other names?" I recited the remaining five names on the list, and he said, "What's Spiegel's first name?"

"William."

"Jeez, that sounds right. But, hell, Jim, I can't be sure."

"I have the crime scene photographs. Maybe if you saw them, it would help jog your memory."

"Bring them down tomorrow," Joe said. "I want to see them."

❏ ❏ ❏

The next morning, I stopped by the post office and mailed nine copies of my Pacek report and its attachments to the Pennsylvania Board of Pardons. I had worked months preparing this material, but I wasn't particularly confident that anyone would read it.

Before I showed Joe Start the crime scene photographs, we talked about what I had found in the crime lab file about Spiegel and if Spiegel could be the moon-faced guy.

"I thought about it all last night," Joe said. "And you know what? I think it's him."

"Why?"

"We had a guy who worked in the Teletype room named Stanley Spiegel. Stanley was president of the German Club. That's how I knew Spiegel was a German name."

"I didn't mention this on the phone," I said, "but there's a problem with the timing."

"What do you mean?"

"They got the hair sample off Spiegel and tested him on the box in July—1958. That was eight months before Charlie confessed. If Spiegel's the man, you had the timing wrong."

Joe didn't say anything for a couple of moments. "It's been a long time," he said.

"When Botula ignored Spiegel, you guys would have argued then. Maybe you knew Botula had his eye on the kid and was going to frame him. Eight months later, you picked up the paper and read about Charlie's confession. Things get twisted over the years."

"I hate to admit it, but I think you're right. It's Spiegel, I'm sure of it. But, Christ, why didn't I do something? I knew who killed Helen Zubryd, and I let Botula put it on the kid."

"That's in the past," I said. "Let's think about now. Let's find out who this Spiegel is, if he's alive, and if so, where. We might get another crack at him."

From Edinboro, I called Commander Ron Shaulis, the Pittsburgh Police Officer in charge of the Allegheny County Identification Center. If William Spiegel was the moon-faced guy, he'd have a record with the city for A & B with intent to ravish, B & E, and perhaps rape. Commander Shaulis came to the phone, and I gave him the name.

"Do you have a date of birth?" he asked.

"No, the best I can do is between 1910 and 1920. He's white, lived on the north side, and spent some time in Woodville. He'll have beefs for A & B, B & E, and maybe rape. In '58 the county had him, but I don't know if he was booked."

"Hold on, I'll check the computer."

A few minutes later, Shaulis came on the line and said, "Nothing. I'm sorry."

"Could you check with the state?"

"Sure, hold on. Maybe we can still pull the rabbit out of the hat."

I couldn't believe this guy didn't have a record and felt like I had my line in a pond that didn't have fish. It seemed like forever before Shaulis got back to the phone, and when he did, he said, "I hate to say this, but I got zero."

"What's the chance this guy was busted but is not on the computer?"

"That depends on when and where he was arrested."

"Pittsburgh. In the fifties and maybe the sixties."

"A lot of that old stuff didn't get put on the computer," Shaulis said.

"If it's not on the computer, where is it?"

"If it hasn't been destroyed, you might get lucky over at the courthouse."

"No one ever gets lucky over at the courthouse," I said.

If William Spiegel was our man, there'd be a record of him at Woodville. For that, I needed Jerry Fielder, so I called him and filled him in on Spiegel and why I thought he might be our killer. When I finished, Fielder asked me the same question Shaulis had: "What's his date of birth?"

"I don't know," I said. "Shaulis has nothing on him. We got a name, let's get a search warrant and hit them with it over at Woodville."

"What's this *we* shit?" Fielder asked. "I don't even have a file number on this case, and you want me to serve search warrants?"

"If Spiegel is the guy, his story is in the files at Woodville. *He* could be at Woodville."

Fielder said that the earliest he could get the warrant would be Monday. "I'm gonna need probable cause," he added. "What's my probable cause?"

"Me," I said. "I'm your probable cause."

❏ ❏ ❏

I had the weekend to kill, so I photocopied one of the crime scene pictures and cut out the section that depicted the handbag. Then I drove down to Catherine Asperger's house to see if the purse found at the crime scene had been hers. Mrs. Asperger looked at the purse and said it hadn't been hers. "I ran over there," she said. "I didn't take my purse, I didn't even take the iron off the board."

That left Janice Todd, so I drove to Bell Acres and showed her my picture of the purse. "Oh, my," she said when she saw it, "I had forgotten that. It was mine. I put it down when I reached for the hatchet. Then I panicked and ran out of there. I wasn't thinking about my purse."

❏ ❏ ❏

Jerry Fielder called Monday morning with news he knew I would not like. "It's gonna take a couple days to get the warrant. If I get it, I'll serve it on Wednesday."

"I'll go over there with you."

"No, you won't."

"That's no way to treat your probable cause."

"I called over there and told them I was going to get a search warrant. They weren't happy about it. I said, 'Hey—just tell me if you have a record on the guy. If you don't—I won't bother with the warrant.'" Fielder paused then said, "So, I get this, 'Oh, we gotta check with our attorney.' So, the lawyer calls. . . . 'You need a court order,' he says." Fielder told the lawyer that court orders are seldom used anymore. "'We do search warrants, and if I get one, I'm coming over there with it.' 'Well, I'm going to be waiting here for you.' he says."

❏ ❏ ❏

Joe Start called to let me know he tried William Spiegel's name on Marie Passmore, the woman who'd worked at the Katherine Walker estate in the late fifties. The name had not registered with her, so she called Mary Colades again. Mary had worked there at the time but didn't remember anyone up there named William Spiegel. Marie reminded him that the Walkers hired many former mental patients and "DPs," and they paid cash, so there were no payroll records.

Joe said he'd been to the public library in Sewickley, where he'd read through the fifty-two editions of the local paper that came out in 1956. He found no mention of a William Spiegel.

I hated to do it, but I had to tell Joe I had struck out with Ron Shaulis at the records center in Pittsburgh.

"I can't believe they don't have a record of him down there," Joe said.

"A lot of that stuff is lost."

"Man, that doesn't seem right."

"How do you feel about Spiegel? Do you still think he's the guy?" I asked.

"Jim, I'm sure of it. His name was William Spiegel."

On Wednesday, I didn't hear from Jerry Fielder, so at four o'clock I called him. He was on the other line and would call me back. An hour later my phone rang, and it was Fielder.

"Did you serve the warrant?" I asked.

"Yeah, there's no one over there with that name. There's never been anyone at Woodville with that name. We checked it under various spellings—nothing. Zip."

"Then Spiegel is not our guy," I said.

"When you called, I was talking to a guy down at the courthouse. He checked the clerk of courts office and found a card on a William Spiegel who'd been busted for A & B."

"When?"

"1952 and 1954. The beef in '52 had to do with an indecent assault on a child. Spiegel was indicted for A & B with intent to commit rape and A & B. He was arrested by the city."

"What about the other arrest?"

"There's not much there. The county detectives had him. Spiegel was charged with indecent assault and A & B with intent to commit rape. He was living at 700 Anderson Street."

"Where is that?"

"On the north side. There's no way to know for sure if this is the Spiegel McInerney had on the lie box," Fielder said.

"Assuming he is the same guy, how come he's not at Woodville? If he wasn't at Woodville, he can't be the moon-faced guy."

"Well, he wasn't at Woodville," Fielder said. "I can tell you that."

"Did they know the name before you went over with the warrant?"

"Yeah," Fielder said. "I said, 'Check to see if you have him, 'cause if you don't, I won't have to get a warrant.'"

"Maybe someone pulled the file before you got there."

"I don't think so," Fielder replied. "Do you want me to stay on the Spiegel thing?"

"I don't know. I'm coming down Friday to dig around the courthouse to see what I can find. Thanks for getting the warrant."

I called Joe Start and gave him the terrible news. At first he didn't know what to say. Finally, he said, "Are you sure?"

"Pretty sure, unless someone over there is playing games."

"I was sure it was Spiegel."

"Fielder did find a couple of busts on the guy — A & B with intent to rape — that kind of thing."

"When?"

"1952 and 1954. One case involved a child."

"Where was he living?"

"On Anderson."

"Shit, that's on the north side."

"I'm going down to the courthouse Friday," I said.

"Nothing at Woodville?" Joe asked.

"Nothing."

"I think I'm losing my mind."

27 William Spiegel

W HEN I GOT HOME FROM SCHOOL ON THURSDAY, MY
wife handed me a letter postmarked Pembroke, Georgia. It
was from a Darla R. Lynn, who was writing to me in response to
Dave Templeton's Easter Sunday article about Chuck Duffy in the
Pittsburgh Press Sunday Magazine.

> My name is Darla (Walk) Lynn. I was not only
> Charlie's neighbor — I am his friend. Tragedy
> not only struck Charlie's life that night, it
> touched all of those around.
>
> No one cared what had happened to me that
> night. No one asked. No one would hear me. I
> was a kid — the same age as Charlie — so I
> wasn't important.
>
> I was never to see Charlie again. Someone
> had taken him away and my mother moved us to
> Los Angeles. . . .
>
> I would like to hear from you. It is important
> to me. I feel I can help to answer some ques-
> tions you may still have. . . . I need, for Chuck as
> well as for me, to finally put a definite "close" to
> his mother's case.

Intrigued by the tone of Darla Lynn's letter, I called and caught
her at home. Darla said she had lived with her parents in a little
house on Barley Road down in the hollow next to the foundation
home of the Skiles family. Mrs. Asperger's house was across the
street, and beyond it, seventy-five yards away, was the little white
house Charlie Zubryd lived in with his mother.

On that cold, rainy night in November, Darla and her baby sister, "Little Hunky," were playing in the outhouse after dark. They noticed that something was going on over at the Zubryds' house: they could see red lights, and they heard men talking. There was suddenly a terrible banging on the outhouse door that froze the girls. When Darla looked through the half-moon window in the door, she saw the eyes of a wild man, a pair of eyes she has never forgotten. The man was breathing hard and talking to himself, trying to see into the outhouse. Finally, their dog came out of the house and chased the man away.

Darla said she still trembles when she thinks of that night and of that man. She knew she had been eyeball to eyeball with the man who had just killed Charlie's mother, a thought that has haunted her ever since. But none of the detectives talked to her or to her parents about that night.

Darla's mother was afraid that the killer, knowing he had been seen, would come back and kill them all. Not long after that, her parents split up, and her mother moved them to L.A. Darla always knew Charlie hadn't killed his mother, and she still has bad dreams about the man. Darla had read the article about the moon-faced man who had confessed to Joe Start and was certain this was the person she had seen that night. She wanted to know if I had identified this man. If so, was he dead or still alive? I told Darla Lynn I was still working on that, and if I did learn who he was, she'd be one of the first to know. "I pray to God he's dead," she said. "Then I can rest."

❑ ❑ ❑

On Friday, I went to Pittsburgh and the Allegheny County Courthouse, where I hoped to get my hands on enough information to determine if William Spiegel was Joe Start's moon-faced killer.

I arrived at the courthouse at ten in the morning; then I spent the next six hours bouncing from clerk to clerk, office to office, ledger to ledger, index to index, and, finally, building to building. Searching for information at the courthouse is like looking for the right path through the woods. There are many dead ends, but once you get onto the right trail, the going gets easier, and you get where you're going. It took a while, but once I got onto Spiegel's paper trail, I got what I wanted — almost.

William P. Spiegel was born on June 21, 1913, in Pittsburgh. (Finally, a date of birth.) The house in which Spiegel was born belonged to his grandfather, Peter Spiegel, who was born in Hess, Germany, and died in 1928 when William was fifteen. The house, located on Woessner Avenue on Pittsburgh's north side, was left to William's Uncle Louis. William's father (also named Peter) was only given five dollars. The old man also left William's Aunt Martha and his Uncle John five dollars. Five bucks apiece, that is. Anyway, his Uncle Louis got the house on Woessner Avenue, a hilly Germany neighborhood that still has cobblestone streets and the look of the old country.

Peter, William's father, was born in 1888. I could not find his death certificate, which meant he died outside of Allegheny County (or he was one hundred three years old; I figured he was dead). In 1912, Peter married Anna Lamm, William's mother. Anna was born in Pittsburgh on April 6, 1887, and, as with her husband, I was unable to document her death. William was their only child.

William Spiegel did have an arrest record, and although sketchy, it painted the picture of a mentally disturbed sex offender. Spiegel was arrested in September 1952 by the Pittsburgh police on a charge of assault and battery with the intent to commit rape, and assault and battery. The victim was listed only as a child. Spiegel would have been thirty-nine years old. I could find no disposition of the case.

The Allegheny County detective's office arrested Spiegel on February 2, 1954, for indecent assault and assault and battery with intent to commit rape. He was living at 700 Anderson Street, an address not far from where Joe Start's moon-faced man had been living when Joe got his confession in July 1958.

Spiegel was arrested again on May 12, 1960, by the Pittsburgh Police Department. He was charged with open lewdness and public indecency. That usually means he had exposed himself to someone. The victim was named Betty Henchar, the forty-one-year-old owner of Henchar's Bar at 1437 Beaver Avenue, another north side address in the old Manchester section of Pittsburgh. Spiegel was indicted on those charges on June 8, 1960; then on May 24, *1968*, the D.A., Robert W. Dugan, had the indictment dropped. I didn't get it. If the D.A. was going to nolle prosequi the true bill, why had he waited eight years? Perhaps Spiegel, during this period, had been in custody somewhere else on another beef.

When Spiegel was arrested in 1954 for assault with intent to commit rape, he was described as a white male, five-foot-eight, one hundred eighty-five pounds, with a light complexion, brown hair, and brown eyes. He certainly met the description of Joe Start's suspect, both physically and with his arrest history of sexual assault. He was also the right age and had lived in the right part of town. In May 1960, he lived in a flophouse at 1550 Beaver Avenue, a couple blocks from Henchar's Bar. The only thing missing was the history of mental illness and the incarceration at Woodville State Hospital.

Spiegel had exposed himself to the Henchar woman in May 1960, roughly two years after Charles McInerney had given him a lie detector test. If he was, in fact, the man who had killed Helen Zubryd, Spiegel was still loose in 1960 victimizing women.

Although I had done better at the courthouse than I had expected, I was disappointed that I hadn't come up with a photograph and had not determined if this man was dead or alive. If he were alive and living in the Pittsburgh area, he had eluded me.

The first thing I did when I got home from Pittsburgh was call Joe Start. I gave him everything I had. It only added to his frustration. "This has got to be the guy," he said. "There's got to be something funny going on at Woodville."

❏ ❏ ❏

I had just gotten off the telephone with Joe Start when Jerry Fielder called. "Hey, Professor," he said, "guess what?"

"What?"

"William Spiegel is dead."

"How do you know?"

"I found his death certificate."

"When did he die?"

"March 7, 1967. He was fifty-three."

"What killed him?" I asked.

"Bilateral pneumonia. Guess where he died?"

"Where?"

"Mayview State Hospital!" So, Joe Start just remembered the wrong hospital. He continued, "Mayview is only five miles up the road from Woodville. I just called over there and asked if I could get his medical records. They told me I need a warrant."

"The guy is dead; who are they protecting?"

"That's what I said."

"You're getting a warrant?"

"The man is dead."

"So what?"

"We have no official interest in the case. How could I justify getting a search warrant?"

"If he's the guy, you can close the Zubryd case. If he's not, then Helen Zubryd's killer might still be alive. You need the warrant to eliminate a suspect. It doesn't matter if he's dead. This is a legitimate investigative lead. When can you get the warrant?"

Fielder relented, "I'll try to get it on Monday."

❑ ❑ ❑

I thought about calling Joe Start, then I decided not to. One more disappointment and Joe would be living at Mayview with William Spiegel's records. Besides, although it was clear that the William Spiegel I had looked up at the courthouse was the man who had died at the Mayview State Mental Institution, there was still a chance that this William Spiegel was not the guy McInerney had tested in July 1958 and, therefore, not Joe's moon-faced guy. If the courthouse-Mayview Spiegel had been incarcerated in November 1956, when Helen Zubryd was murdered, or locked up at the time of the polygraph test, he could not be our man.

Jerry Fielder called late Monday afternoon and said he'd been to Mayview with the warrant, and now he had everything they had on Spiegel. Considering Spiegel had spent seventeen years, in three stints, in the institution, it wasn't much, but it was enough.

William Spiegel was a schizophrenic who, in 1939 at age twenty-six, was initially admitted to the hospital. That was the connection I had been looking for. According to Charles McInerney's polygraph report, that William Spiegel "had been treated for mental illness since 1939." They were probably one and the same. Moreover, Spiegel was not a patient from February 1954 to May 26, 1960, the period covering the Zubryd murder and McInerney's polygraph test. I was therefore certain I had the name, date of birth, criminal history, and mental records of Joe Start's moon-faced confessor.

After pulling a false fire alarm in December 1939, Spiegel was put into Mayview and stayed there almost ten years. He was readmitted for child molestation on July 23, 1952, and released in February 1954, when he was forty-one. He was out of the institution for six years, then in May 1960, he was readmitted. This must have been prompted by his arrest for open lewdness and public indecency in connection with Betty Henchar. Spiegel never got out after that. He died March 7, 1967, of double pneumonia. That's why the D.A. had dropped the Henchar indictment. The D.A. was probably keeping the case open as long as Spiegel stayed put.

It wasn't much of a life. According to Spiegel's death certificate, he was a Catholic and, as such, was buried by the Catholic Charities Society of St. Vincent DePaul in Pittsburgh. Otherwise, his body would have been shipped to Philadelphia to be used as a medical school cadaver. He was buried March 11, 1967, in an unmarked grave at Calvary Cemetery on Hazelwood Avenue in Pittsburgh.

Spiegel had never been married, had an eighth-grade education, and had worked on and off as a farm laborer. This was the kind of work he had done for Katherine Walker at the Walker estate in Sewickley.

Spiegel's file contained a few cryptic handwritten notes, made by his doctors. On February 8, 1961, a doctor had written: "Uncooperative, argumentative, very hostile and threatening. Prognosis poor." On March 18, 1965: "Patient remains psychotic. Progress guarded." On July 26, 1966: "Prognosis poor. Condition essentially unchanged. Requires institutional care."

❏ ❏ ❏

One of Spiegel's unidentified physicians had made the following undated note, a message that told it all: "Patient always answers questions with this phrase — 'She was awful snotty that day.'"

❏ ❏ ❏

Joe Start had not lost his mind after all. There was a moon-faced confessor, and he was William P. Spiegel, just as Joe — minus the name — had remembered him. Spiegel had been one hell of a suspect. He hated women, was a sex offender, was mentally ill and violent, had been in Ambridge on the day of the murder applying for unemployment benefits, met the description of the wild-eyed man who'd gotten on the bus that night near Helen's house, and had confessed. Why Ted Botula had dismissed this man was something I will never fully understand. After a suspect like this, how could Botula have gone after the boy?

I called Joe Start, gave him the news, and he was ecstatic. "You don't know what this means to me," he said.

"If it hadn't been for Jerry Fielder," I replied, "none of this would have been possible."

"I hope you tell him how much I appreciate it," Joe said. "This case has been bothering me for over thirty years. Now I can let it go. What are you going to do with yourself now that it's over?" he asked.

"I'm not quite finished with it," I said. "I'd like to find Betty Henchar, the woman Spiegel exposed himself to in 1960. Besides you, she's the only person I know of who actually met the man. She might like to know he's dead."

"She may be dead too," Joe said.

"Do you think Helen Zubryd had run into Spiegel before the night he killed her?" I asked.

"I doubt it," Joe replied, "unless they had worked together up at the Walkers."

"According to Catherine Asperger, something had been bothering Helen on the afternoon prior to her death."

"I guess we'll never know that," Joe said. "I wonder how many other women he'd victimized."

"We'll never know that, either," I said.

28 A Living Witness

BETTY HENCHAR, THE WOMAN SPIEGEL HAD, I SUS-pected, exposed himself to in the bar, still lived in the Pitts-burgh area, and she agreed to talk to me about the incident. She was a little reluctant to see me until I told her Spiegel was dead. On May 4, 1991, a Saturday, Sue and I drove to Pittsburgh to talk with Betty Henchar.

Mrs. Henchar, a seventy-two-year-old woman who reminded me a great deal of Catherine Asperger, right down to her Eastern Euro-pean accent, said that in 1960 she and her husband, Jack, now deceased, owned Henchar's Bar at 1437 Beaver Avenue in the Manchester section of Pittsburgh. The building they occupied had three floors. The bar was on the first, the Henchars lived on the second, and they rented out an apartment on the third. Besides tending bar, Jack Henchar worked at the Fort Pitt Manufacturing Company, a factory located a few blocks away. They had a small lunch trade, and at eleven o'clock on workdays, Jack would walk home from the factory to prepare lunch for their customers. They had opened the bar in 1957, and business had been slow.

One morning in May, at ten-thirty, when Betty Henchar was working behind the bar alone, a man walked into the tavern and approached the bar. The man just stood there, staring at her in a way that immediately frightened her. Betty had seen hard characters come and go, but there was something about this man that was very frightening. "What would you like?" she asked.

"A glass of beer," he replied; then he sat down on one of the bar stools. This man was stocky, had light brown hair, a full face, and crazy eyes he never took off her.

Betty was terrified and didn't want this man to know that her husband was at work, so she yelled up at the ceiling for Jack to come down to the bar. With that, the stocky man got up and walked out of the tavern, leaving Betty Henchar shaken and fearful.

A week later, at ten-thirty in the morning when no one was in the bar but Betty, the man came back. "What do you want?" she asked.

"A glass of beer," the man said, taking a seat at the bar.

Betty poured the man his beer then walked into the kitchen where she could watch him without being seen. The man drank his beer then began to shake violently as he sat there. Betty thought he was sick or something, so she came out of the kitchen to walk behind the bar. "Mister," she said, "you all right?" Betty then realized the man had taken his penis out of his trousers and was playing with himself.

"I'll be all right," the man said, "when I get finished with you."

Betty ran to the front of the bar, out the door, and to the other side of Beaver Avenue. As she ran she screamed for help. Once on the other side of Beaver Avenue, she sat on the steps of the building across the street and watched as the man strolled out the front door of her bar. He pointed to her and shouted, "I'll get you someday, you fucking bitch."

When Jack came home for lunch, Betty told him she wasn't working in the bar anymore; she was too afraid. But she worked the bar anyway because she had to.

Two days later, the man came back. It was ten-thirty, and she was alone in the bar. He asked for a beer. Terrified, Betty walked into the kitchen to find something to protect herself with but decided against that. When she stepped back into the bar to fetch him his beer, she noticed that he had shut and bolted the front door.

This time, Betty fled the building through the kitchen door and then sat crying in the alley, where she waited for Jack to come home from the factory.

By the time Jack got back, the man was gone. It was Jack who called the police. Two cops came to the bar, took their complaint, then went out and arrested the man. Betty said she has a vague memory of testifying before the grand jury, but she doesn't remember doing anything more on the case.

The man did not come back to the bar, but about a month later, Betty saw him walking along Beaver Avenue. She saw him a few more times during the week that followed then didn't see him again.

It took years for Betty to get over the fear of working in the bar alone. She said that just telling the story brought back the fear. She could still feel it.

As Sue and I drove home that day, I was struck by how many people William Spiegel had victimized and how many lives he had permanently changed.

The next day, Sunday, I called Chuck Duffy to tell him about William Spiegel and was surprised by his reaction, which was quite emotional. "It's finally over," he said. "It was so senseless, it's frightening. I've been thinking a lot about my mother lately. Most of my life I spent trying to forget her, now I can remember. Thank you."

29 A Pardon and a Death

JERRY PACEK, ON MAY 13, 1991, HAD HIS FOURTH AND LAST session with Dr. Russell Scott and Dr. Kay Thompson. Clara Pacek died on February 15, 1991, of a massive heart attack.

On July 1, 2, and 3, 1991, producer Janet Tamaro from *Inside Edition* came to Western Pennsylvania to film a segment about Chuck Duffy and the Zubryd murder case. On this occasion, Chuck had a tearful reunion with Elaine Asperger and Darla Lynn (neé Walk).

Jerry Pacek's *Inside Edition* segment aired on July 24, 1991, and on August 1, three members of the Pennsylvania Board of Pardons voted to grant Jerry a pardon hearing. On September 12, 1991, after hearing Jerry's appeal, the five-member Board of Pardons voted unanimously to recommend a pardon for Jerry. Lieutenant Governor Mark Singel, chairman of the Board of Pardons, said the detectives on Jerry's case had committed a "monumental injustice" in jailing him. "It's time to free Jerry Pacek," he said.

"I've been a member of the criminal justice system for thirty-five years," said board member Thomas G. Frame. "And I've never seen a more atrocious miscarriage of justice than I've seen here. On behalf of the system, Jerry, I'd like to apologize."

"This day should have happened thirty-three years ago," said Jerry. "The justice system finally apologized and freed me from the embarrassment and humiliation. I had resigned myself to taking my innocence to my grave."

Dave Templeton, the writer for the *Pittsburgh Press*, did a follow-up article on Chuck Duffy and the Zubryd case. The article came out on September 16, 1991, and featured the material about William Spiegel. Ted Botula was asked to comment, and he said, "If Fisher thinks he has a solution, more power to him." Botula didn't recall Spiegel and noted that second-guessing the police was becoming a national habit. When asked if he had been comfortable with Chuck

Duffy as the murderer, Botula said, "I never felt comfortable on any case that I worked on. There is always a little vacuum that goes unexplained in a murder investigation." In April 1995, Ted Botula passed away.

When Joe Start was asked if he thought William Spiegel had killed Helen Zubryd, he said, "I'd bet my life on it."

Inside Edition aired the Chuck Duffy segment on October 21, 1991. Jim Flevaris, the part-time township cop who told Sue and me that he knew from the beginning that Charlie had killed his mother, told Janet Tamaro that he knew the night of the murder that her killer was a sex maniac.

Governor Robert Casey, on November 15, 1991, granted Jerry Pacek a pardon, the first pardon of its kind in the history of Pennsylvania. The pardon came eighteen months after my first visit with Jerry. When he heard the news, Jerry said, "I don't know how to describe this. I just want to thank everybody—friends, family, strangers, news people, especially Jim Fisher. . . . It's the best feeling in the world."

As of this writing, Jerry Pacek lives with his wife and daughter near Kittanning, Pennsylvania. He has built a new house and has been promoted to a position at the carpet company that does not require physical labor. His days installing carpet—the trade he learned in prison—are over.

Chuck Duffy and Jerry Pacek each filed a lawsuit against Allegheny County. Although the suits were based on different causes of action, they both stemmed from their having been—as boys—wrongfully and maliciously accused and punished for murders they did not commit.

Chuck Duffy died on October 9, 1993, from an AIDS-related illness. He was forty-five. Florence Duffy, living in Virginia near her sister, had passed away only two days earlier. Chuck had made the arrangements for his own funeral, including the writing of two obituaries—one for the newspaper in Columbus, Ohio, and the other for the *Pittsburgh Post-Gazette*. These separate obituaries reflect the double life Chuck had lived following his adoption in 1959. For thirty years, he had kept Charles Zubryd a secret. Those who knew Chuck during his last months in life recognized how knowing the truth about his mother's murder had changed him for the better. Chuck's lawsuit was dropped.

Jim Gibson, one of Chuck's longtime friends and a former business associate, said of him: "I've never known anyone like Chuck Duffy—he was one of a kind."

The murder of Lillian Stevick has never been solved.

Notes on the Text

Prologue

The scene depicting the girls trapped in the outhouse by the wild-eyed man is based upon interviews with Darla R. Lynn, née Walk, on April 24, May 2, and July 1, 1991. On April 17, 1991, Mrs. Lynn wrote me a letter after having read a magazine article about my involvement in the Zubryd case. She said she had lost contact with her childhood neighbor and friend, Charlie Zubryd, and wanted to know how to get in touch with him. She also wrote: "Tragedy not only struck Charlie's life that night, it touched all of those around.

"No one cared what had happened to me that night. No one asked — no one would hear me. I was a kid — the same age as Charlie — so I wasn't important."

1. Introduction

The March 15, 1959, article that got me interested in the Zubryd case read as follows:

ERIE DAILY TIMES
March 15, 1959
1956 MURDER SOLVED
Boy, 10, Admits Slaying Mother

PITTSBURGH (AP) — Dist. Atty. Edward C. Boyle said Saturday the 1956 slaying of Helen Zubryd, a Sewickley Twp. mother was solved. He said her 10-year-old son, Charles, signed a statement admitting the killing.

Boyle said the youth admitted striking his mother on the head with a hatchet. Her blood soaked body was found in the basement of the home she and her son occupied.

Mrs. Zubryd, a widow, was employed as a part-time maid in two Sewickley homes.

The son told the police at the time of the slaying that he returned from a visit to the home of a neighbor and found the body.

Boyle said the youth told police that the night of the killing his mother was about to punish him with an Army belt that had a big buckle on it. The boy, according to Boyle, ran to the cellar. The 41-year-old mother followed.

Boyle said:

"Charles said he picked up a hatchet. She tried to run from him, but he caught up with her."

The boy, according to Boyle, first used the blunt end of the hatchet and felled the mother. The sharp edge of the hatchet still was embedded in the head when the body was found.

County detectives have been questioning the boy periodically ever since, Boyle said.

He added:

"We have questioned about 1,500 persons in this and it always came back to the home. Detectives were always puzzled by the belt found near the body. They never felt it was an instrument to protect herself from an attacker."

2. "Yes, I Killed My Mother"

The accounts of the Zubryd murder and the cited newspaper quotes are from the November to 21–27, 1956, editions of the *Pittsburgh Post-Gazette*, the *Pittsburgh Press*, the *Pittsburgh Sun-Telegraph*, and the *Daily Citizen* (now the *Beaver County Times*).

The depiction of Charlie's confession and the events surrounding it are from the various newspaper accounts on March 15 and 16, 1959. The reference to Charlie having taken a polygraph test in 1957 is in the March 16, 1959, edition of the *Pittsburgh Sun-Telegraph*, page one.

References to the obliterated fingerprints, the removal of the hatchet from Helen Zubryd's head, and the fact that Charlie Zubryd was never a suspect in the murder are in the March 16, 1959, edition of the *Daily Citizen*, page one.

Helen Zubryd's six brothers, pallbearers at her funeral, were Wash Sudik, Mike Sudik, Peter Sudik, George Sudik, John Sudik, and Nicholas Sudik, Sr.

The condition and appearance of the Skiles home on Barley Road is based upon interviews with Catherine Asperger, James Flevaris, Joe Start, Nick Schifino, Ted Botula, and Janice Todd.

Janice and John Todd are not real names. I have used fictitious names in this instance to protect the privacy of these people. These are the only fictitious names in the book.

3. "Charge the Boy, or Release Him"

The background material on Edward C. Boyle is from a profile of him in the July 31, 1975, edition of the *Pittsburgh Press* called "Ex-D.A. Boyle Recalls Old Friends," by Rich Gigler, and his July 2, 1981, obituary in the *Pittsburgh Post-Gazette*. John Nee, formerly a criminal justice professor at Mercyhurst College in Erie and a twenty-year member of the Pittsburgh Police Department, told me much about Edward Boyle. John Nee died in October 1991. I also talked with Sheriff Gene Coon of Allegheny County, his chief deputy, John McNamara, and former Pittsburgh police officer John McMahon.

The description of the squad room in the Allegheny County detective's office is based upon information from former county detectives Joe Start and Ted Botula. The county detective's office, as an arm of the county D.A.'s office, was disbanded in 1974. It has been replaced by the Allegheny County Homicide Bureau attached to the Allegheny County Police Department, a more autonomous law enforcement agency. Employees of the D.A.'s office now occupy the space once used by Henry Pieper and his detectives. Today the D.A. does oversee an investigative branch, however, these men and women, about a dozen investigators, seldom handle murder cases.

The depiction of Henry Pieper is based upon interviews with Joe Start, John Nee, and Ted Botula.

The account of how Louis Glasso got involved in Charlie Zubryd's case is based upon interviews with Marge Zubryd and Genevieve Settino. Glasso's background came from Yolanda Glasso, his daughter.

The account of Charlie's hearing before Judge John Duff is based upon newspaper reportage and Chuck Duffy's memory of it. Lou Glasso's initial visit with Charlie at the Juvenile Detention Center is based upon Chuck Duffy's memory.

4. Strangers Bearing Gifts

The newspaper interview of Marion Stetter appeared in the March 17, 1959, edition of the *Pittsburgh Sun-Telegraph*.

The background and profile of Dr. William McCabe is based upon the interviews of several former detectives who knew him.

The description of Charlie's stay at the private hospital, including the nature of the tests he was given, is based upon newspaper reportage and Chuck Duffy's vivid memory of this period in his life.

Doctor McCabe's statements that Charlie Zubryd was a normal kid who was not strong enough to commit the murder are direct quotes from Pittsburgh's newspapers.

The scene describing Charlie's first visit with his family at the hospital is based upon Chuck Duffy's memory of it.

5. Helen and Joe

The description of Helen Zubryd's early life comes from interviews with Janice Todd, Karen DePalma, Mary Sudik, and Mrs. Louis Mayes. The details of the suicide of Chuck Duffy's grandfather came from Mrs. Louis Mayes, Chuck's aunt. Chuck's adoption has kept him in the dark about certain aspects of his family's history. No one had ever told him about his grandfather's suicide.

The account of Joe Zubryd's life is based upon information provided by Janice Todd, Marjorie Zubryd, Harry Zubryd, Maureen Zubryd, Olga DeRamo, and Joe Zubryd's obituary.

Accounts of the Chervenak and Geyer cases are based upon reportage of these homicides in Pittsburgh's area newspapers.

6. The Aspergers

The detective I was asked to call at Mrs. Asperger's house was Nick Bruich. My interview with Catherine Asperger and her daughter Elaine took place on February 12, 1989. I talked to Mrs. Asperger three times after that, and I interviewed Elaine a dozen or more times.

On July 1, 1991, Elaine and Charlie (Chuck Duffy) would meet in front of Charlie's old house on Barley Road. It was the first time they had seen each other since Charlie's Aunt Marge had brought him back into the neighborhood a year after the murder.

7. *True Detective*

Of the three accounts of the Zubryd case published in the true-crime magazines, the July 1959 account in *True Detective* was the most complete and balanced. The article, by D. L. Champion, was called "Pennsylvania's Incredible Axe Murder." Champion wrote, "Within 18 months he lost both parents. Two years later the tragic boy is still haunted by the unsolved murder of his mother."

Dr. Jim Drane's psychiatric analysis of Charlie Zubryd and the murder of his mother was presented as part of a video documentary I made on the case and showed at Edinboro's Annual Academic Festival held on February 20, 1989.

Dr. John Gaydos was interviewed at his home on March 5 and 7, 1989.

The detective I called regarding the police files on the Zubryd case was Detective Nick Bruich, a homicide detective with the Allegheny County Police Department. The chief deputy D.A. I talked to at the Allegheny County Courthouse was Robert Vincler. I spoke to him on four occasions.

8. John Syka

John Syka was interviewed on March 19, 1989, and then again on October 2, 1989.

While I was with him, he gave me several photographs, including one of Helen in her coffin at the funeral home.

9. Marge Zubryd

The article about the Zubryd case, "He Could Stare a Hole Through You," by Bruce McIntyre, appeared in the June 1959 edition of *Inside Detective*. The *True Detective* article came out the following month, along with an account by Seymour Ettmann in *Startling Detective*. Ettmann, calling his piece "A Hatchet for Helen," made Ted Botula took like Sherlock Holmes:

> On the first anniversary of the murder, it was announced
> that the investigation had already cost the county more than
> $100,000. The police had put in a total of 14,000 man-hours
> on the case. In all they interrogated 1,300 persons, conducted
> polygraph examinations of some 75 possible leads, checked
> the names, addresses, occupations, and work schedules of
> the 2,365 persons living in Sewickley Township.
>
> Further, the Allegheny County Police investigated every
> former resident who moved out of the community within the
> year. These families were traced clear across the country to
> California where they were questioned by Los Angeles and
> Fresno detectives.

Harry Zubryd was interviewed on March 1 and 14, 1989. His wife, Maureen, was interviewed on March 14 and 23, 1989.

I talked to Jim Flevaris on March 18, 1989, and again on April 12, 1989. Flevaris was working at George's Used Appliance Center in Ambridge. Flevaris was wrong about the Skiles brothers. At the time of my interview with Flevaris, James was still alive, as was his mother, Margaret. Margaret Skiles died in 1991. I had asked Floyd Skiles for an interview on June 3, 1989, but Floyd, one of Elmer and Margaret Skiles' younger sons, said he didn't "want to get involved."

On July 1, 1991, I talked to Irene (Skiles) Belfiore, the oldest of the Skiles children. She told me that her mother had recently passed away and that her brother James was still in a home. I talked to her brother Fritz Skiles on August 15, 1991.

I talked to Marge Zubryd on March 18, 1989. I spoke with her again on November 24, 1989, and on April 9, 1990.

10. Ted Botula

The people I spoke to about Ted Botula were John Nee, Gene Coon, John McMahon, John McNamara, William Fera, Nick Schifino, and Joe Start.

I first interviewed Ted Botula at his home on February 8, 1989. I talked to him again on February 10 and videotaped the interview. After that, I spoke with him on ten other occasions, the last being on January 10, 1991.

11. The Futile Paper Chase and Janice Todd

John Nee and I visited District Attorney Bob Colville on July 27, 1989. Chris Conrad, an assistant D.A., was one of the two members of his staff who searched the sixth floor that day for the Zubryd file.

I talked to Genevieve Settino in Ambridge on June 14, 1989, and spoke to Yolanda Glasso the next day. I called Lou Glasso's former legal secretary, Bernice Hummert, on June 15, 1989.

I first called Janice Todd on March 9, 1989; and my wife and I visited her and her husband on March 12, 1989. I would later talk to Janice ten more times.

12. Joe Start

The people I talked to about Joe Start were Ted Botula, John Nee, William Fera, and Nick Schifino; with the exception of John Nee, all were Allegheny County detectives. John Nee had been with the Pittsburgh Police Department.

I first interviewed Joe Start on February 17, 1989. After that, we spoke about the Zubryd case on twenty-four separate occasions.

13. The Moon-Faced Guy

I told Ted Botula about Joe Start's moon-faced man on March 4, 1989.

The man I talked to at the Bellevue Police Department was Chief of Police

Michael Bookser. One of the old-time cops who had worked the north side for the Pittsburgh Police Department was John McMahon.

Joe Start was hypnotized on March 22, 1990.

John Nee called Commander Ron Shaulis of the Allegheny County Identification Center on March 28, 1990.

14. A Complete Reversal

Joe Start's forensic hypnosis, performed on March 22, 1990, and the discovery of the Allegheny County Coroner's file on March 29, 1990, took place almost a year after these events are depicted in the story. These events occurred after, not before, my initial contact with Chuck Duffy. I did this to keep the story line intact.

The presence of semen on Helen Zubryd's blue jeans is documented in a four-page Allegheny County Crime Lab report called, "Preliminary Report — Confidential Report of Laboratory Findings." Dated November 29, 1956, and numbered Case 6659, it was submitted by Wilkaan Fong, microanalyst. The 23-inch tear mark in Helen Zubryd's blue jeans and the finger gouges in the skin at her waist are also noted in this report. Also mentioned are the traces of blood and tissue found under the victim's fingernails and the pubic hair, not hers, found near her body.

According to the four Receipt for Exhibits logs attached to the crime lab report (documents listing the items sent to the crime lab for examination), nothing on the clothing of Elmer, Jr., and James Skiles connected them to the crime.

According to the Receipt for Exhibits log, the following item was recovered at the crime scene by Wilkaan Fong and Irving Botton: "One lift of possible fabric impression on the side of heater next to body." There was no mention of this impression, however, in the crime lab report. Ted Botula had mentioned such an impression in one of my early talks with him, and according to his recollection, this impression had matched the shirt Charlie Zubryd had been wearing on the day of the murder.

Dr. Theodore Helmbold's five-page autopsy report was numbered C-56-109 and dated November 21, 1956. The autopsy had been performed at 1:10 A.M.

Nick Schifino's interview took place on March 30, 1990.

The material regarding the establishment of the Allegheny County Crime Laboratory and the background of Charles A. McInerney is from interviews of Ted Botula, Joe Start, and John Nee, plus: Joseph D. Nicol, "Facilities and Organization of the Allegheny County Crime Laboratory," *Proceedings of the American Academy of Forensic Sciences* (March 1951, pp. 134–135); and David Dillon, *History of Criminalistics in the U.S. 1850–1950.* Ph.D. dissertation, University of California, Berkeley, 1977.

15. The Walker Estate

I informed Ted Botula of the evidence I had found in the coroner's file on March 31, 1990. This phone interview was taped. I told Marge Zubryd of the semen and other crime scene evidence on April 9, 1990. Both of these interviews were conducted about a year after my initial contact with Chuck Duffy.

16. "You Didn't Kill Your Mother"

My initial telephone call to Chuck Duffy was made on the day depicted — March 25, 1989. My wife and I were invited by Chuck to visit him at his apartment in Columbus; we went on March 31 and April 1, 1989.

17. Chuck Duffy

I interviewed Chuck Duffy in Columbus on March 31 and April 1, 1989. The entire interview was audiotaped. At the time of the interview, Chuck was not employed. He was thinking about starting a new business.

Chuck Duffy visited us at our house on two occasions, and on December 19, 1990, I returned to Columbus to visit and reinterview him. After March 1989, I spoke to Chuck about the case and his life on at least two dozen occasions.

Jim Wise, Chuck Duffy's best friend in junior and senior high school, confirmed that Chuck had confided to him about being accused of his mother's murder. Chuck told Jim about this and his adoption when they were in the ninth grade. Mr. Wise said that Chuck was an ordinary, fun-loving kid who had a lot of friends.

When I spoke to Jim Wise on December 11, 1991, he said he had lost touch with Chuck in the summer of 1968, following their sophomore year in college. Years later, Jim tried to find Chuck but had no idea where he was or where his mother was living. In October 1991, when the television show *Inside Edition* aired Chuck's story, Mr. Wise got in touch with me and I directed him to Chuck. In November 1991, the two men were reunited after twenty-two years. Jim Wise is now the pastor of a church in Youngstown, Ohio. He attended Chuck's funeral, held in Columbus, Ohio.

18. Winding Down to a Stop

My talk with Joe Start about Chuck Duffy's attitude toward him took place on April 10, 1989.

Chuck Duffy called his Uncle Mike on March 27, 1989, and he visited his old house on Barley Road and Janice and John Todd in Bell Acres on June 3, 1989.

19. The Murder of Lillian Stevick

The account of the Stevick case is based principally on reportage in the three greater Pittsburgh area newspapers plus the *Valley Daily News* (now called the *Valley News Dispatch*). The account is also informed in a few places by the Pacek trial transcript, interviews with four of the Pacek trial jurors, and Paul Moses, who, as an attorney just out of law school, had attended the nine-day trial.

I talked to Paul Moses on May 12, 1990, and the four jurors on May 12, May 18, and May 19, 1990. The four jurors are Steve Hanus, Harry Weber, Walter R. Brooks, and Joseph Hergenroeder.

Jerry Pacek's initial statement, given to police officers on the night of the murder, follows.

> November 17, 1958 (11:50 P.M.)
> I was walking home and when I was at the corner of Sixth Ave. and Morgan St. I heard some moaning and went to see. I was at the bottom of the steps when I saw someone get up and run. I ran over to Morgan St. and saw a young man run across the road into the weeds. I tried to stop some cars but I had no results so I stood on Morgan St. for about two minutes and then I saw a person run from the weeds and back across the road up onto Crescent St. So I went to the house and knocked on the door a few times and a man came to the door and I explained what happened. He went upstairs and did something and he told me to wait on the porch. He came down and we went around the front of the house. We went up the steps and saw her laying beside the steps. He told me to wait there and he went to call the police. He came back out and we were talking about it. While I was waiting for him, I went around the front of the house and then I saw a fellow about six foot standing at the top of the steps and when he saw me he ran. He was a white man about 18 or 19 years old with black shiny hair and he had on gray pants and a white or grey sweat-shirt. He (Mr. DeLeonardis) told me to tell his wife to call an ambulance. I was going around the side of the house when I saw his wife. So I told her to call an ambulance and she said she didn't need to because the police

was coming and then I said that her husband said to call an ambulance and she went back to the house. And she came back out and her husband told her to get an old blanket. She went to get one and I stayed there with him then he told me to go get the blanket from her. I went to the front of the house and as I was coming up on the porch she was coming out of the house. I told her that her husband told me to get the blanket. I took the blanket and I walked around the side of the house and the man's wife was behind me. And as I got to the back of the house another woman came out of the back door. She went up the steps in front of me and I handed the man the blanket. He covered her over and we waited for the police to come.

[Signed]   Jerry Joseph Pacek
                                               1031 Nesbit Street
                                               Brackenridge, Pa.

Jerry Pacek's first signed confession follows.

November 19, 1958 (12:45)

I Jerry Pacek age 13, 1031 Nesbit St. make this statement of my own free will without any force, threats or promises made to me. On Monday evening Nov. 17, 1958 I was standing at the top of Morgan St. Hill waiting for Mrs. Stevick. She came down to Morgan St. and I followed her. And then I started to talk to her. I said to her it was a nice evening and she said yes. I asked her where she was going. She said she was going home. Then I started to get smart with her and she rejected [me]. I pushed her down and hit her with the pipe and then I drug her over to the steps. I had my penius [*sic*] out and got on top of her. She pushed me away and then I hit her with the pipe. It was a steel pipe. It was about eighteen inches long and I found it along Crescent St. Then I kept hitting her for about seven or eight times. I cut her pants with a pen-knife which I gave to Mr. Vrotney. I dragged her by the fingers over to the steps. When I hit her the second time by the steps she put her hands on top of her head. I left her and took the clothes which were in the bag and put them in Mrs. Vic's trash-can and then I started down Seventh Avenue. I was running. I through [*sic*] the pipe by a pair of steps that went up to Webster St. Then I came down by the old brewery on Sixth Ave. and went home that way. I walked around the neighborhood. I walked from the brewery to Mile Lock Lane on Sixth Ave. Then I walked over Mile Lock Lane to Third Ave.

[Page 2]
I walked down Third Ave. to Cherry St. Then I walked over Cherry St. to Fifth Ave. Then I walked up Fifth to Morgan St. I stood there on the corner and thought about what I had done. And I felt sorry for the woman. And then I decided to help her and blamed it on Jim Bauman because he had a record. I went up there and looked at her and she was still there so I went to the house and told them about the woman being in the back yard.

[Signed]   Jerry Joseph Pacek
                     1031 Nesbit Street
                     Brackenridge, Pa.

The newspaper account of Jerry Pacek's crime scene reenactment appeared in the November 20, 1958, edition of the *Valley Daily News*. The piece was written by staff writer Walter M. Dear and appeared under the headline "YOUTHFUL SLAYER REENACTS CRIME WITH WOMAN COP."

Ted Botula's quote: "There's no doubt. He's the one," is in the November 20, 1958, edition of the *Pittsburgh Sun-Telegraph*.

Alvin Rosensweet's article, "2 STRIKES ON BOY SLAYER," appeared in the November 21, 1958, edition of the *Pittsburgh Post-Gazette*.

Ted Botula's investigation of Jerry Pacek's background was reported in the November 21, 1958, edition of the *Pittsburgh Sun-Telegraph*.

Coroner McClelland's quote after the inquest is from the December 11, 1958, edition of the *Pittsburgh Press*. The quote regarding the two murder weapons introduced at the inquest is from the *Valley Daily News* on December 12, 1958.

The fact that the Pacek trial jury knew that Mary Daley was pregnant was verified by Paul Moses, the young attorney who attended the trial, and by the four jurors I interviewed. Prosecutor Strauss's reference to alibi testimony as being "pregnant" with falsehood was also recalled by these people and is recorded in the Pacek trial transcript.

The confidential Allegheny County Behavior Clinic report regarding Jerry Pacek appeared in the April 14, 1959, edition of the *Pittsburgh Sun-Telegraph*.

The United States Supreme Court case that, in my opinion, supports the legal view that Jerry Pacek had been denied due process, is *Haley v. State of Ohio* 68 S.Ct. 302 (1948).

20. The Evidence

I talked to Joe Start about Jerry Pacek on March 3, 1989. The interview in the book takes place one year later (a change in time done for dramatic effect). I had talked to Joe about the Pacek case shortly after I had initially read about it in the newspapers.

Nick Schifino was interviewed on May 1, 1990, and I talked to Art Sabulsky on May 24, 1990. I asked Ted Botula about the Pacek case on May 1, 1990.

I received the coroner's file on the Stevick murder case from John Thompson on April 23, 1990.

Some of the people who helped me look for the Pacek trial transcript were Tom Yaken, a former Allegheny County clerk of courts; Bill Quest, a clerk at the Allegheny County Clerk's Office; Edward Aul, a former chief county court reporter; Phyllis Pugliese, Allegheny County Court Reporter's Office; Bob Best, Harrisburg Records Center; Patty McClair, state Parole Board, Harrisburg; Jerry Long, Allegheny County Clerk's Office; and Lydia A. King, Allegheny County coordinator.

I called District Attorney Bob Colville on May 17, 1990; and on May 24, 1990, he called me back to say he had found the Pacek trial transcript and had a copy for me.

21. Jerry Pacek

Pat McCormick's testimony can be found on pages 474–480 in the trial transcript. Ted Botula's testimony begins on pages 243, 402, and 486.

I talked to Chuck Duffy about the Pacek case on May 4, 1990.

Jerry Pacek called me for the first time on May 8, 1990.

The court document containing Attorney John Snee's withdrawal of Jerry's appeal is his "Petition for Counsel Fees and Expenses," which, under item number eight, reads:

> An appeal was filed in the Supreme Court of Pennsylvania on August 8, 1960, from the judgment of the Court of Oyer and Terminer. The expenses of this appeal and subsequent Non Pros will be paid for by Petitioner.
>
> The Non Pros was entered by the Supreme Court on Petitioner's request after reviewing the record and reviewing the testimony consisting of 996 pages. Petitioner entered the Non Pros on September 25, 1961, because in his opinion the appeal would not be successful.

I obtained the above document, among others, on May 17, 1990, at the Allegheny County Court Clerk's Office. County Coordinator Lydia A. King and Jerry Long of the clerk's office helped me find the court papers pertaining to the Pacek case.

On July 10, 1990, I spoke to Pittsburgh attorney Paul Moses about John Snee's failings as a lawyer. Mr. Moses knew Snee and had witnessed his performance at the Pacek trial. According to Moses, Snee had probably withdrawn Jerry's appeal because he did not have the energy, desire, or wherewithal to file a winning appellate brief.

22. A New Investigation

Steve Hanus, one of the Pacek trial jurors, remembered that Jerry Pacek had been "out prowling that night looking into windows." Mr. Hanus said that Sam Strauss had Jerry's clothing laid out on a table, and the boy's underwear had been "filthy." He recalled that when Jerry testified, the boy never looked at the jury, and that's one of the reasons they didn't believe him. Hanus remembered Ted Botula, who was in the courtroom every day looking quite dapper in his expensive clothes. Hanus felt that John Snee fought hard for Jerry but was no match for Strauss, who acted like he felt sorry for the boy.

According to Mr. Hanus, Judge O'Brien was "one hell of a gentleman," who was "very distinguished and friendly." Every morning the judge asked the jury if they had had a good night. The jurors' reunion never took place. Mr. Hanus said the jury voted for murder two because Jerry was so young, figuring ten years in prison would straighten him out, and because the boy needed to get away from his parents and his environment.

I talked to Mr. Hanus on May 18, 1990. He was sixty-four, thirty-three when he sat on the jury.

I talked to another former juror, Joseph Hergenroeder, on May 19, 1990. Mr. Hergenroeder described Jerry as "a rough character, a bad boy, and cocky. The boy's attitude turned us against him." He said that Sam Strauss had all the jurors spellbound, that Strauss "made Jerry Pacek seem guilty." At one point, Strauss had said, "I could have been more severe with Jerry — but due to his age I took it easy on him." Mr. Hergenroeder said, "Every time Snee would make a point, Strauss would step on it — stamp it out."

Mr. Hergenroeder was forty-eight at the time of the trial.

Robert K. Morehead, formerly a reporter for the *Valley Daily News*, now called the *Valley News Dispatch*, had covered the Pacek case. I interviewed him at his home in Tarentum on August 10, 1990.

Paul Moses was interviewed at his office in downtown Pittsburgh on July 25, 1990.

I talked to Ed Vrotney, the former Brackenridge chief of police, on July 13, 1990. His wife, who had been ill at that time, died on January 16, 1991.

I talked to Ted Botula about the Pacek case on July 10, 1990.

I reported my Stevick case findings to District Attorney Bob Colville on July 16, 1990.

23. The Media Spread the Stories

Tony Klimko's December 29 – 30, 1990, article in the *Valley News Dispatch* is not excerpted in the book.

Tony Klimko, in a *Valley News Dispatch* article that came out on January 5, 1991, quoted Ralph Yovetich who, uncharacteristically, had much to say about the Pacek case:

> "We know when she got off the bus from the hospital she came down Morgan St., stopped at the store for a loaf of bread and was seen by people at the garage," Yovetich said. "Then her body and the bag with the bread is found here. Later a bag of old clothes she was carrying is found in a garbage can on the next street up the hill. " . . .
>
> "That's one of the things that doesn't add up about this case. There's an awful lot of unanswered questions on this one," said Yovetich, who toured the crime scene at the request of the *Valley News Dispatch.*
>
> A 21-year Pittsburgh policeman, Yovetich was first a narcotics detective then had the elite homicide squad. He eventually became assistant police superintendent.
>
> Yovetich has headed the D.A.'s investigators for the past 15 years.
>
> "One of the things that really bothered me about this case is the total lack of physical evidence against Pacek," Yovetich said.
>
> "No trace of the victim's blood, hair, or textile fibers were found on Pacek and no murder weapon was ever found.
>
> "With the wounds she had and there's no trace of blood on him? No way," said Yovetich who has seen scores of murder scene victims. . . .
>
> "That confession would never have been allowed to stand as evidence under today's rules," Yovetich said.
>
> "Pacek said he confessed because police wore him down after 17 hours of questioning.

"I don't condone it but that's the way things were done in those days," Yovetich said. "Then we could arrest a man on suspicion of a felony and hold him for 72 hours. You didn't have to name the felony or have probable cause. You could make the arrest as long as the suspect was in proximity to where a felony might have occurred.

"Sounds like Russia, doesn't it," he asked.

Does Yovetich feel Pacek is innocent?

"Our job in this isn't to find Jerry Pacek innocent. I want to find out who committed the murder if he didn't. I will not be convinced he didn't do it until I find out who did," Yovetich said.

To do this Yovetich and his investigators are going back and checking out anybody whose name ever came up in connection with the murder.

"This time we're going to do it right," he said.

Dave Templeton, the feature writer for the *Pittsburgh Press Sunday Magazine*, interviewed me on January 7, 1991.

Television producer Steve Oppenheim is no longer with *Inside Edition*. The article containing Oppenheim's quote about Jerry Pacek appeared in the January 12, 13, 1991, editions of the *Valley News Dispatch*.

24. Hypnosis

District Attorney Bob Colville pledged his support for Jerry and Jerry's application for a pardon on March 11, 1991.

25. The Threads of Two Investigations

Tony Klimko's article about Jerry Pacek's session with Drs. Scott and Thompson was published in the March 26, 1991, edition of the *Valley News Dispatch*. On March 27, 1991, Klimko's *Valley News Dispatch* article about Jerry Pacek's application for a pardon with Colville's support came out.

I got my first look at the crime lab file on the Zubryd case on April 10, 1991. According to the "Supplemental Confidential Report of Laboratory Findings," dated June 6, 1957, and styled "Helen Zubryd—Murder, Laboratory Case Number 6659," thirty-seven people were examined by polygraph operator Charles A. McInerney between the dates November 24, 1956, and March 22, 1957. Above the list of names and dates of people tested, the report read: "The following subjects were brought to this laboratory for the purpose of taking polygraph examinations in connection with the murder of Helen Zubryd in Sewickley Township on November 20, 1956."

The people on that list familiar to me were

James Flevaris	December 26, 1956
Floyd Skiles	December 26, 1956
Mike Zubryd	January 2, 1957
Margaret Skiles	January 17, 1957
Charles Zubryd	March 4, 1957

At the end of McInerney's June 6, 1957, report, following the list of people tested, he wrote: "On the polygraph records of these subjects there were no significant emotional disturbances indicative of deception on questions pertaining to the crime."

26. Woodville

Eddie Boyle's quote about the army belt appeared in the March 15, 1959, edition of the *Pittsburgh Sun-Telegraph*.

The article about Charlie's murder reenactment in District Attorney Boyle's office was in the March 16, 1959, edition of the *Pittsburgh Sun-Telegraph*.

Ted Botula's list of factors suggesting Charlie Zubryd's guilt was published in the March 16, 1959, edition of the *Pittsburgh Post-Gazette*.

I mailed my Pacek report to the Pennsylvania Board of Pardons on Thursday, April 11, 1991.

I talked to Catherine Asperger about the crime scene purse on May 1, 1991, and spoke to Janice Todd about it on May 5, 1991.

27. William Spiegel

Darla Lynn's letter to me is dated April 17, 1991.

Besides the information on William Spiegel I obtained from the courthouse, I acquired a great deal more from Norma Chase, a Pittsburgh attorney. Norma is an expert at this kind of thing and accessed sources of information I would have missed.

Some of the documents upon which I have based my Spiegel profile are

— Death Certificate Number 136135, dated May 14, 1968
— Petition for Discharge of Legacy in the Estate of Peter Spiegel dated April 8, 1941
— Motion of District Attorney for Nolle Prosequi dated May 24, 1968

— Court of Quarter Sessions of the Peace, O&T 63 Number 171, page 235
 Docket Book: and transcript of docket, May 13, 1960
— Constable's Subpoena Service Certification (Grand Jury) Number 2381,
 June 8, 1960
— Court of Quarter Sessions of the Peace, Number 457 and Number 491,
 September 1952.

Norma Chase located Spiegel's burial site at Calvary Cemetery on Hazelwood Avenue in Pittsburgh. He's buried in Section 29, Row 5, Grave 46.

Late in 1991, the Woodville State Hospital closed its doors for good. Most of
the patients were moved to Mayview.

28. A Living Witness

John Henchar, Betty Henchar's son, was present for the interview with
Betty Henchar at her home on May 4, 1991; he had been helpful in arranging for
the interview.

Index

JIM FISHER, a law school graduate, former FBI agent, investigator of last resort, and author, teaches criminal investigation at Edinboro University of Pennsylvania. This is his third book.